"Truly a classic—clear, concise, and warm in its presentation of historic Reformed theology. This latest edition is even better than the original." —R. C. Sproul

"One could hardly wish for a better study resource to show the five points' faithfulness to Scripture. The fullness of the bibliographies gives this book special value. In days like ours, when fuzzy theology flourishes, this disciplined display of the heart of the gospel calls for three of the loudest cheers we can give." —J. I. Packer

"I was first introduced to this splendid guidebook as a teenager. Now, almost four decades later, it is a privilege to commend this enlarged and revised edition to a new generation. It is a model of clarity, full of biblical teaching, and will help you through the vast maze of Christian books to some of the very best." —Sinclair B. Ferguson

"Next to the doctrine of salvation, the sovereignty of God has, to me, been the most powerfully comforting truth from the Word of God. To understand God's hand in my hardship as a quadriplegic has dissipated the darkness of despair and hopelessness. My thanks to P&R Publishing for issuing a new edition of this excellent book." —Joni Eareckson Tada

"An invaluable resource to students of Reformed theology for forty years. This new and expanded edition should prove even more helpful to anyone wishing to understand or teach the biblical basis of the doctrines of grace. The appendices are much more than additional, interesting information. They serve to deepen one's understanding of what true Calvinism is all about." —Jerry Bridges

"A classic exposition and defe   is new and improved edition wi   believes that in Christ, God s   vill not save themselves. The authors clearly prove the sovereignty of God's grace from the Scriptures and show how this leads to a life in godliness. Simply put, *The Five Points of Calvinism* is the best and the most complete short introduction to the doctrines of grace." —Philip G. Ryken

"I am delighted to see this masterpiece in its new, revised edition, as its original version had a formative influence on my own thinking and ministry. Now, in its updated and enlarged form, it is even better. For anyone seeking to understand, teach, and enjoy the doctrines of grace, this book is quite simply a 'must.'" —John Blanchard

"I've always liked its concise and uncluttered presentation, its down-to-earth explanation, its usable collection of Bible passages and recommended titles, and that excellent supplemental article on foreknowledge. There is no telling how many times I have given copies away or recommended its use to others. But now, without losing any of its essential character, it's even better!" —Jim Elliff

"A powerful reaffirmation of the 'heart and soul' of classic Calvinism. The authors' scholarship is extensive, they never fudge an issue, and they carry their readers along in an inoffensive way to their conclusions. A superb depiction of Calvinistic soteriology, this edition will continue to be a valuable aid in the spread of biblical Christianity." —Robert L. Reymond

"We are excited about this revised and expanded edition. I have personally seen our sovereign God at work in a gracious way in the life and ministry of my friend Curtis Thomas. I pray that this new edition will be widely used to bring glory to the God of our salvation." —Robert C. (Ric) Cannada Jr.

"A standby for many years, *The Five Points of Calvinism* has been enlarged and revised—a fact that only makes it even more valuable." —Jay E. Adams

THE
FIVE
POINTS OF
CALVINISM

THE
FIVE
POINTS OF
CALVINISM

DEFINED, DEFENDED, AND DOCUMENTED

SECOND EDITION

DAVID N. STEELE
CURTIS C. THOMAS
S. LANCE QUINN

PUBLISHING
P.O. BOX 817 • PHILLIPSBURG • NEW JERSEY 08865-0817

Unless otherwise indicated, all Scripture quotations are from The Holy Bible, English Standard Version, copyright © 2001 by Crossway Bibles, a division of Good News Publishers. Used by permission. All rights reserved.

Italics within Scripture quotations indicate emphasis added.

Page design and typesetting by Lakeside Design Plus

Printed in the United States of America

Library of Congress Cataloging-in-Publication Data
Steele, David N.
    The five points of Calvinism : defined, defended, and documented,
  by David N. Steele, Curtis C. Thomas, S. Lance Quinn—2nd ed.
        p. cm.
    Includes bibliographical references and index.
    ISBN 0-87552-827-9 (pbk.)
    1. Calvinism. I. Thomas, Curtis C., 1937– II. Quinn, S. Lance.
  III. Title.

BX9422.3.S74 2004
230'.42—dc22

                                                    2003065963

It is with deep gratitude that we dedicate this book to the memory of

Dr. Loraine Boettner

in appreciation of his writing ministry, kind encouragement, and sacrificial Christian example.

CONTENTS

PART ONE
THE FIVE POINTS DEFINED:
THEIR ORIGIN AND CONTENTS

PART TWO

THE FIVE POINTS DEFENDED:
THEIR BIBLICAL SUPPORT

PART THREE

THE FIVE POINTS DOCUMENTED:
RECOMMENDED READING

⸙

APPENDICES

FOREWORD

It gives me great pleasure to commend this new edition of *The Five Points of Calvinism*, as I did the first edition. For forty years, I made frequent use of the original edition, and I found it both accurate and convenient. It offered a clear and concise definition of the Calvinistic position, provided a conspectus of the biblical foundation for each point, and gave a brief review of the literature available in English on the whole subject and on each point. I wrote at the time, "To get this in compact form at a readily accessible price is certainly a most desirable project. Far from duplicating existing materials, this present work may be viewed as filling an unfortunate lacuna."

In this new edition, the qualities of the earlier one have been carefully maintained. The biblical support for each point not only records the reference, but actually gives the written text of the relevant passage. The bibliography, while useful in the first edition, has been greatly developed and updated with a listing of 328 sources, as compared with 104 in the earlier edition. Only three ancient works that are difficult to secure and nineteen pamphlets of lesser importance have been deleted, and some 246 titles have been added.

In addition to the previous appendix on "The Meaning of 'Foreknew' in Romans 8:29," the new edition contains seven new appendices, the longest one detailing some of the historical vicissitudes of the struggle between Calvinism and Arminianism, by whatever name they may have been known. The last two examples of this struggle relate to recent controversies of a somewhat different nature within the evangelical community, the last one actually relating to the defense of God's exhaustive foreknowledge that embraces even the future decisions of moral agents.

In the foreword to the first edition, I responded to the objection that the five points of Calvinism are an artificial division by saying:

> To be sure, this structure has its historical origin . . . in the necessity to counter the objections of the Remonstrance (1610), which were formulated along five main heads of doctrine. Nevertheless, and in part, on account of these historical moorings, the five points provide a classic framework, which is quite well adapted for the expression of certain distinguishing emphases of Calvinism. Furthermore, they are well suited for the exhibition of the inner correlation between Calvinistic tenets, since each of them may well be viewed as an aspect of the sovereign grace of God.

I would like in this new foreword to say a word about the nomenclature of the five points. Ever since the appearance of Loraine Boettner's magisterial *The Reformed Doctrine of Predestination,* it has been customary to refer to the five points according to the acrostic TULIP:

1. **T**otal Depravity
2. **U**nconditional Election
3. **L**imited Atonement
4. **I**rresistible Grace
5. **P**erseverance of the Saints

This has been convenient and to a large extent appropriate. Each of the terms, however, may lead to some misapprehension that needs to be corrected. Therefore, I have suggested some alternative language that, in my judgment, specifies more accurately the issues in view. It is as follows:

1. Radical and Pervasive Depravity
2. Sovereign, Divine Election
3. Definite Atonement (or Particular Redemption)
4. Effectual, Saving Grace
5. Perseverance of God with the Saints

This does not constitute an acrostic. If one be required, I would propose the following one, which emphasizes that all five points are really an articulation of the doctrine of grace:

GRACE is:
1. **O**bligatory (that is, indispensable)
2. **S**overeign (in choice)
3. **P**articular (in redemption)
4. **E**ffectual (in operation)
5. **L**asting (that is, secure)

This is discussed in my book *Our Sovereign Saviour* (Fearn, U.K.: Christian Focus, 2002) on pages 47–56. It is my modest contribution to the present fine volume.

Roger Nicole

PREFACE
TO THE SECOND EDITION

It has now been forty years since the first edition of this work was published. As I look back from the fortieth anniversary, several things have occurred, including the sudden calling home to heaven in 1991 of my previous coauthor, David Steele. In addition, the work has been translated into several foreign languages, plus braille, and this English edition has been reprinted over and over again. The interest in the work has been surprising and has far exceeded our expectations.

I welcome my new coauthor, Lance Quinn, my friend and pastor at The Bible Church of Little Rock. It was he who suggested that we produce a new edition on the fortieth anniversary of this work. He not only encouraged me to do so, but also wanted to be a part of the project, for which I am most grateful. To have Lance as my pastor, friend, and now coauthor, is a continual reminder of God's wonderful grace.

While our theology, as expressed in this small volume, has not changed, we have long thought that the book needed changes in several areas. First, a number of important works have been published since our first edition appeared in 1963. Some of these are reprints and others are new books and booklets. We have therefore included a number of additional titles in "Part Three: The Five Points Documented: Recommended Reading." The inclusion of the additional material is Lance's work. He has a masterful knowledge of printed resources, thanks to his extensive library and voracious reading. Lance has also written appendix G.

Second, in the first edition of the book, in the section dealing with "The Perseverance of the Saints or the Security of Believers," our primary emphasis was on God's *preservation*, and hence our security as believers, rather than on the believer's *perseverance*. This distinction is now highlighted because there are many who profess to be Christians, but give little or no evidence of a changed life. Many have placed their hope in some emotional decision or hazy commitment that they once made, with little regard to their present lifestyle. Therefore, we have added an appendix on "Perseverance and Preservation" to demonstrate the other side of this wonderful doctrine. We are not only *preserved* by God for salvation, but required by Him to *persevere* in the faith, striving continually toward a holy life. Without our *perseverance*, we can have no assurance of His *preservation*.

A third difference from the first edition is that all the biblical quotations in Part Two are now from the English Standard Version.[1]

Among the seven new appendices is an article written by James McGuire, senior pastor of Ward Evangelical Presbyterian Church in Northville, Michigan, entitled "A Kinder, Gentler Calvinism." The wonderful doctrines of grace known as Calvinism have on occasion been harmed by the spirit in which they have been expressed. In this article, Dr. McGuire points out: "It is so much easier to be lost in the beauty, the faithfulness, the cohesiveness, the clarity of sound Reformed theology than to be lost in the practice of love, which is, after all, the

---

1. Other versions we recommend include the New American Standard Bible, the New International Version, The New King James Version, The Berkeley Version, the Amplified New Testament, *The New Testament: A Translation in the Language of the People*, by Charles B. Williams, *The New Testament: An Expanded Translation*, by Kenneth S. Wuest, and the New English Bible.

great aim of orthodox theology. Galatians 5:6b says, *'The only thing that counts is faith expressing itself through love.'*" He concludes with this very appropriate appeal: "We need a kinder, gentler Calvinism because truth fueled by love is the most liberating force known to man." We heartily agree, and suggest that you read Dr. McGuire's appendix before reading the rest of this book.

The other appendices include "A Defense of Calvinism," by C. H. Spurgeon; "The Practical Applications of Calvinism," by Curt Daniel; "The Practical Importance of the Doctrine [of Predestination]," by Loraine Boettner; and "Calvinism and Arminianism Before and After: A Brief Historical Sketch," by Lance Quinn. You will find each of these appendices to be a valuable contribution to your understanding and appreciation of Calvinism.

Dr. Curt Daniel, who has done extensive research into the history and theology of Calvinism, graciously reviewed the list of works in Part Three for completeness and accuracy. He has also given us permission to include chapter 73 of his work, *The History and Theology of Calvinism*, as the appendix mentioned above. For his assistance, we acknowledge our indebtedness and appreciation.

A special word of thanks also goes to Richard Fulenwider, whose personal ministry is to help those who are computer illiterate. He provided valuable help in putting the old edition into digital form, answering many calls for urgent help, and personally overseeing our getting the new edition computer-ready for the publisher.

And last, to my faithful, patient, and helpful wife, Betty, who joyfully shares and lives these wonderful truths, I express my love and profound admiration. Without her help on this new edition (not to mention the first one), you might have already laid it aside.

Curtis C. Thomas

I would like to express my thanks to and for my wife, Beth, who labors tirelessly in our home in order to allow writing projects like this to come to fruition. She is a true servant of the Lord on my behalf. For her, proclaiming the message of God's sovereignty in salvation is worth every sacrifice. I would also like to acknowledge our eight children (Lacey, Lancer, Logan, Lindsey, Lauren, Lucas, Lexa, and Lisa), with the prayer that they will all one day embrace the sweet doctrines of God's sovereign grace.

I would also like to thank the elders and members of The Bible Church of Little Rock, for whom the truths taught in this book are precious. They have greatly encouraged their pastor-teacher to preach these doctrines of grace. May we all live in the fullness of the grace we have received.

S. Lance Quinn

Soli Deo Gloria!

PREFACE
TO THE FIRST EDITION

This work has been designed to serve as an *introductory survey* of that system of theology known as "the five points of Calvinism." As we shall see, each of the five points, which make up this historic system, constitutes a distinct and important biblical doctrine. Viewed together, these five doctrines form the basic framework of God's plan for saving sinners.

The purpose of this survey is threefold: We wish first to *define*, second to *defend*, and third to *document* the "five points." In order to do this, we have divided the material into three separate parts, each of which forms an independent unit of study.

Part One deals with the *history* and *contents* of the system. The sole function of this section is to explain what Calvinism is. In order to show how and why the five-point structure of Calvinism was developed, we have discussed the origin and contents of "the five points of Arminianism." These two opposing systems are contrasted, point by point, so that it might be clearly understood wherein and to what extent they differ in their interpretation of the biblical plan of salvation. The basic concepts of each system are analyzed, but no attempt whatsoever is made in Part One to defend the truthfulness of Calvinism.

Part Two is devoted to a *biblical defense* of the five points of Calvinism. After each point has been introduced and related to the overall system, some of the more important verses in which it is taught are given. The various passages appealed to in the support of each point are classified under appropriate headings. Approximately 250 passages (consisting of well over 400 verses) are quoted in full. Great care has been exercised to avoid quoting verses out of their context. Before considering the biblical defense presented in Part Two, the reader should clearly understand the contents of Calvinism discussed in Part One.

Part Three is designed to *encourage* and *aid* the reader to make *a thorough investigation of Calvinistic theology.* We have *listed* and carefully *documented* (giving the author's full name, the title, the publisher's name and address, the date of publication, and the number of pages) *over 90 works* dealing with Calvinism and the individual doctrines contained within the system. Included in this list of titles are 60 separate books plus 15 reference works (systematic theologies, etc.), in addition to information concerning the Calvinistic contents of the great Protestant confessions of faith, and a number of booklets and tracts. Over 50 of the individual books (not including the reference works) are briefly introduced; we have indicated such things as the nature of their contents, their value, and their style. Many of these works have been written by the foremost theologians of both the past and the present. They set forth and defend, explain and clarify, state and answer objections to, as well as show the influence and value of, Calvinistic theology.[1]

It is our hope that the material contained in this survey will help to promote the spread of Calvinism and that many will thus be led to understand, to believe, and to propagate this biblical system of doctrine, which ascribes *all the glory* for the salvation of sinners *to God alone!*

---

1. Parts One and Two of this work were first published as an appendix to *Romans: An Interpretive Outline.* These two parts, along with the material contained in Part Three, are being published in this paperback edition in order to make it available at a more accessible price.

It is no novelty, then, that I am preaching; no new doctrine. I love to proclaim these strong old doctrines, that are called by nickname *Calvinism*, but which are surely and verily the revealed truth of God as it is in Christ Jesus. By this truth I make a pilgrimage into [the] past, and as I go, I see father after father, confessor after confessor, martyr after martyr, standing up to shake hands with me. . . . Taking these things to be the standard of my faith, I see the land of the ancients peopled with my brethren; I behold multitudes who confess the same as I do, and acknowledge that this is the religion of God's own church.

Charles Haddon Spurgeon
"Election," *The Metropolitan Tabernacle*

THE FIVE POINTS DEFINED:
THEIR ORIGIN AND CONTENTS

To understand how and why the system of theology known to history as Calvinism came to bear this name and to be formulated in five points, one must understand the theological conflict which occurred in Holland during the first quarter of the seventeenth century.

POINTS OF CONTENTION

The Protest of the Arminian Party

In 1610, just one year after the death of James Arminius (a Dutch seminary professor), his followers drew up *five articles of faith* based on his teachings. The Arminians, as his followers came to be called, presented these five doctrines to the State of Holland in the form of a "Remonstrance" (i.e., a protest). The Arminian party insisted that the Belgic Confession of Faith and the Heidelberg Catechism (the official expression of the doctrinal position of the Church of Holland) be changed to conform to the doctrinal views contained in the

1

Remonstrance. The Arminians objected to the doctrines upheld in both the Confession and the Catechism relating to divine sovereignty, human inability, unconditional election or pre-destination, particular redemption, irresistible grace, and the perseverance of the saints. They wanted the official standards of the Church of Holland revised on these subjects.

The Five Points of Arminianism

Roger Nicole summarizes the five articles contained in the Remonstrance as follows:

> I. God elects or reproves on the basis of foreseen faith or unbelief. II. Christ died for all men and for every man, although only believers are saved. III. Man is so depraved that divine grace is necessary unto faith or any good deed. IV. This grace may be resisted. V. Whether all who are truly regenerate will certainly persevere in the faith is a point which needs further investigation.[1]

The last article was later altered so as definitely to teach that the truly regenerate believer could lose his faith and thus lose his salvation. However, Arminians have not been in agreement on this point. Some have held that all who are regenerated by the Spirit of God are eternally secure and can never perish.

The Philosophical Basis of Arminianism

J. I. Packer, in analyzing the system of thought embodied in the Remonstrance, observes:

1. Roger Nicole, "Arminianism," in *Baker's Dictionary of Theology,* ed. Everett F. Harrison (Grand Rapids: Baker, 1960), 64.

The theology which it contained (known to history as Arminianism) stemmed from two philosophical principles: first, that divine sovereignty is not compatible with human freedom, nor therefore with human responsibility; second, that ability limits obligation. . . . From these principles, the Arminians drew two deductions: first, that since the Bible regards faith as a free and responsible act, it cannot be caused by God, but is exercised independently of Him; second, that since the Bible regards faith as obligatory on the part of all who hear the gospel, ability to believe must be universal. Hence, they maintained, Scripture must be interpreted as teaching the following positions: (1.) Man is never so completely corrupted by sin that he cannot savingly believe the gospel when it is put before him, nor (2.) is he ever so completely controlled by God that he cannot reject it. (3.) God's election of those who shall be saved is prompted by His foreseeing that they will of their own accord believe. (4.) Christ's death did not ensure the salvation of anyone, for it did not secure the gift of faith to anyone (there is no such gift); what it did was rather to create a possibility of salvation for everyone if they believe. (5.) It rests with believers to keep themselves in a state of grace by keeping up their faith; those who fail here fall away and are lost. Thus, Arminianism made man's salvation depend ultimately on man himself, saving faith being viewed throughout as man's own work and, because his own, not God's in him.[2]

A Five-Point Response to Arminianism

A national synod was called to meet in Dort in 1618 for the purpose of examining the views of Arminius in the light of

2. James I. Packer, "Introductory Essay," in *The Death of Death in the Death of Christ*, by John Owen (London: Banner of Truth, 1959), 3–4.

Scripture. The Great Synod was convened by the States-General of Holland on November 13, 1618. Among the 84 Dutch delegates were 18 secular commissioners. Included were 27 delegates from various German states, Switzerland, England, and Scotland. There were 154 sessions held during the seven months that the Synod met to consider these matters, the last of which was on May 9, 1619.

Warburton writes:

> The Synod had given a very close examination to the "five points" which had been advanced by the Remonstrants, and had compared the teaching advanced in them with the testimony of Scripture. Failing to reconcile that teaching with the Word of God, which they had definitely declared could alone be accepted by them as the rule of faith, they had unanimously rejected them. They felt, however, that a mere rejection was not sufficient. It remained for them to set forth the true Calvinistic teaching in relationship to those matters which had been called into question. This they proceeded to do, embodying the Calvinistic position in five chapters which have ever since been known as "the five points of Calvinism."[3]

The name *Calvinism* derives from John Calvin (1509–1564), the great French Reformer who did so much to expound and defend these views.

No doubt it will seem strange to many in our day that the Synod of Dort rejected as heretical the five doctrines advanced by the Arminians, for these doctrines have gained wide acceptance in the modern church. In fact, they are seldom questioned

3. Ben A. Warburton, *Calvinism* (Grand Rapids: Eerdmans, 1955), 61. Although there were five Calvinistic articles, there were only four chapters. This was because the third and fourth articles were combined into one chapter. Consequently, the third chapter is always designated as Chapter III–IV.

in our generation. But the vast majority of the Protestant theologians of that day took a much different view of the matter. They maintained that the Bible set forth a system of doctrine quite different from that advocated by the Arminian party. Salvation was viewed by the members of the Synod as *a work of grace from beginning to end;* they did not believe that the sinner saved himself or contributed to his salvation in any sense. Adam's fall had completely ruined the race. All men were by nature spiritually dead, and their wills were in bondage to sin and Satan. The ability to believe the gospel was itself a gift from God, bestowed only upon those whom He had chosen to be the objects of His unmerited favor. It was not man, but God, who determined which sinners would be shown mercy and saved. This, in essence, is what the members of the Synod of Dort understood the Bible to teach.

CALVINISM AND ARMINIANISM COMPARED

In the chart which follows, the five points of Arminianism (rejected by the Synod) and the five points of Calvinism (set forth by the Synod) are given, side by side, so that it might be readily seen wherein and to what extent these two systems of doctrine differ.

THE FIVE POINTS OF ARMINIANISM	THE FIVE POINTS OF CALVINISM
1. Free Will or Human Ability Although human nature was seriously affected by the Fall, man has not been left in a state of total spiritual helplessness. God graciously enables every sinner to repent and believe, but He does so in such a manner as not to interfere with man's freedom. Each sinner possesses a free will, and his eternal destiny depends on how he uses it.	**1. Total Inability or Total Depravity** Because of the Fall, man is unable of himself to savingly believe the gospel. The sinner is dead, blind, and deaf to the things of God; his heart is deceitful and desperately corrupt. His will is not free; it is in bondage to his evil nature. Therefore, he will not—indeed, he cannot—choose good over evil in the spiritual realm. Consequently, it

Man's freedom consists of his ability to choose good over evil in spiritual matters; his will is not enslaved to his sinful nature. The sinner has the power either to cooperate with God's Spirit and be regenerated or to resist God's grace and perish. The lost sinner needs the Spirit's assistance, but he does not have to be regenerated by the Spirit before he can believe, for faith is man's act and precedes the new birth. Faith is the sinner's gift to God; it is man's contribution to salvation.

takes much more than the Spirit's assistance to bring a sinner to Christ. It takes regeneration, by which the Spirit makes the sinner alive and gives him a new nature. Faith is not something man contributes to salvation, but is itself a part of God's gift of salvation. It is God's gift to the sinner, not the sinner's gift to God.

2. Conditional Election

God's choice of certain individuals for salvation before the foundation of the world was based upon His foreseeing that they would respond to His call. He selected only those whom He knew would of themselves freely believe the gospel. Election therefore was determined by, or conditioned upon, what man would do. The faith which God foresaw, and upon which He based His choice, was not given to the sinner by God (it was not created by the regenerating power of the Holy Spirit), but resulted solely from man's will. It was left entirely up to man to determine who would believe and therefore who would be elected for salvation. God chose those whom He knew would, of their own free will, choose Christ. Thus, the sinner's choice of Christ, not God's choice of the sinner, is the ultimate cause of salvation.

2. Unconditional Election

God's choice of certain individuals for salvation before the foundation of the world rested solely in His own sovereign will. His choice of particular sinners was not based on any foreseen response or obedience on their part, such as faith, repentance, etc. On the contrary, God gives faith and repentance to each individual whom He selected. These acts are the result, not the cause, of God's choice. Election, therefore, was not determined by, or conditioned upon, any virtuous quality or act foreseen in man. Those whom God sovereignly elected He brings through the power of the Spirit to a willing acceptance of Christ. Thus, God's choice of the sinner, not the sinner's choice of Christ, is the ultimate cause of salvation.

3. Universal Redemption or General Atonement

Christ's redeeming work made it possible for everyone to be saved,

3. Particular Redemption or Limited Atonement

Christ's redeeming work was intended to save the elect only and but did not actually secure the salvation of anyone. Although Christ died for all men and for every man, only those who believe in Him are saved. His death enabled God to pardon sinners on the condition that they believe, but it did not actually put away anyone's sins. Christ's redemption becomes effective only if man chooses to accept it.

actually secured salvation for them. His death was a substitutionary endurance of the penalty of sin in the place of certain specified sinners. In addition to putting away the sins of His people, Christ's redemption secured everything necessary for their salvation, including faith, which unites them to Him. The gift of faith is infallibly applied by the Spirit to all for whom Christ died, thereby guaranteeing their salvation.

4. The Holy Spirit Can Be Effectually Resisted

The Spirit calls inwardly all those who are called outwardly by the gospel invitation; He does all that He can to bring every sinner to salvation. But inasmuch as man is free, he can successfully resist the Spirit's call. The Spirit cannot regenerate the sinner until he believes; faith (which is man's contribution) precedes and makes possible the new birth. Thus, man's free will limits the Spirit in the application of Christ's saving work. The Holy Spirit can only draw to Christ those who allow Him to have His way with them. Until the sinner responds, the Spirit cannot give life. God's grace, therefore, is not invincible; it can be, and often is, resisted and thwarted by man.

4. The Efficacious Call of the Spirit or Irresistible Grace

In addition to the outward general call to salvation, which is made to everyone who hears the gospel, the Holy Spirit extends to the elect a special inward call that inevitably brings them to salvation. The external call (which is made to all without distinction) can be, and often is, rejected. However, the internal call (which is made only to the elect) cannot be rejected; it always results in conversion. By means of this special call, the Spirit irresistibly draws sinners to Christ. He is not limited in His work of applying salvation by man's will, nor is He dependent upon man's cooperation for success. The Spirit graciously causes the elect sinner to cooperate, to believe, to repent, to come freely and willingly to Christ. God's grace, therefore, is invincible; it never fails to result in the salvation of those to whom it is extended.

5. Falling from Grace

Those who believe and are truly saved can lose their salvation by failing to keep up their faith, etc.

5. Perseverance of the Saints

All who are chosen by God, redeemed by Christ, and given faith by the Spirit, are eternally saved.

All Arminians have not been agreed on this point; some have held that believers are eternally secure in Christ—that once a sinner is regenerated, he can never be lost.

They are kept in faith by the power of almighty God, and thus persevere to the end.

According to Arminianism:
Salvation is accomplished through the combined efforts of God (who takes the initiative) and man (who must respond)—man's response being the determining factor. God has provided salvation for everyone, but His provision becomes effective only for those who, of their own free will, choose to cooperate with Him and accept His offer of grace. At the crucial point, man's will plays a decisive role; thus, *man,* not God, determines who will be the recipients of the gift of salvation.

According to Calvinism:
Salvation is accomplished by the almighty power of the triune God. The Father chose a people, the Son died for them, and the Holy Spirit makes Christ's death effective by bringing the elect to faith and repentance, thereby causing them to willingly obey the gospel. The entire process (election, redemption, regeneration) is the work of God and is by grace alone. Thus, *God,* not man, determines who will be the recipients of the gift of salvation.

REJECTED
by the Synod of Dort
This was the system of thought contained in the "Remonstrance" (though the "five points" were not originally arranged in this order). It was submitted by the Arminians to the Church of Holland in 1610 for adoption, but was rejected by the Synod of Dort in 1619 on the ground that it was unscriptural.

REAFFIRMED
by the Synod of Dort
This system of theology was reaffirmed by the Synod of Dort in 1619 as the doctrine of salvation contained in the Holy Scriptures. The system was at that time formulated in "five points" (in answer to the five points submitted by the Arminians) and has ever since been known as "the five points of Calvinism."

THE HISTORICAL ROOTS OF EACH SYSTEM

The basic concepts of each system are much older than the Synod of Dort. Neither John Calvin nor James Arminius originated the basic concepts which undergird the two systems that bear their names.

The Controversy Between Pelagius and Augustine

The fundamental principles of each system can be traced back many centuries prior to the time when Calvin and Arminius lived. For example, the basic doctrines of the Calvinistic position had been vigorously defended by Augustine against Pelagius in the fifth century. Cunningham writes:

> As there was nothing new in substance in the Calvinism of Calvin, so there was nothing new in the Arminianism of Arminius.... The doctrines of Arminius can be traced back as far as the time of Clemons Alexandrinus, and seem to have been held by many of the fathers of the third and fourth centuries, having been diffused in the church through the corrupting influence of pagan philosophy. Pelagius and his followers, in the fifth century, were as decidedly opposed to Calvinism as Arminius was, though they deviated much further from sound doctrine than he did.[4]

Pelagius denied that human nature had been corrupted by sin. He maintained that the only ill effect which the race had suffered as the result of Adam's transgression was the bad example which he had set for mankind. According to Pelagius, every infant comes into the world in the same condition as Adam was before the Fall. His leading principle was that *man's will is absolutely free*. Hence, everyone has the power, within himself, to believe the gospel, as well as to keep the law of God perfectly.

Augustine, on the other hand, maintained that human nature had been so completely corrupted by Adam's fall that no one, in himself, has the ability to obey either the law or the gospel. Divine grace is essential if sinners are to believe and be saved, and this grace is extended only to those whom God pre-

4. William Cunningham, *Historical Theology* (London: Banner of Truth, 1960), 2:374.

destined to eternal life before the foundation of the world. The act of faith, therefore, results, not from the sinner's free will (as Pelagius taught), but from God's free grace, which is bestowed on the elect only.

Semi-Pelagianism, the Forerunner of Arminianism

Smeaton, in showing how Semi-Pelagianism (the forerunner of Arminianism) originated, states:

> Augustine's unanswerable polemic had so fully discredited Pelagianism in the field of argument, that it could no longer be made plausible to the Christian mind. It collapsed. But a new system soon presented itself, teaching that *man with his own natural powers is able to take the first step towards his conversion,* and that this obtains or merits the Spirit's assistance. Cassian . . . was the founder of this middle way, which came to be called SEMI-PELAGIANISM, because it occupied intermediate ground between Pelagianism and Augustinianism, and took in elements from both. He acknowledged that Adam's sin extended to his posterity, and that human nature was corrupted by original sin. But, on the other hand, he held a system of universal grace for all men alike, making the final decision in the case of every individual dependent on the exercise of free-will.

Speaking of those who followed Cassian, Smeaton continues:

> They held that the first movement of the will in the assent of faith must be ascribed to the natural powers of the human mind. This was their primary error. Their maxim was: *"It is mine to be willing* to believe, and it is the part of God's grace to assist." They asserted the sufficiency of Christ's grace for all, and that every one

according to his own will obeyed or rejected the invitation, while God equally wished and equally aided all men to be saved. . . . The entire system thus formed is a half-way house containing elements of error and elements of truth, and not at all differing from the Arminianism which, after the resuscitation of the doctrines of grace by the Reformers, diffused itself in the very same way through the different Churches.[5]

Calvinism, the Theology of the Reformation

The leaders of the Protestant Reformation of the sixteenth century rejected Pelagianism and Semi-Pelagianism on the ground that both systems were unscriptural. Like Augustine, the Reformers held to the doctrines of the sovereignty of God, the total depravity of man, and unconditional election. As Boettner shows, they stood together in their view of predestination:

It was taught not only by Calvin, but by Luther, Zwingli, Melanchthon (although Melanchthon later retreated toward the Semi-Pelagian position), by Bullinger, Bucer, and all of the outstanding leaders in the Reformation. While differing on some other points they agreed on this doctrine of Predestination and taught it with emphasis. Luther's chief work, *The Bondage of the Will*, shows that he went into the doctrine as heartily as did Calvin himself.[6]

5. George Smeaton, *The Doctrine of the Holy Spirit*, 2d ed. (1889; reprint, London: Banner of Truth, 1974), 338–39. Italics and capitalizations are his. Semi-Pelagianism was repudiated by the Synod of Orange in A.D. 529, just as Arminianism was repudiated by the Synod of Dort almost eleven hundred years later.

6. Loraine Boettner, *The Reformed Doctrine of Predestination* (Philadelphia: Presbyterian and Reformed, 1963), 1.

Packer states:

All the leading Protestant theologians of the first epoch of the Reformation, stood on precisely the same ground here. On other points, they had their differences; but in asserting the helplessness of man in sin, and the sovereignty of God in grace, they were entirely at one. To all of them, these doctrines were the very life-blood of the Christian faith. . . . To the Reformers, the crucial question was not simply, whether God justifies believers without works of law. It was the broader question, whether sinners are wholly helpless in their sin, and whether God is to be thought of as saving them by free, unconditional, invincible grace, not only justifying them for Christ's sake when they come to faith, but also raising them from the death of sin by His quickening Spirit in order to bring them to faith. Here was the crucial issue: whether God is the author, not merely of justification, but also of faith; whether, in the last analysis, Christianity is a religion of utter reliance on God for salvation and all things necessary to it, or of self-reliance and self-effort.[7]

Thus, it is evident that the five points of Calvinism, drawn up by the Synod of Dort in 1619, were by no means a new sys-

---

7. James I. Packer and O. R. Johnston, "Historical and Theological Introduction," in *The Bondage of the Will*, by Martin Luther (Westwood, N.J.: Revell, 1957), 58–59. In speaking of the English Reformation, Buis shows that "the advocates of that Reformation were definitely Calvinistic." To substantiate this, he quotes the following from Fisher: "The Anglican Church agreed with the Protestant Churches on the continent on the subject of predestination. On this subject, for a long period, the Protestants generally were united in opinion. The leaders of the English Reformation, from the time when the death of Henry VIII placed them firmly upon Protestant grounds, profess the doctrine of absolute as distinguished from conditional predestination." Harry Buis, *Historic Protestantism and Predestination* (Philadelphia: Presbyterian and Reformed, 1958), 87.

tem of theology. On the contrary, as Dr. Wyllie asserts of the Synod, "It met at a great crisis and it was called to review, re-examine and authenticate over again, in the second generation since the rise of the Reformation, that body of truth and system of doctrine which that great movement had published to the world."[8]

THE DIFFERENCE BETWEEN CALVINISM AND ARMINIANISM

The issues involved in this historic controversy are indeed grave, for they vitally affect the Christian's concept of God, of sin, and of salvation. Packer, in contrasting these two systems, is certainly correct in asserting,

> The difference between them is not primarily one of emphasis, but of content. One proclaims a God Who saves; the other speaks of a God Who enables man to save himself. One view [Calvinism] presents the three great acts of the Holy Trinity for the recovering of lost mankind—election by the Father, redemption by the Son, calling by the Spirit—as directed towards the same persons, and as securing their salvation infallibly. The other view [Arminianism] gives each act a different reference (the objects of redemption being all mankind, of calling, those who hear the gospel, and of election, those hearers who respond), and denies that any man's salvation is secured by any of them. The two theologies thus conceive the plan of salvation in quite different terms. One makes salvation depend on the work of God,

8. Quoted by Warburton, *Calvinism*, 58. Smeaton says of the work of the Synod of Dort that "it may be questioned whether anything more valuable as an ecclesiastical testimony for the doctrines of sovereign, special, efficacious grace was ever prepared on this important theme since the days of the apostles" (Smeaton, *The Doctrine of the Holy Spirit*, 359).

the other on a work of man; one regards faith as part of
God's gift of salvation, the other as man's own contribution to salvation; one gives all the glory of saving
believers to God, the other divides the praise between
God, Who, so to speak, built the machinery of salvation,
and man, who by believing operated it. Plainly, these
differences are important, and the permanent value of
the "five points," as a summary of Calvinism, is that they
make clear the points at which, and the extent to which,
these two conceptions are at variance.[9]

THE *ONE* POINT OF CALVINISM

While recognizing the permanent value of the five points as
a summary of Calvinism, Packer warns against simply equating
Calvinism with the five points. He gives several excellent reasons
why such an equation is incorrect, one of which we quote:

The very act of setting out Calvinistic soteriology [the
doctrine of salvation] in the form of five distinct points
(a number due, as we saw, merely to the fact that there
were five Arminian points for the Synod of Dort to
answer) tends to obscure the organic character of
Calvinistic thought on this subject. For the five points,
though separately stated, are really inseparable. They
hang together; you cannot reject one without rejecting
them all, at least in the sense in which the Synod meant
them. For to Calvinism there is really only *one* point to
be made in the field of soteriology: the point that *God
saves sinners. God*—the Triune Jehovah, Father, Son and
Spirit; three Persons working together in sovereign wisdom, power and love to achieve the salvation of a chosen people, the Father electing, the Son fulfilling the

9. Packer, "Introductory Essay," 4–5.

Father's will by redeeming, the Spirit executing the purpose of Father and Son by renewing. *Saves*—does everything, first to last, that is involved in bringing man from death in sin to life in glory: plans, achieves and communicates redemption, calls and keeps, justifies, sanctifies, glorifies. *Sinners*—men as God finds them, guilty, vile, helpless, powerless, unable to lift a finger to do God's will or better their spiritual lot. *God saves sinners*—and the force of this confession may not be weakened by disrupting the unity of the work of the Trinity, or by dividing the achievement of salvation between God and man and making the decisive part man's own, or by soft-pedalling the sinner's inability so as to allow him to share the praise of his salvation with his Saviour. This is the one point of Calvinistic soteriology which the "five points" are concerned to establish and Arminianism in all its forms to deny: namely, that sinners do not save themselves in any sense at all, but that salvation, first and last, whole and entire, past, present and future, is of the Lord, to whom be glory for ever; amen.[10]

This brings to completion Part One of our survey. No attempt whatsoever has been made in this section to prove the truthfulness of the Calvinistic doctrines. Our sole purpose has been to give a brief history of the system and to explain its contents. We are now ready to consider its biblical support.

10. Ibid., 6. Italics are his.

Part Two

THE FIVE POINTS DEFENDED: THEIR BIBLICAL SUPPORT

The question of supreme importance is not how the system under consideration came to be formulated in five points, or why it was named Calvinism, but rather *whether it is supported by Scripture.* The final court of appeal for determining the validity of any theological system is the inspired, authoritative Word of God. If Calvinism can be verified by clear and explicit declarations of Scripture, then it must be received by Christians; if not, it must be rejected. For this reason, biblical passages are given below in support of the five points.

After each point has been introduced, some of the more important verses in which it is taught are quoted (from the ESV). In each case, the italics within the verses are ours. Apart from the remarks contained in the headings under which the verses are given, there are no explanatory comments as to their meaning. This procedure was necessary because of the limited design of this introductory survey. To compensate for this, we have recommended a number of works in Part Three which deal with these as well as with many other passages of Scripture related to Calvinism.

Although the five points are dealt with below under separate headings, and texts are classified in support of each of them individually, they must not be evaluated on a purely individual basis. For these five doctrines are not presented in the Bible as separate and independent units of truth. On the contrary, in the biblical message they are woven into one harmonious, interrelated system in which God's plan for recovering lost sinners is marvelously displayed. In fact, these doctrines are so inseparably connected that no one of them can be fully appreciated unless it is properly related to, and viewed in light of, the other four; for *they mutually explain and support one another.* To judge these doctrines individually, without relating each to the others, would be like attempting to evaluate one of Rembrandt's paintings by looking at only one color at a time and never viewing the work as a whole. Do not, therefore, merely judge the biblical evidence for each point separately; rather, consider carefully the collective value of the evidence when these five doctrines are viewed together as a system. When thus properly correlated, they form a fivefold cord of unbreakable strength.

TOTAL DEPRAVITY OR TOTAL INABILITY

The view one takes concerning salvation will be determined, to a large extent, by the view one takes concerning sin and its effects on human nature. It is not surprising, therefore, that the first article dealt with in the Calvinistic system is the biblical doctrine of total inability or total depravity.

When Calvinists speak of man as being totally depraved, they mean that man's nature is corrupt, perverse, and sinful throughout. The adjective "total" does not mean that each sinner is as totally or completely corrupt in his actions and thoughts as it is possible for him to be. Instead, the word "total" is used to indicate that the *whole* of man's being has been affected by sin. The corruption extends to *every part* of man, his body and soul; sin has affected all (the totality) of man's faculties—his mind, his will, etc.

As a result of this inborn corruption, the natural man is totally unable to do anything spiritually good; thus, Calvinists speak of man's "total inability." The inability intended by this terminology is *spiritual inability;* it means that the sinner is so spiritually bankrupt that *he can do nothing pertaining to his salvation.* It is quite evident that many unsaved people, when judged by man's standards, do possess admirable qualities and do perform virtuous acts. But in the spiritual realm, when judged by God's standards, the unsaved sinner is incapable of good. The natural man is enslaved to sin; he is a child of Satan, rebellious toward God, blind to truth, corrupt, and unable to save himself or to prepare himself for salvation. In short, the unregenerate man is *dead in sin,* and *his will is enslaved* to his evil nature.

Man did not come from the hands of his Creator in this depraved, corrupt condition. God made Adam upright; there was no evil whatsoever in his nature. Originally, Adam's will was free from the dominion of sin; he was under no natural compulsion to choose evil, but through his fall he brought spiritual death upon himself and all his posterity. He thereby plunged himself and the entire race into spiritual ruin and lost for himself and his descendants the ability to make right choices in the spiritual realm. His descendants are still free to choose— every man makes choices throughout life—but inasmuch as Adam's offspring are born with sinful natures, they do not have the *ability* to choose spiritual good over evil. Consequently, man's will is no longer free (i.e., free from the dominion of sin) as Adam's will was free before the Fall. Instead, man's will, as the result of inherited depravity, is in bondage to his sinful nature.

The Westminster Confession of Faith gives a clear, concise statement of this doctrine. "Man, by his fall into a state of sin, hath wholly lost all ability of will to any spiritual good accompanying salvation: so as, a natural man, being altogether averse from that good, and dead in sin, is not able, by his own strength, to convert himself, or to prepare himself thereunto."[1]

Spiritual Deadness

As the result of Adam's transgression, men are born in sin and by nature are spiritually dead; therefore, if they are to become God's children and enter His kingdom, they must be born anew of the spirit.

1. When Adam was placed in the Garden of Eden, he was warned not to eat of the fruit of the tree of the knowledge of good and evil on the threat of immediate *spiritual* death.

> GENESIS 2:16–17: "And the LORD God commanded the man, saying, 'You may surely eat of every tree of the garden, but of the tree of the knowledge of good and evil you shall not eat, for in the day that you eat of it you *shall surely die.'*"

2. Adam disobeyed and ate of the forbidden fruit (Genesis 3:1–7); consequently, he brought spiritual death upon himself and upon the race.

> ROMANS 5:12: "Therefore, just as sin came into the world through one man [Adam, see vs. 14], and *death through sin,* and so death *spread to all men* because *all sinned . . .*"

> EPHESIANS 2:1–3: "And you were *dead in the trespasses and sins* in which you once walked, following the course of this world, following the prince of the power of the air, the spirit that is now at work in the sons of disobedience—among whom we all once lived in the passions of our flesh, carrying out the desires of the body and the

1. Chap. IX, sect. 3.

mind, and we were *by nature* children of wrath, like the rest of mankind."

COLOSSIANS 2:13: "And you, who were *dead* in your trespasses and the uncircumcision of your flesh, God *made alive* together with him, having forgiven us all our trespasses."

3. David confessed that he, as well as all other men, was born in sin.

PSALM 51:5: "Behold, I was *brought forth in iniquity,* and *in sin* did my mother conceive me."

PSALM 58:3: "The wicked are estranged from the womb; they go astray from birth, speaking lies."

4. Because men are born in sin and are by nature spiritually dead, Jesus taught that men must be born anew if they are to enter God's kingdom.

JOHN 3:5–7: "Jesus answered, 'Truly, truly, I say to you, unless one is born of water and the Spirit, he cannot *enter* the kingdom of God. That which is born of the flesh is flesh, and that which is born of the Spirit is spirit. Do not marvel that I said to you, *"You must be born again."'"*

Compare John 1:12–13.

Darkened Minds and Corrupt Hearts

As the result of the Fall, men are blind and deaf to spiritual truth. Their minds are darkened by sin; their hearts are corrupt and evil.

GENESIS 6:5: "The LORD saw that the wickedness of man was great in the earth, and that *every intention of the thoughts of his heart was only evil continually.*"

GENESIS 8:21: "The intention of man's *heart* is *evil* from his youth."

ECCLESIASTES 9:3: "The *hearts* of the children of man are *full of evil,* and madness is in their hearts while they live."

JEREMIAH 17:9: "The *heart is deceitful above all things, and desperately sick;* who can understand it?"

MARK 7:21–23: "For from within, *out of the heart of man,* come evil thoughts, sexual immorality, theft, murder, adultery, coveting, wickedness, deceit, sensuality, envy, slander, pride, foolishness. All these evil things come from within, and they defile a person."

JOHN 3:19: "And this is the judgment: the light has come into the world, and *people loved the darkness* rather than the light because their deeds were evil."

ROMANS 8:7–8: "For the *mind* that is set on the flesh is hostile to God, for *it* does not submit to God's law; indeed, *it cannot.* Those who are in the flesh *cannot please God.*"

1 CORINTHIANS 2:14: "The natural person does not accept the things of the Spirit of God, for they are folly to him, and *he is not able to understand them* because they are spiritually discerned."

EPHESIANS 4:17–19: "Now this I say and testify in the Lord, that you must no longer walk as the Gentiles do, in the futility of their minds. They are *darkened in their understanding,* alienated from the life of God because of the ignorance that is in them, *due to their hardness of heart.* They have become callous and have given themselves up to sensuality, greedy to practice every kind of impurity."

EPHESIANS 5:8: "... for at one time you were *darkness,* but now you are light in the Lord."

TITUS 1:15: "To the pure, all things are pure, but to the defiled and unbelieving, nothing is pure; *but both their minds and their consciences are defiled.*"

Bondage to Sin and Satan

Before sinners are born into God's kingdom through the regenerating power of the Spirit, they are children of the devil and under his control; they are slaves to sin.

JOHN 8:44: "You are of *your father the devil,* and *your will* is to do your father's desires."

EPHESIANS 2:1–2: "And you were dead in the trespasses and sins in which you once walked, following the course of this world, *following the prince of the power of the air,* the spirit that is now at work in the sons of disobedience."

2 TIMOTHY 2:25–26: "God may perhaps grant them repentance leading to a knowledge of the truth, and they may escape from *the snare of the devil,* after being *captured by him to do his will.*"

1 JOHN 3:10: "By this it is evident who are the children of God, and who are the *children of the devil:* whoever does not practice righteousness is not of God, nor is the one who does not love his brother."

1 JOHN 5:19: "We know that we are from God, and the whole world lies *in the power of the evil one.*"

JOHN 8:34: "Jesus answered them, 'Truly, truly, I say to you, everyone who commits sin is *a slave to sin.*'"

ROMANS 6:20: "When you were slaves of sin, you were free in regard to righteousness."

Titus 3:3: "For we ourselves were once foolish, disobedient, led astray, *slaves* to various passions and pleasures, passing our days in malice and envy, hated by others and hating one another."

A Universal Bondage

The reign of sin is universal; all men are under its power. Consequently, none is righteous—not even one!

2 Chronicles 6:36: ". . . for there is *no one* who does not sin."

Compare 1 Kings 8:46.

Job 15:14–16: "What is man, that he can be pure? Or he who is born of a woman, that he can be righteous? Behold, God puts no trust in his holy ones, and the heavens are not pure in his sight; how much less one *who is abominable and corrupt,* a man who drinks injustice like water!"

Psalm 130:3: "If you, O Lord, should mark iniquities, O Lord, *who could stand?*"

Psalm 143:2: "Enter not into judgment with your servant, for *no one living* is righteous before you."

Proverbs 20:9: "*Who* can say, 'I have made my heart pure; I am clean from my sin'?"

Ecclesiastes 7:20: "Surely there is *not a righteous man on earth* who does good and never sins."

Ecclesiastes 7:29: "See, this alone I found, that God made man upright, but *they* have sought out many schemes."

ISAIAH 53:6: *"All* we like sheep have gone astray; we have turned every one to his own way."

ISAIAH 64:6: "We have *all* become like one who is unclean, and all our righteous deeds are like a polluted garment. We all fade like a leaf, and our iniquities, like the wind, take us away."

ROMANS 3:9–12: "What then? Are we Jews any better off? No, not at all. For we have already charged that *all*, both Jews and Greeks, are *under the power of sin*, as it is written: '*None* is righteous, no, *not one; no one* understands; *no one* seeks for God. *All* have turned aside; together they have become worthless; *no one* does good, *not even one.'*"

JAMES 3:2, 8: "For we *all* stumble in many ways, and if anyone does not stumble in what he says, he is a perfect man, able also to bridle his whole body. . . . *no human being* can tame the tongue. It is a restless evil, full of deadly poison."

1 JOHN 1:8, 10: "If we say we have no sin, we deceive ourselves, and the truth is not in us. . . . If we say we have not sinned, we make him a liar, and his word is not in us."

Inability to Change

Men left in their dead state are unable of themselves to repent, to believe the gospel, or to come to Christ. They have no power within themselves to change their nature or to prepare themselves for salvation.

JOB 14:4: "Who can bring a clean thing out of an unclean? There is *not one.*"

JEREMIAH 13:23: "Can the Ethiopian change his skin or the leopard his spots? Then also you can do good who are *accustomed to do evil.*"

MATTHEW 7:16–18: "You will recognize them by their fruits. Are grapes gathered from thornbushes, or figs from thistles? So, every healthy tree bears good fruit, but the diseased tree bears bad fruit. A healthy tree cannot bear bad fruit, *nor can a diseased tree bear good fruit.*"

MATTHEW 12:33: "Either make the tree good and its fruit good, or make the tree bad and its fruit bad, for the tree is known by its fruit."

JOHN 6:44: *"No one can come to me unless* the Father who sent me *draws him.* And I will raise him up on the last day."

JOHN 6:65: "And he said, 'This is why I told you that *no one can come to me unless it is granted him* by the Father.'"

ROMANS 11:35–36: "'Or *who has given a gift to him* that he might be repaid?' For *from him* and *through him* and *to him* are all things. To *him* be glory forever. Amen."

1 CORINTHIANS 2:14: *"The natural person* does not accept the things of the Spirit of God, for they are folly to him; and *he is not able to understand them* because they are spiritually discerned."

1 CORINTHIANS 4:7: "For who sees *anything different in you?* What do you have that you did not receive? If then you received it, *why do you boast as if you did not receive it?"*

2 CORINTHIANS 3:5: "Not that we are *sufficient in ourselves* to claim anything as coming from us, but our sufficiency is *from* God."

For further biblical confirmation that men are unable of themselves to do anything to gain salvation, see the Scriptures given below under "The Efficacious Call of the Spirit or Irresistible

Grace." Note especially those verses which state that *God* gives faith, grants repentance, creates a new heart within the sinner, and does similar things.

UNCONDITIONAL ELECTION

Because of Adam's transgression, his descendants enter the world as guilty, lost sinners. As fallen creatures, they have no desire to have fellowship with the Creator. He is holy, just, and good, whereas they are sinful, perverse, and corrupt. Left to their own choices, they inevitably follow the god of this world and do the will of their father, the devil. Consequently, men have cut themselves off from the Lord of heaven and have forfeited all rights to His love and favor. It would have been perfectly just for God to have left all men in their sin and misery and to have shown mercy to none. God was under no obligation whatsoever to provide salvation for anyone. It is in this context that the Bible sets forth the doctrine of election.

The doctrine of election declares that God, before the foundation of the world, chose certain individuals from among the fallen members of Adam's race to be the objects of His undeserved favor. These, and these only, He purposed to save. God could have chosen to save all men (for He had the power and authority to do so) or He could have chosen to save none (for He was under no obligation to show mercy to any)—but He did neither. Instead, He chose to save some and to exclude others. His eternal choice of particular sinners for salvation was not based upon any foreseen act or response on the part of those selected, but was based solely on His own good pleasure and sovereign will. Thus, election was not determined by, or conditioned upon, anything that men would do, but resulted entirely from God's self-determined purpose.

Those who were not chosen for salvation were passed by and left to their own evil devices and choices. It is not within the creature's jurisdiction to call into question the justice of the Creator for not choosing everyone for salvation. It is enough to know that the Judge of the earth has done right. It should, however, be kept in mind that if God had not graciously chosen a people for Himself and sovereignly determined to provide salvation for them and apply it to them, none would be saved. The fact that He did this for some, to the exclusion of others, is in no way unfair to the latter group, unless of course one maintains that God was under obligation to provide salvation for sinners—a position which the Bible utterly rejects.

The doctrine of election should not only be viewed against the backdrop of human depravity and guilt, but should also be studied in connection with the eternal covenant or agreement made between the members of the Godhead. For it was in the execution of this covenant that the Father chose out of the world of lost sinners a definite number of individuals and gave them to the Son to be His people. The Son, under the terms of this compact, agreed to do all that was necessary to save those "chosen" and "given" to Him by the Father. The Spirit's part in the execution of this covenant was to apply to the elect the salvation secured for them by the Son.

Election, therefore, is but one aspect (though an important aspect) of the saving purpose of the triune God, and thus must not be viewed as salvation. For the act of election itself saved no one; what it did was to mark out certain individuals for salvation. Consequently, the doctrine of election must not be divorced from the doctrines of human guilt, redemption, and regeneration, or else it will be distorted and misrepresented. In other words, if the Father's act of election is to be kept in its proper biblical balance and correctly understood, it must be related to the redeeming work of the Son, who gave Himself to save the elect, and to the renewing work of the Spirit, who brings the elect to faith in Christ.

A Chosen People

There are general statements in Scripture that God has an elect people, and that He predestined them to salvation, and thus to eternal life.

DEUTERONOMY 10:14–15: "Behold, to the LORD your God belong heaven and the heaven of heavens, the earth with all that is in it. Yet *the LORD set his heart in love* on your fathers and *chose* their offspring after them, you above all peoples, as you are this day."

PSALM 33:12: "Blessed is the nation whose God is the LORD, the people whom he has *chosen* as his heritage!"

PSALM 65:4: "Blessed is the one you *choose* and bring near, to dwell in your courts! We shall be satisfied with the goodness of your house, the holiness of your temple!"

PSALM 106:5: ". . . that I may look upon the prosperity of your *chosen ones,* that I may rejoice in the gladness of your nation, that I may glory with your inheritance."

HAGGAI 2:23: "On that day, declares the LORD of hosts, I will take you, O Zerubbabel my servant, the son of Shealtiel, declares the LORD, and make you like a signet ring, for I have *chosen* you, declares the LORD of hosts."

MATTHEW 11:27: "No one knows the Father except the Son and anyone to whom the Son *chooses* to reveal him."

MATTHEW 22:14: "For many are called, but few are *chosen.*"

MATTHEW 24:22, 24, 31: "And if those days had not been cut short, no human being would be saved. But for the sake of *the elect* those days will be cut short. . . . For false christs and false prophets will arise and perform great signs and wonders, so as to lead astray, if possible, even *the elect.* . . . And he will send out his angels with a loud trumpet call, and they will gather *his elect* from the four winds, from one end of heaven to the other."

LUKE 18:7: "And will not God give justice to *his elect,* who cry to him day and night?"

ROMANS 8:28–30: "And we know that for those who love God all things work together for good, for those who are *called according to his purpose.* For those whom he foreknew he also *predestined* to be conformed to the image of his Son, in order that he might be the firstborn among many brothers. And those whom he *predestined* he also called, and those whom he called he also justified, and those whom he justified he also glorified."

ROMANS 8:33: "Who shall bring any charge against *God's elect?*"

ROMANS 11:28: "As regards the gospel, they are enemies of God for your sake. But as regards *election,* they are beloved for the sake of their forefathers."

COLOSSIANS 3:12: "Put on then, as *God's chosen ones,* holy and beloved . . ."

1 THESSALONIANS 5:9: "For God has not *destined* us for wrath, but *to obtain salvation* through our Lord Jesus Christ."

TITUS 1:1: "Paul, a servant of God and an apostle of Jesus Christ, for the sake of the faith of *God's elect* and their knowledge of the truth, which accords with godliness."

1 PETER 1:1–2: "To those who are *elect* exiles . . . *according to the foreknowledge* of God the Father, in the sanctification of the Spirit, for obedience to Jesus Christ and for sprinkling with his blood . . ."

1 PETER 2:8–9: "They stumble because they disobey the word, as they were *destined* to do. But you are a *chosen* race, a royal priesthood, a holy nation, a people for his own possession, that you may proclaim the excellencies of him who *called* you out of darkness into his marvelous light."

REVELATION 17:14: "They will make war on the Lamb, and the Lamb will conquer them, for he is Lord of lords and King of kings, and those with him are *called* and *chosen* and faithful."

Election Not Based on Foreseen Responses

Before the foundation of the world, God chose particular individuals for salvation. His selection was *not based upon any foreseen response or act* performed by those chosen. Faith and good works are the *result*, not the *cause*, of God's choice.

1. God did the choosing.

MARK 13:20: "And if the Lord had not cut short the days, no human being would be saved. But for the sake of *the elect, whom he chose,* he shortened the days."

See also 1 Thessalonians 1:4 and 2 Thessalonians 2:13, quoted below.

2. God's choice was made before the foundation of the world.

EPHESIANS 1:4: ". . . even as he *chose* us in him *before the foundation of the world,* that we should be holy and blameless before him."

See 2 Thessalonians 2:13, 2 Timothy 1:9, Revelation 13:8, and Revelation 17:8, quoted below.

3. God chose particular individuals for salvation—their names were written in the book of life before the foundation of the world.

> REVELATION 13:8: "And all who dwell on earth will worship it, everyone whose *name* has not been *written before the foundation of the world* in the book of life of the Lamb that was slain."

> REVELATION 17:8: "And the dwellers on earth whose *names* have not been *written* in the book of life *from the foundation of the world* will marvel to see the beast, because it was and is not and is to come."

4. God's choice was not based upon any foreseen merit residing in those whom He chose, nor was it based on any foreseen good works performed by them.

> ROMANS 9:11–13: "Though they were *not yet born and had done nothing either good or bad*—in order that God's purpose of *election* might continue, not because of works but because of his call—she was told, 'The older will serve the younger.' As it is written, 'Jacob I loved, but Esau I hated.'"

> ROMANS 9:16: "So then it depends *not on human will or exertion,* but on *God, who has mercy.*"

> ROMANS 10:20: "I have been found by those who did not seek me; I have shown myself to those who did not ask for me."

> 1 CORINTHIANS 1:27–29: "But *God chose* what is *foolish* in the world to shame the wise; *God chose* what is *weak* in the world to shame the strong; *God chose* what is *low and despised* in the world, even things that are not, to bring to nothing things that are, *so that no human being might boast in the presence of God.*"

2 TIMOTHY 1:9: ". . . who saved us and called us to a holy calling, not because of *our works* but because of *his own purpose* and *grace*, which he gave us in Christ Jesus before the ages began."

5. Good works are the result, not the ground, of predestination.

EPHESIANS 2:10: "For we are his workmanship, created in Christ Jesus *for good works*, which *God prepared* beforehand, that we should walk in them."

JOHN 15:16: "You did not choose me, but *I chose you* and *appointed you* that you should go and bear fruit and that your fruit should abide, so that whatever you ask the Father in my name, he may give it to you."

6. God's choice was not based upon foreseen faith. Faith is the result and therefore the evidence of God's election, not the cause or ground of His choice.

ACTS 13:48: "And when the Gentiles heard this, they began rejoicing and glorifying the word of the Lord, and as many as were *appointed* to eternal life *believed.*"

ACTS 18:27: "He greatly helped those who *through grace had believed.*"

PHILIPPIANS 1:29: "For it has been *granted* to you that for the sake of Christ you should not only *believe* in him but also suffer for his sake."

PHILIPPIANS 2:12–13: "Therefore, my beloved, as you have always obeyed, so now, not only as in my presence but much more in my absence, work out your own salvation with fear and trembling, *for it is God who works in you, both to will and to work for his good pleasure.*"

1 THESSALONIANS 1:4–5: "For we *know,* brothers loved by
God, that *he has chosen you, because our gospel came to
you* not only in word, but also *in power* and *in the Holy
Spirit* and *with full conviction."*

2 THESSALONIANS 2:13–14: *"God chose you as the first fruits
to be saved, through sanctification* by the Spirit and *belief
in the truth.* To this he called you through our gospel, so
that you may obtain the glory of our Lord Jesus Christ."

JAMES 2:5: "Has not *God chosen* those who are poor in
the world *to be rich in faith and heirs of the kingdom,*
which he has promised to those who love him?"

See appendix C, "The Meaning of 'Foreknew' in Romans
8:29." See also those verses quoted below under "The
Efficacious Call of the Spirit or Irresistible Grace,"
which teach that faith and repentance are the gifts of
God and are wrought in the soul by the regenerating
power of the Holy Spirit.

7. It is by faith and good works that one confirms his calling
and election.

2 PETER 1:5–11: "For this very reason, make every effort
to supplement your faith with virtue, and virtue with
knowledge, and knowledge with self-control, and self-
control with steadfastness, and steadfastness with godliness, and godliness with brotherly affection, and brotherly affection with love. For if these qualities are yours
and are increasing, they keep you from being ineffec-
tive or unfruitful in the knowledge of our Lord Jesus
Christ. For whoever lacks these qualities is so near-
sighted that he is blind, having forgotten that he was
cleansed from his former sins. Therefore, brothers, be
all the more diligent to *make your calling and election
sure,* for if you practice these qualities you will never

fall. For in this way there will be richly provided for you an entrance into the eternal kingdom of our Lord and Savior Jesus Christ."

Election Precedes Salvation

Election is not salvation, but is *for* salvation. Just as the president-elect does not become the president of the United States *until* he is inaugurated, so those chosen for salvation are not saved *until* they are regenerated by the Spirit and justified by faith in Christ.

> ROMANS 11:7: "What then? Israel failed to obtain what it was seeking. *The elect obtained it,* but the rest were hardened."

> 2 TIMOTHY 2:10: "Therefore I endure everything for the sake of *the elect,* that they also *may obtain the salvation* that is in Christ Jesus with eternal glory."

> See Acts 13:48, 1 Thessalonians 1:4, and 2 Thessalonians 2:13–14, quoted above. Compare Ephesians 1:4 with Romans 16:7. In Ephesians 1:4, Paul shows that men were *chosen* "in Christ" before the world began. From Romans 16:7, it is clear that men are not *actually* "in Christ" until their conversion.

Sovereign Mercy

Election was based on the sovereign, distinguishing mercy of almighty God. It was not man's will, but God's will, that determined which sinners would be shown mercy and saved.

> EXODUS 33:19: "I will be gracious to whom I will be gracious, and will show mercy on whom I will show mercy."

> DEUTERONOMY 7:6–7: "For you are a people holy to the LORD your God. The LORD your God *has chosen* you to

be a people for his treasured possession, out of all the peoples who are on the face of the earth. It was not because you were more in number than any other people that the LORD set his love on you and *chose you*, for you were the fewest of all peoples."

MATTHEW 20:15: "Am I not allowed to do what *I choose* with what belongs to me?"

ROMANS 9:10–24: "And not only so, but also when Rebecca had conceived children by one man, our forefather Isaac, though they were not yet born and had done nothing either good or bad—in order that God's purpose of election might continue, not because of works but because of his call—she was told, 'The older will serve the younger.' As it is written, 'Jacob I loved, but Esau I hated.' What shall we say then? Is there injustice on God's part? By no means! For he says to Moses, *'I will have mercy on whom I have mercy, and I will have compassion on whom I have compassion.'* So then it depends not on human will or exertion, but *on God, who has mercy.* For the Scripture says to Pharaoh, 'For this very purpose I have raised you up, that I might show my power in you, and that my name might be proclaimed in all the earth.' So then he has mercy *on whomever he wills,* and he hardens whomever he wills. You will say to me then, 'Why does he still find fault? For who can resist his will?' But who are you, O man, to answer back to God? Will what is molded say to its molder, 'Why have you made me like this?' *Has the potter no right over the clay,* to make out of the same lump one *vessel for honored use* and another for dishonorable use? What if God, desiring to show his wrath and to make known his power, has endured with much patience vessels of wrath prepared for destruction, in order to make known the riches of his glory for *vessels of mercy, which he has pre-*

pared beforehand for glory—even us whom he has called, not from the Jews only but also from the Gentiles?"

ROMANS 11:4–6: "But what is God's reply to him? 'I have kept for myself seven thousand men who have not bowed the knee to Baal.' So too at the present time there is a remnant, *chosen by grace*. But if it is by grace, it is no longer on the basis of works; otherwise grace would no longer be grace."

Compare 1 Kings 19:10, 18.

ROMANS 11:33–36: "Oh, the depth of the riches and wisdom and knowledge of God! How unsearchable are his judgments and how inscrutable his ways! 'For who has known the mind of the Lord, or who has been his counselor?' 'Or who has given a gift to him that he might be repaid?' For from him and through him and to him are all things. To him be glory forever. Amen."

EPHESIANS 1:5: "He predestined us for adoption through Jesus Christ, according to the purpose of his will."

Sovereignty over All Things

The doctrine of election is but a part of the much broader biblical doctrine of God's absolute sovereignty. The Scriptures teach not only that God predestined certain individuals to eternal life, but that all events, both small and great, come about as the result of God's eternal decree. The Lord God rules over heaven and earth with absolute control; nothing comes to pass apart from His eternal purpose.

1 CHRONICLES 29:10–12: "Therefore David blessed the LORD in the presence of all the assembly. And David said: 'Blessed are you, O LORD, the God of Israel our father, forever and ever. Yours, O LORD, is the greatness and the power and the glory and the victory and the majesty, for

all that is in the heavens and in the earth is yours. Yours is the kingdom, O LORD, and you are exalted as head above all. Both riches and honor come from you, and you rule over all. In your hand are power and might, and in your hand it is to make great and to give strength to all.'"

JOB 42:1–2: "Then Job answered the LORD and said: 'I know that you can do all things, and that no purpose of yours can be thwarted.'"

PSALM 115:3: "Our God is in the heavens; he does all that he pleases."

PSALM 135:6: "Whatever the LORD pleases, he does, in heaven and on earth, in the seas and all deeps."

ISAIAH 14:24, 27: "The LORD of hosts has sworn: 'As I have planned, so shall it be, and as I have purposed, so shall it stand. . . . For the LORD of hosts has purposed, and who will annul it? His hand is stretched out, and who will turn it back?'"

ISAIAH 46:9–11: "Remember the former things of old; for I am God, and there is no other; I am God, and there is none like me, declaring the end from the beginning and from ancient times things not yet done, saying, 'My counsel shall stand, and I will accomplish all my purpose,' calling a bird of prey from the east, the man of my counsel from a far country. I have spoken, and I will bring it to pass; I have purposed, and I will do it."

ISAIAH 55:11: ". . . so shall my word be that goes out from my mouth; it shall not return to me empty, but it shall accomplish that which I purpose, and shall succeed in the thing for which I sent it."

JEREMIAH 32:17: "Ah, Lord GOD! It is you who has made the heavens and the earth by your great power and by your outstretched arm! Nothing is too hard for you."

DANIEL 4:35: "All the inhabitants of the earth are accounted as nothing, and he does according to his will among the host of heaven and among the inhabitants of the earth; and none can stay his hand or say to him, 'What have you done?'"

MATTHEW 19:26: "With God all things are possible."

PARTICULAR REDEMPTION OR LIMITED ATONEMENT

As was observed above, election itself saved no one; it only marked out particular sinners for salvation. Those *chosen* by the Father and given to the Son had to be *redeemed* if they were to be saved. In order to secure their redemption, Jesus Christ came into the world and took upon Himself human nature so that He might identify Himself with His people and act as their legal representative or substitute. Christ, acting on behalf of His people, kept God's law perfectly and thereby worked out a perfect righteousness which is imputed or credited to them the moment they are brought to faith in Him. Through what He did, they are constituted righteous before God. They are also freed from all guilt and condemnation as the result of what Christ suffered for them. Through His substitutionary sacrifice, He endured the penalty of their sins and thus removed their guilt forever. Consequently, when His people are joined to Him by faith, they are credited with perfect righteousness and are freed from all guilt and condemnation. They are saved, not because of what they themselves have done or will do, but solely on the ground of Christ's redeeming work.

Historical or mainline Calvinism has consistently maintained that Christ's redeeming work was definite in *design* and *accomplishment*—that it was intended to render complete satisfaction for certain specified sinners, and that it actually secured salvation for these individuals and for no one else. The salvation which Christ earned for His people includes everything involved in bringing them into a right relationship with God, including the gifts of faith and repentance. Christ did not die simply to make it possible for God to pardon sinners. Neither does God leave it up to sinners to decide whether or not Christ's work will be effective. On the contrary, all for whom Christ sacrificed Himself will be saved infallibly. Redemption, therefore, was designed to bring to pass God's purpose of election.

All Calvinists agree that Christ's obedience and suffering were of infinite value, and that if God had so willed, the satisfaction rendered by Christ would have saved every member of the human race. It would have required no more obedience, nor any greater suffering, for Christ to have secured salvation for every man, woman, and child who ever lived than it did for Him to secure salvation for the elect only. But He came into the world to represent and save only those given to Him by the Father. Thus, Christ's saving work was limited in that it was designed to save some and not others, but it was not limited in value, for it was of infinite worth and would have secured salvation for everyone if this had been God's intention.

The Arminians also place a limitation on the atoning work of Christ, but one of a much different nature. They hold that Christ's saving work was designed to make possible the salvation of all men on the condition that they believe, but that Christ's death *in itself* did not actually secure or guarantee salvation for anyone.

Since not all men will be saved as the result of Christ's redeeming work, a limitation must be admitted. Either the atonement was limited in that it was *designed to secure* salvation for certain sinners, but not for others, or it was limited in that it was not intended to secure salvation for any, but was *designed only to make it possible* for God to pardon sinners on the condition that they believe. In other words, one must limit its design either in *extent* (it was not intended for all) or in *effectiveness* (it did not secure salvation for any). As Boettner so aptly observes, for the Calvinist, the atonement "is like a narrow bridge which goes all the way across the stream; for the Arminian it is like a great wide bridge that goes only half-way across."[2]

Jesus Actually Saves

The Scriptures describe the end intended and accomplished by Christ's work as the full salvation (actual reconciliation, justification, and sanctification) of His people.

1. The Scriptures state that Christ came, not to enable men to save themselves, but to *save* sinners.

> MATTHEW 1:21: "She will bear a son, and you shall call his name Jesus, for he will *save his people* from their sins."

2. Loraine Boettner, *The Reformed Doctrine of Predestination* (Philadelphia: Presbyterian and Reformed, 1963), 153. Spurgeon's comments as to whether it is the Calvinists or the Arminians who limit the Atonement, are to the point. "We are often told that we limit the atonement of Christ, because we say that Christ has not made a satisfaction for all men, or all men would be saved. Now, our reply to this is, that, on the other hand, our opponents limit it: we do not. The Arminians say, Christ died for all men. Ask them what they mean by it. Did Christ die so as to secure the salvation of all men? They say, 'No, certainly not.' We ask them the next question—Did Christ die so as to secure the salvation of any man in particular? They answer, 'No.' They are obliged to admit this, if they are consistent. They say, 'No. Christ has died that any man may be saved if'—and then follow certain conditions of salvation. Now, who is it that limits the death of Christ? Why, you. You say that Christ did not die so as infallibly to secure the salvation of anybody. We beg your pardon, when you say we limit Christ's death; we say, 'No, my dear sir, it is you that do it.' We say Christ so died that he infallibly secured the salvation of a multitude that no man can number, who through Christ's death not only may be saved, but are saved and cannot by any possibility run the hazard of being anything but saved. You are welcome to your atonement; you may keep it. We will never renounce ours for the sake of it." Quoted from James I. Packer, "Introductory Essay," in *The Death of Death in the Death of Christ,* by John Owen (London: Banner of Truth, 1959), 14.

LUKE 19:10: "For the Son of man came to seek and to *save* the lost."

2 CORINTHIANS 5:21: "For our sake he [God] made him [Christ] to be sin who knew no sin, so that in him *we might become* the righteousness of God."

GALATIANS 1:3–4: "Grace to you and peace from God our Father and the Lord Jesus Christ, *who gave himself* for our sins *to deliver us* from the present evil age, according to the will of our God and Father."

1 TIMOTHY 1:15: "The saying is trustworthy and deserving of full acceptance, that Christ Jesus came into the world to *save* sinners, of whom I am the foremost."

TITUS 2:14: ". . . who *gave himself* for us *to redeem us* from all lawlessness and *to purify* for himself a people for his own possession who are zealous for good works."

1 PETER 3:18: "For *Christ* also *suffered* once for sins, the righteous for the unrighteous, *that he might bring us to God,* being put to death in the flesh but made alive in the spirit."

2. The Scriptures declare that, as the result of what Christ did and suffered, His people are reconciled to God, justified, and given the Holy Spirit, who regenerates and sanctifies them. All these blessings were secured by Christ Himself for His people.

a. Christ, by His redeeming work, secured *reconciliation* for His people.

ROMANS 5:10: "For if while we were enemies we were *reconciled* to God *by the death of his Son,* much more, now that we are reconciled, shall we be saved by his life."

2 CORINTHIANS 5:18–19: "All this is from God, who through Christ *reconciled* us to himself and gave us the ministry of reconciliation; that is, in Christ God was reconciling the world to himself, not counting their trespasses against them, and entrusting to us the message of reconciliation."

EPHESIANS 2:15–16: ". . . by abolishing the law of commandments and ordinances, that he might create in himself one new man in place of the two, so making peace, and might *reconcile us* both to God in one body through the cross, thereby killing the hostility."

COLOSSIANS 1:21–22: "And you, who once were alienated and hostile in mind, doing evil deeds, *he has now reconciled* in his body of flesh by his death, *in order to* present you holy and blameless and above reproach before him."

b. Christ secured the righteousness and pardon needed by His people for their *justification*.

ROMANS 3:24–25: ". . . and are *justified* by his grace as a gift, *through the redemption that is in Christ Jesus*, whom God put forward as a propitiation by his blood, to be received by faith. This was to show God's righteousness, because in his divine forbearance he had passed over former sins."

ROMANS 5:8–9: "But God shows his love for us in that *while we were still sinners, Christ died for us*. Since, therefore, we have now been *justified by his blood*, much more shall we be saved by him from the wrath of God."

1 CORINTHIANS 1:30: "He is the source of your life in Christ Jesus, whom God made our wisdom and our *righteousness* and sanctification and redemption."

GALATIANS 3:13: "Christ *redeemed* us from the curse of the law by becoming a curse for us."

COLOSSIANS 1:13–14: "He has delivered us from the domain of darkness and transferred us to the kingdom of his beloved Son, in whom *we have redemption*, the forgiveness of sins."

HEBREWS 9:12: "He entered once for all into the holy places, not by means of the blood of goats and calves *but by means of his own blood, thus securing an eternal redemption.*"

1 PETER 2:24: "He himself *bore our sins* in his body on the tree, that we might die to sin and live to righteousness. By his wounds *you have been healed.*"

c. Christ secured the gift of the Spirit, which includes *regeneration* and *sanctification* and all that is involved in them.

EPHESIANS 1:3–4: "Blessed be the God and Father of our Lord Jesus Christ, who has blessed us in Christ *with every spiritual blessing* in the heavenly places, even as he chose us in him before the foundation of the world, that we should be holy and blameless before him."

PHILIPPIANS 1:29: "For it has been *granted to you* that for the sake of Christ you should not only *believe* in him but also suffer for his sake."

ACTS 5:31: "God exalted him at his right hand as Leader and Savior, *to give repentance* to Israel and forgiveness of sins."

TITUS 2:14: ". . . who gave himself for us to *redeem us* from all lawlessness and to *purify* for himself a people for his own possession who are zealous for good works."

Titus 3:5–6: "He saved us, not because of works done by us in righteousness, but according to his own mercy, by the washing of *regeneration* and *renewal* of the Holy Spirit, whom he poured out on us richly *through* Jesus Christ our Savior."

Ephesians 5:25–26: "Husbands, love your wives, as Christ loved the church and gave himself up for her, that he might *sanctify* her, having cleansed her by the washing of water with the word."

1 Corinthians 1:30: "He is the source of your life in Christ Jesus, whom God made our wisdom and our righteousness and *sanctification* and redemption."

Hebrews 9:14: ". . . how much more will the *blood of Christ,* who through the eternal Spirit offered himself without blemish to God, *purify* our conscience from dead works to serve the living God."

Hebrews 13:12: "So Jesus also *suffered* outside the gate *in order to sanctify* the people through his own blood."

1 John 1:7: "But if we walk in the light, as he is in the light, we have fellowship with one another, and *the blood of Jesus* his Son *cleanses* us from all sin."

Jesus Fulfills the Eternal Covenant

Scripture represents the Lord Jesus Christ, in all that He did and suffered for His people, as fulfilling the terms of a gracious compact or arrangement which He had entered into with His heavenly Father before the foundation of the world.

1. Jesus was sent into the world by the Father to save the people whom the Father had given to Him. Those given to Him by the Father come to Him (see and believe in Him), and none of them shall be lost.

JOHN 6:35–40: "Jesus said to them, 'I am the bread of life;
whoever comes to me shall not hunger, and whoever
believes in me shall never thirst. But I said to you that
you have seen me and yet do not believe. *All that the
Father gives me will come to me,* and whoever comes to
me I will never cast out. For I have come down from
heaven, not to do my own will but *the will of him who
sent me.* And this is the will of him who sent me, *that I
should lose nothing of all that he has given me,* but raise
it up on the last day. For this is the will of my Father,
that everyone who looks on the Son and believes in him
should have eternal life, and I will raise him up on the
last day.'"

2. Jesus, as the good shepherd, lays down His life for His sheep.
All who are "His sheep" are brought by Him into the fold and
are made to hear His voice and follow Him. Notice that the
Father had given the sheep to Christ!

JOHN 10:11, 14–18: "I am the good shepherd. The good
shepherd lays down his life for *the sheep. . . .* I am the
good shepherd. *I know my own* and my own know me,
just as the Father knows me and I know the Father; and
I lay down my life for the sheep. And I have *other sheep*
that are not of this fold. *I must bring them also,* and they
will listen to my voice. So there will be one flock, one
shepherd. For this reason the Father loves me, because
I lay down my life that I may take it up again. No one
takes it from me, but I lay it down of my own accord. I
have authority to lay it down, and I have authority to
take it up again. *This charge I have received from my
Father."*

JOHN 10:24–29: "[The unbelieving Jews demanded of
Him,] 'If you are the Christ, tell us plainly.' Jesus
answered them, 'I told you, and you do not believe. The

works that I do in my Father's name bear witness about me, but you do not believe *because you are not part of my flock*. My sheep hear my voice, and *I know them*, and *they follow me. I give them eternal life,* and *they* will never perish, and no one will snatch *them* out of my hand. *My Father, who has given them to me,* is greater than all, and no one is able to snatch them out of the Father's hand.'"

3. Jesus, in His High Priestly Prayer, prays not for the world, but for those given to Him by the Father. In fulfillment of the Father's charge, Jesus had accomplished the work the Father had sent Him to do—to make God known to His people and to give them eternal life.

> JOHN 17:1–11, 20, 24–26: "When Jesus had spoken these words, he lifted up his eyes to heaven, and said, 'Father, the hour has come; glorify your Son that the Son may glorify you, *since you have given him authority over all flesh, to give eternal life to all whom you have given him.* And this is eternal life, that they know you the only true God, *and Jesus Christ whom you have sent.* I glorified you on earth, having *accomplished the work that you gave me to do.* And now, Father, glorify me in your own presence with the glory that I had with you before the world existed. I have *manifested your name to the people whom you gave me out of the world.* Yours they were, and you gave them to me, and they have kept your word. Now they know that everything that you have given me is from you. For I have given them the words that you gave me, and they have received them and have come to know in truth that I came from you; and they have believed that you sent me. *I am praying for them. I am not praying for the world but for those whom you have given me,* for they are yours. All mine are yours, and yours are mine, and I am glorified in them. And I am no longer in the world, but they are in the world, and I am

coming to you. Holy Father, *keep them* in your name, *which you have given me,* that they may be one, even as we are one. . . . I do not ask for these only, but *also for those who will believe in me* through their word. . . . Father, I desire that they also, *whom you have given me,* may be with me where I am, to see my glory that you have given me because you loved me *before the foundation of the world.* O righteous Father, even though the world does not know you, I know you, and *these know that you have sent me.* I made known to them your name, and I will continue to make it known, that the love with which you have loved me may be in them, and I in them.'"

4. Paul declares that all of the spiritual blessings which the saints inherit, such as sonship, redemption, the forgiveness of sin, etc., result from their being "in Christ," and he traces these blessings back to their ultimate source in the eternal counsel of God—to that great blessing of their having been chosen in Christ before the foundation of the world and destined to be God's sons through Him.

> EPHESIANS 1:3–12: "Blessed be the God and Father of our Lord Jesus Christ, *who has blessed us* in Christ *with every spiritual blessing* in the heavenly places, *even as he chose us in him before the foundation of the world,* that we should be holy and blameless before him. In love he *predestined us for adoption through Jesus Christ, according to the purpose of his will,* to the praise of his glorious grace, with which he has blessed us in the Beloved. In him we have *redemption* through his blood, *the forgiveness of our trespasses,* according to the riches of his grace, which he lavished upon us, in all wisdom and insight making known to us the mystery of his will, according to his purpose, which he set forth in Christ as a plan for the fullness of time, to unite all things in

him, things in heaven and things on earth. In him we have obtained an inheritance, having been predestined *according to the purpose of him who works all things according to the counsel of his will,* so that we who were the first to hope in Christ might be to the praise of his glory."

5. The parallel which Paul draws between the condemning work of Adam and the saving work of Jesus Christ, the "second man" and the "last Adam," can best be explained on the principle that both stood in covenant relation to "their people" (Adam stood as the federal head of the race, and Christ stood as the federal head of the elect). As Adam involved his people in death and condemnation by his sin, even so Christ brought justification and life to His people through His righteousness.

> ROMANS 5:12, 17–19: "Therefore, just as sin came into the world through one man [Adam], and death through sin, and so death spread to all men because all sinned— . . . If, because of one man's trespass, death reigned through that one man, much more will those who receive the abundance of grace and the free gift of righteousness reign in life through the one man Jesus Christ. Therefore, as one trespass led to condemnation for all men, *so one act of righteousness leads to justification and life for all men.* For as by the one man's disobedience the many were made sinners, so *by the one man's obedience the many will be made righteous.*"

How Jesus Died for "All" and Yet for a Particular People

Some passages speak of Christ's dying for "all" men and of His death as saving the "world," yet others speak of His death as being definite in design and of His dying for particular people and securing salvation for them.

1. There are two classes of texts that speak of Christ's saving work in *general terms:* (a) those containing the word "world"— e.g., John 1:9, 29; 3:16–17; 4:42; 2 Corinthians 5:19; 1 John 2:1–2; 4:14, and (b) those containing the word "all"—e.g., Romans 5:18; 2 Corinthians 5:14–15; 1 Timothy 2:4–6; Hebrews 2:9; 2 Peter 3:9.

One reason for the use of these expressions was to correct the false notion that salvation was for the Jews alone. Such phrases as "the world," "all men," "all nations," and "every crea-ture" were used by the New Testament writers to emphatically correct this mistake. These expressions are intended to show that Christ died for all men without *distinction* (i.e., He died for Jews and Gentiles alike), but they are not intended to indi-cate that Christ died for all men without *exception* (i.e., He did not die for the purpose of saving each and every lost sinner).

2. There are other passages which speak of His saving work in *definite terms* and show that it was intended to infallibly save a particular people, namely, those given to Him by the Father.

MATTHEW 1:21: ". . . for he will save *his people* from their sins."

MATTHEW 20:28: "The Son of man came not to be served but to serve, and to give his life as a *ransom for many.*"

MATTHEW 26:28: ". . . for this is my blood of the covenant, which is poured out *for many* for the forgiveness of sins."

JOHN 10:11: "I am the good shepherd. The good shepherd lays down his life for *the sheep.*"

JOHN 11:50–53: "'Nor do you understand that it is better for you that one man should die for *the people,* not that the whole nation should perish.' He did not say this of his own accord, but being high priest that year he proph-esied that Jesus would die for the nation, and not for the nation only, but also to gather into one *the children of God who are scattered abroad.* So from that day on they made plans to put him to death."

Acts 20:28: "Pay careful attention to yourselves and to all the flock, in which the Holy Spirit has made you overseers, to care for the *church* of God, *which he obtained with his own blood.*"

Ephesians 5:25–27: "Husbands, love your wives, *as Christ loved the church and gave himself up for her,* that he might sanctify *her,* having cleansed *her* by the washing of water with the word, so that *he might present the church to himself* in splendor, without spot or wrinkle or any such thing, that *she* might be holy and without blemish."

Romans 8:32–34: "He who did not spare his own Son but gave him up *for us all,* how will he not also with him graciously *give us* all things? Who shall bring any charge against *God's elect?* It is God who justifies. Who is to condemn?"

Hebrews 2:17; 3:1: "Therefore he had to be made like his brothers in every respect, so that he might become a merciful and faithful high priest in the service of God, to make propitiation *for the sins of the people.* . . . Therefore, holy brothers, you *who share in a heavenly calling,* consider Jesus, the apostle and high priest of our confession . . ."

Hebrews 9:15: "Therefore he is the mediator of a new covenant, so that *those who are called* may receive the promised eternal inheritance, since a death has occurred that *redeems them* from the transgressions committed under the first covenant."

Hebrews 9:28: ". . . Christ, having been offered once to bear the sins of *many* . . ."

REVELATION 5:9: "And they sang a new song, saying, 'Worthy are you to take the scroll and to open its seals, for you were slain, and by your blood you *ransomed people* for God *from every tribe and language and people and nation.'*"

Review also the verses quoted above under "Jesus Fulfills the Eternal Covenant," points 1, 2, and 3.

THE EFFICACIOUS CALL OF THE SPIRIT OR IRRESISTIBLE GRACE

Each member of the Trinity—the Father, the Son, and the Holy Spirit—participates in, and contributes to, the salvation of sinners. As was shown above, the Father, before the foundation of the world, marked out those who were to be saved and gave them to the Son to be His people. At the appointed time, the Son came into the world and secured their redemption. But these two great acts—election and redemption—do not complete the work of salvation, because included in God's plan for recovering lost sinners is the renewing work of the Holy Spirit, by which the benefits of Christ's obedience and death are applied to the elect. It is with this phase of salvation (its application by the Spirit) that the doctrine of irresistible or efficacious grace is concerned. Simply stated, this doctrine asserts that the Holy Spirit never fails to bring to salvation those sinners whom He personally calls to Christ. He inevitably applies salvation to every sinner whom He intends to save, and it is His intention to save all the elect.

The *gospel invitation extends a call* to salvation to every one who hears its message. It invites all men without distinction to drink freely of the water of life and live. It promises salvation to all who repent and believe. But this outward general call, extended to the elect and nonelect alike, will not bring sinners to Christ. Why? Because men are by nature dead in sin and are under its power. They are of themselves unable and unwilling to forsake their evil ways and to turn to Christ for mercy. Consequently, the unregenerate will not respond to the gospel call to repentance and faith. No amount of external threatenings or promises will cause blind, deaf, dead, rebellious sinners to bow before Christ as Lord and to look to Him alone for salvation. Such an act of faith and submission is contrary to the lost man's nature.

Therefore, the *Holy Spirit*, in order to bring God's elect to salvation, extends to them *a special inward call* in addition to the outward call contained in the gospel message. Through this special call, the Holy Spirit performs a work of grace within the sinner, which inevitably brings him to faith in Christ. The inward change wrought in the elect sinner enables him to understand and believe spiritual truth; in the spiritual realm, he is given the seeing eye and the hearing ear. The Spirit creates within him a new heart or a new nature. This is accomplished through regeneration or the new birth by which the sinner is made a child of God and is given spiritual life. His will is renewed through this process, so that the sinner spontaneously comes to Christ of his own free choice. Because he is given a new nature so that he loves righteousness, and because his mind is enlightened so that he understands and believes the biblical gospel, the renewed sinner freely and willingly turns to Christ as Lord and Savior. Thus, the once dead sinner is drawn to Christ by the inward, supernatural call of the Spirit, who through regeneration makes him alive and creates faith and repentance within him.

Although the general outward call of the gospel can be, and often is, rejected, the special inward call of the Spirit never fails to result in the conversion of those to whom it is made. This special call is not made to all sinners, but is issued to the elect only. The Spirit is in no way dependent upon their help or cooperation for success in His work of bringing them to Christ. It is for this reason that Calvinists speak of the Spirit's call and of God's grace in saving sinners as being "efficacious," "invincible," or "irresistible." The grace which the Holy Spirit extends to the elect cannot be thwarted or refused; it never fails to bring them to true faith in Christ.

The doctrine of irresistible or efficacious grace is set forth in the Westminster Confession of Faith in these words: "All those whom God hath predestinated unto life, and those only, He is pleased, in His appointed and accepted time, effectually to call, by His Word and Spirit, out of that state of sin and death, in which they are by nature, to grace and salvation, by Jesus Christ; enlightening their minds spiritually and savingly to understand the things of God, taking away their heart of stone, and giving unto them an heart of flesh; renewing their wills, and by His almighty power, determining them to that which is good, and effectually drawing them to Jesus Christ: yet so, as they come most freely, being made willing by His grace."[3]

The Spirit Saves

Scripture affirms that salvation is the work of the Spirit as well as that of the Father and the Son.

ROMANS 8:14: "For all who are *led by the Spirit* of God are sons of God."

1 CORINTHIANS 2:10–13: "For the *Spirit searches* every-thing, even the depths of God. For who knows a person's thoughts except the spirit of that person, which is in him? So also no one comprehends the thoughts of God *except the Spirit of God*. Now we have received not the spirit of the world, but the Spirit who is from God, that we might understand the things freely given us by God. And we impart this in words not taught by human wis-dom but *taught by the Spirit*, interpreting spiritual truths to those who are spiritual."

3. Chap. X, sect. 1.

1 CORINTHIANS 6:11: "But you were washed, you were sanctified, you were justified in the name of the Lord Jesus Christ and *by the Spirit of our God.*"

1 CORINTHIANS 12:3: "Therefore I want you to understand that no one speaking in the Spirit of God ever says 'Jesus is accursed!' and no one can say 'Jesus is Lord' *except in the Holy Spirit.*"

2 CORINTHIANS 3:6: "The letter kills, but *the Spirit gives life.*"

2 CORINTHIANS 3:17–18: "Now the Lord is the Spirit, and where the Spirit of the Lord is, there is freedom. And we all, with unveiled face, beholding the glory of the Lord, are being transformed into the same image from one degree of glory to another. For this comes *from the Lord who is the Spirit.*"

1 PETER 1:1–2: "To those who are elect exiles . . . according to the foreknowledge of God the Father, in the *sanctification of the Spirit,* for obedience to Jesus Christ and for sprinkling with his blood: May grace and peace be multiplied to you."

The Spirit Gives New Birth

Through regeneration or the new birth, sinners are given spiritual life and made God's children. The Bible describes this process as a spiritual resurrection, a creation, the giving of a new heart, etc. The inward change, which is thus wrought through the Holy Spirit, results from God's power and grace, and in no way is He dependent upon man's help for success in this work.

1. Sinners, through regeneration, are brought into God's kingdom and are made His children. The *author* of this "second"

birth is the Holy Spirit; the *instrument* which He uses is the word of God.

> JOHN 1:12–13: "But to all who did receive him, who believed in his name, he gave the right to become children of God, *who were born,* not of blood nor of the will of the flesh nor of the will of man, but *of God."*

> JOHN 3:3–8: "Jesus answered him, 'Truly, truly, I say to you, unless one is *born again* he cannot *see* the kingdom of God.' Nicodemus said to him, 'How can a man be born when he is old? Can he enter a second time into his mother's womb and be born?' Jesus answered, 'Truly, truly, I say to you, unless one is born of water and the Spirit, he cannot *enter* the kingdom of God. That which is born of the flesh is flesh, and that which is *born of the Spirit* is spirit. Do not marvel that I said to you, "You must be born again." The wind blows where it wishes, and you hear its sound, but you do not know where it comes from or where it goes. So it is with everyone who is born of the Spirit.'"

> TITUS 3:5: "He saved us, not because of works done by us in righteousness, but according to his own mercy, by the washing of *regeneration* and *renewal of the Holy Spirit."*

> 1 PETER 1:3: "Blessed be the God and Father of our Lord Jesus Christ! According to his great mercy, he has caused us to *be born again* to a living hope through the resurrection of Jesus Christ from the dead."

> 1 PETER 1:23: "You have been *born again,* not of perishable seed but of imperishable, through the living and abiding *word of God."*

> 1 JOHN 5:4: "For everyone who has been *born of God* overcomes the world. And this is the victory that has overcome the world—our faith."

2. Through the Spirit's work, the dead sinner is given a new heart (nature) and made to walk in God's law. In Christ he becomes a new creation.

> DEUTERONOMY 30:6: "And the LORD your God will *circumcise your heart* and the heart of your offspring, so that you will love the LORD your God with all your heart and with all your soul, that you may live."

> EZEKIEL 36:26–27: "And I will give you a *new heart,* and a *new spirit* I will put within you. And I will remove the heart of stone from your flesh and give you a heart of flesh. And I will put my Spirit within you, and cause you to walk in my statutes and be careful to obey my rules."

> Compare Ezekiel 11:19.

> GALATIANS 6:15: "For neither circumcision counts for anything, nor uncircumcision, but a *new creation.*"

> EPHESIANS 2:10: "For we are his workmanship, *created* in Christ Jesus for good works, which God prepared beforehand, that we should walk in them."

> 2 CORINTHIANS 5:17–18: "Therefore, if anyone is in Christ, *he is a new creation.* The old has passed away; behold, the new has come. All this is from God, who through Christ reconciled us to himself and gave us the ministry of reconciliation."

3. The Holy Spirit raises the sinner from his state of spiritual death and makes him alive.

> JOHN 5:21: "For as the Father raises the dead and *gives them life,* so also the Son *gives life* to whom he will."

> EPHESIANS 2:1, 5: "And you were dead in the trespasses and sins in which you once walked. . . . even when we

were dead in our trespasses, [God] made us *alive* together with Christ."

COLOSSIANS 2:13: "And you, who were dead in your trespasses and the uncircumcision of your flesh, *God made alive* together with him, having forgiven us all our trespasses."

The Spirit Reveals the Secrets of God

God makes known to His chosen ones the secrets of the kingdom through the inward personal revelation given by the Spirit.

MATTHEW 11:25–27: "At that time Jesus declared, 'I thank you, Father, Lord of heaven and earth, that you have hidden these things from the wise and understanding and revealed them to little children; yes, Father, for such was your gracious will. All things have been handed over to me by my Father, and no one knows the Son except the Father, and no one *knows the Father* except the Son and anyone to whom the Son *chooses to reveal him.*'"

LUKE 10:21: "In that same hour he rejoiced in the Holy Spirit and said, 'I thank you, Father, Lord of heaven and earth, that you have hidden these things from the wise and understanding and *revealed* them to little children; yes, Father, for such was your gracious will.'"

MATTHEW 13:10–11, 16: "Then the disciples came and said to him, 'Why do you speak to them in parables?' And he answered them, 'To you it has been *given to know the secrets* of the kingdom of heaven, but to them it has not been given. . . . But blessed are your eyes, for they *see*, and your ears, for they *hear.*'"

LUKE 8:10: "To you it has been *given to know the secrets* of the kingdom of God, but for others they are in parables, so that 'seeing they may not see, and hearing they may not understand.'"

MATTHEW 16:15–17: "He said to them, 'But who do you say that I am?' Simon Peter replied, 'You are the Christ, the Son of the living God.' And Jesus answered him, 'Blessed are you, Simon Bar-Jonah! For flesh and blood has not *revealed* this to you, but *my Father* who is in heaven.'"

JOHN 6:37, 44–45: "All that the Father *gives me will come to me*, and whoever comes to me I will never cast out. . . . No one can come to me unless the Father who sent me *draws* him. And I will raise him up on the last day. It is written in the Prophets, 'And they will all be taught by God.' Everyone who has *heard* and *learned from the Father* comes to me."

JOHN 6:64–65: "'But there are some of you who do not believe.' (For Jesus knew from the beginning who those were who did not believe, and who it was who would betray him.) And he said, 'This is why I told you that no one can come to me unless it is *granted* him *by the Father.*'"

1 CORINTHIANS 2:14: "The natural person does not accept the things of the Spirit of God, for they are folly to him, and he is not able to understand them because they are *spiritually discerned.*"

EPHESIANS 1:17–18: ". . . that the God of our Lord Jesus Christ, the Father of glory, *may give you* a *spirit of wisdom and of revelation* in the knowledge of him, *having the eyes of your hearts enlightened*, that you may *know* what is the hope to which he has called you . . ."

See also John 10:3–6, 16, 26–29.

The Spirit Gives Faith and Repentance

Faith and *repentance* are *divine gifts* and are wrought in the soul through the regenerating work of the Holy Spirit.

ACTS 5:31: "God exalted him at his right hand as Leader and Savior, to *give repentance* to Israel and forgiveness of sins."

ACTS 11:18: "When they heard these things they fell silent. And they glorified God, saying, 'Then to the Gentiles also God has *granted repentance* that leads to life.'"

ACTS 13:48: "And when the Gentiles heard this, they began rejoicing and glorifying the word of the Lord, and as many as were *appointed* to eternal life *believed*."

ACTS 16:14: "One who heard us was a woman named Lydia, from the city of Thyatira, a seller of purple goods, who was a worshiper of God. *The Lord opened her heart* to *pay attention* to what was said by Paul."

ACTS 18:27: "And when he wished to cross to Achaia, the brothers encouraged him and wrote to the disciples to welcome him. When he arrived, he greatly helped those *who through grace had believed*."

EPHESIANS 2:8–9: "For by grace you have been saved through faith. And this is not your own doing; *it is the gift of God*, not a result of works, so that no one may boast."

PHILIPPIANS 1:29: "For it has been *granted to you* that for the sake of Christ you should not only *believe* in him but also suffer for his sake."

2 TIMOTHY 2:25–26: "God may perhaps *grant* them *repentance* leading to a *knowledge* of the truth, and they may escape from the snare of the devil, after being captured by him to do his will."

The Spirit Effectually Calls

The gospel invitation extends a general outward call to salvation to all who hear the message. In addition to this external call, the Holy Spirit extends a special inward call to the elect only. The general call of the gospel can be, and often is, rejected, but the special call of the Spirit cannot be rejected; it always results in the conversion of those to whom it is made.

ROMANS 1:6–7: ". . . including you who are *called* to belong to Jesus Christ, To all those in Rome who are loved by God and *called* to be saints . . ."

ROMANS 8:30: "And those whom he predestined he also *called*, and those whom he *called* he also justified, and those whom he justified he also glorified."

ROMANS 9:23–24: ". . . in order to make known the riches of his glory for vessels of mercy, which he has prepared beforehand for glory—even us whom he has *called*, not from the Jews only but also from the Gentiles."

1 CORINTHIANS 1:1–2, 9, 23–31: "Paul, *called* by the will of God to be an apostle of Christ Jesus, and our brother Sosthenes, To the church of God that is in Corinth, to those sanctified in Christ Jesus, called to be saints. . . . God is faithful, by whom you were *called* into the fellowship of his Son, Jesus Christ our Lord. . . . but we preach Christ crucified, a stumbling block to Jews and folly to Gentiles, but to those who are *called*, both Jews and Greeks, Christ the power of God and the wisdom of God. For the foolishness of God is wiser than men, and the weakness of God is stronger than men. For consider your *calling*, brothers: not many of you were wise according to worldly standards, not many were powerful, not many were of noble birth. But God chose what is foolish in the world to shame the wise; God chose what is weak in the world to shame the strong; God

chose what is low and despised in the world, even things
that are not, to bring to nothing things that are, so that
no human being might boast in the presence of God. He
is the source of your life in Christ Jesus, whom God
made our wisdom and our righteousness and sanctification and redemption. Therefore, as it is written, 'Let
the one who boasts, boast in the Lord.'"

GALATIANS 1:15–16: "But when he who had set me apart
before I was born, and who *called* me by his grace, was
pleased to reveal his Son to me, in order that I might
preach him among the Gentiles, I did not immediately
consult with anyone."

EPHESIANS 4:4: "There is one body and one Spirit—just
as you were *called* to the one hope that belongs to your
call."

2 TIMOTHY 1:9: ". . . who saved us and *called* us to a holy
calling, not because of our works but because of his own
purpose and grace, which he gave us in Christ Jesus
before the ages began."

HEBREWS 9:15: "Therefore he is the mediator of a new
covenant, so that those who are *called* may receive the
promised eternal inheritance."

JUDE 1: ". . . To those who are *called*, beloved in God the
Father and kept for Jesus Christ . . ."

1 PETER 1:15: "But as he who *called* you is holy, you also
be holy in all your conduct."

1 PETER 2:9: "But you are a chosen race, a royal priesthood, a holy nation, a people for his own possession,
that you may proclaim the excellencies of him who *called*
you out of darkness into his marvelous light."

1 PETER 5:10: "And after you have suffered a little while, the God of all grace, who has *called* you to his eternal glory in Christ, will himself restore, confirm, strengthen, and establish you."

2 PETER 1:3: "His divine power has granted to us all things that pertain to life and godliness, through the knowledge of him who *called* us to his own glory and excellence."

REVELATION 17:14: "They will make war on the Lamb, and the Lamb will conquer them, for he is Lord of lords and King of kings, and those with him are *called* and chosen and faithful."

Salvation, Given by a Sovereign God

The application of salvation is all of grace and is accomplished solely through the almighty power of God.

ISAIAH 55:11: ". . . so shall my word be that goes out from my mouth; it shall not return to me empty, but it shall *accomplish* that which *I purpose,* and shall succeed in the thing for which I sent it."

JOHN 3:27: "John answered, 'A person cannot receive even one thing unless it is *given* him from heaven.'"

JOHN 17:2: ". . . since you have given him authority over all flesh, to *give* eternal life to all whom you have given him."

ROMANS 9:16: "So then it depends not on human will or exertion, but on *God, who has mercy.*"

1 CORINTHIANS 3:6–7: "I planted, Apollos watered, but *God gave the growth.* So neither he who plants nor he who waters is anything, but only *God who gives the growth.*"

1 Corinthians 4:7: "For who sees anything different in you? What do you have that you did not *receive?* If then you received it, why do you boast as if you did not receive it?"

Philippians 2:12–13: "Therefore, my beloved, as you have always obeyed, so now, not only as in my presence but much more in my absence, work out your own salvation with fear and trembling, for it is *God who works in you*, both to *will* and to *work* for his good pleasure."

James 1:18: *"Of his own will* he brought us forth by the word of truth, that we should be a kind of firstfruits of his creation."

1 John 5:20: "And we know that the Son of God has come and has *given us understanding, so that we may know* him who is true; and we are in him who is true, in his Son Jesus Christ. He is the true God and eternal life."

THE PERSEVERANCE OF THE SAINTS OR THE SECURITY OF BELIEVERS

The elect are not only redeemed by Christ and renewed by the Spirit, but also *kept* in faith by the almighty power of God. All those who are spiritually united to Christ through regeneration are eternally secure in Him. Nothing can separate them from the eternal and unchangeable love of God. They have been predestined to eternal glory and are therefore assured of heaven.

The doctrine of the perseverance of the saints does not maintain that all who *profess* the Christian faith are certain of heaven. It is *saints*—those who are set apart by the Spirit—who *persevere* to the end. It is *believers*—those who are given true, living faith in Christ—who are *secure* and safe in Him. Many who profess to believe fall away, but they do not fall from grace, for they were never in grace. True believers do fall into temptations, and they do commit grievous sins, but these sins do not cause them to lose their salvation or separate them from Christ.

The Westminster Confession of Faith gives the following statement of this doctrine: "They, whom God hath accepted in His Beloved, effectually called, and sanctified by His Spirit, can neither totally nor finally fall away from the state of grace, but shall certainly persevere therein to the end, and be eternally saved."[4]

Boettner is certainly correct in asserting:

This doctrine does not stand alone but is a necessary part of the Calvinistic system of theology. The doctrines of Election and Efficacious Grace logically imply the certain salvation of those who receive these blessings. If God has chosen men absolutely and unconditionally to eternal life, and if His Spirit effectively applies to them the benefits of redemption, the inescapable conclusion is that these persons shall be saved.[5]

The following verses show that God's people are given *eternal life* the moment they believe. They are *kept by God's power* through faith and *nothing can separate them from His love*. They have been *sealed* with the Holy Spirit, who has been given as the *guarantee* of their salvation, and they are thus assured of an eternal inheritance.

ISAIAH 43:1–3: "But now thus says the LORD, he who created you, O Jacob, he who formed you, O Israel: 'Fear not, for I have redeemed you; I have called you by name, you are mine. When you pass through the waters, I will be with you; and through the rivers, they shall not overwhelm you; when you walk through fire you shall not be

4. Chap. XVII, sect. 1.
5. Boettner, *The Reformed Doctrine of Predestination*, 182.

burned, and the flame shall not consume you. For I am the LORD your God, the Holy One of Israel, your Savior.'"

ISAIAH 54:10: "'For the mountains may depart and the hills be removed, but my steadfast love shall not depart from you, and my covenant of peace shall not be removed,' says the LORD, who has compassion on you."

JEREMIAH 32:40: "I will make with them an everlasting covenant, that I will not turn away from doing good to them. And I will put the fear of me in their hearts, that they may not turn from me."

MATTHEW 18:12–14: "What do you think? If a man has a hundred sheep and one of them has gone astray, does he not leave the ninety-nine on the mountains and go in search of the one that went astray? And if he finds it, truly, I say to you, he rejoices over it more than over the ninety-nine that never went astray. So it is not the will of my Father who is in heaven that *one* of these little ones *should perish*."

JOHN 3:16: "For God so loved the world, that he gave his only Son, that whoever believes in him *should not perish* but have eternal life."

JOHN 3:36: "Whoever believes in the Son has *eternal life*."

JOHN 5:24: "Truly, truly, I say to you, whoever hears my word and believes him who sent me *has eternal life*. He *does not come into judgment*, but *has passed from death to life*."

JOHN 6:35–40: "Jesus said to them, 'I am the bread of life; whoever comes to me shall *not hunger*, and whoever believes in me shall *never thirst*. But I said to you that you have seen me and yet do not believe. All that the Father gives me will come to me, and whoever comes to me *I will never cast out.* For I have come down from heaven, not to do my own will but the will of him who sent me. And this is the will of him who sent me, that I should *lose nothing* of all that he has given me, but raise it up on the last day. For this is the will of my Father, that everyone who looks on the Son and believes in him should have eternal life, and I will raise him up on the last day.'"

JOHN 6:47: "Truly, truly, I say to you, whoever believes *has eternal life.*"

JOHN 10:27–30: "My sheep hear my voice, and I know them, and they follow me. I give them *eternal life, and they will never perish,* and *no one will snatch them out of my hand.* My Father, who has given them to me, is greater than all, and no one is able to snatch them out of the Father's hand. I and the Father are one."

JOHN 17:11–12, 15: "And I am no longer in the world, but they are in the world, and I am coming to you. Holy Father, *keep them* in your name, which you have given me, that they may be one, even as we are one. While I was with them, *I kept them* in your name, which you have given me. I have guarded them, and *not one of them has been lost* except the son of destruction, that the Scripture might be fulfilled. . . . I do not ask that you take them out of the world, but that you *keep them from the evil one.*"

ROMANS 5:8–10: "But God shows his love for us in that while we were still sinners, Christ died for us. Since, therefore, we have now been *justified by his blood,* much more *shall we be saved by him from the wrath of God.* For if while we were enemies we were reconciled to God by the death of his Son, much more, now that we are reconciled, shall we be *saved by his life.*"

Romans 8:1: "There is therefore now *no condemnation* for those who are in Christ Jesus."

Romans 8:29–30: "For those whom he *foreknew* he also *predestined* to be conformed to the image of his Son, in order that he might be the firstborn among many brothers. And those whom he predestined he also *called*, and those whom he called he also *justified*, and those whom he justified he also *glorified*."

Romans 8:35–39: "Who shall separate us from the love of Christ? Shall tribulation, or distress, or persecution, or famine, or nakedness, or danger, or sword? As it is written, 'For your sake we are being killed all the day long; we are regarded as sheep to be slaughtered.' No, in all these things we are *more than conquerors through him* who loved us. For I am sure that neither death nor life, nor angels nor rulers, nor things present nor things to come, nor powers, nor height nor depth, *nor anything else in all creation, will be able to separate us from the love of God in Christ Jesus our Lord*."

1 Corinthians 1:7–9: ". . . so that you are not lacking in any spiritual gift, as you wait for the revealing of our Lord Jesus Christ, who will *sustain you to the end, guiltless* in the day of our Lord Jesus Christ. *God is faithful*, by whom you were called into the fellowship of his Son, Jesus Christ our Lord."

1 Corinthians 10:13: "No temptation has overtaken you that is not common to man. God is faithful, and he will *not let you be tempted beyond your ability*, but with the temptation he will also provide the way of escape, that you may be *able to endure it*."

2 Corinthians 4:14, 17: ". . . knowing that he who raised the Lord Jesus *will raise us* also with Jesus and bring us with you into his presence. . . . For this slight momen-

tary affliction is preparing for us an eternal weight of glory beyond all comparison."

EPHESIANS 1:5, 13–14: "He predestined us for adoption through Jesus Christ, according to the purpose of his will. . . . In him you also, when you heard the word of truth, the gospel of your salvation, and believed in him, were *sealed* with the promised Holy Spirit, who is *the guarantee of our inheritance* until we acquire possession of it, to the praise of his glory."

EPHESIANS 4:30: "And do not grieve the Holy Spirit of God, by whom you were *sealed* for the day of redemption."

COLOSSIANS 3:3–4: "For you have died, and your life is hidden with Christ in God. When Christ who is your life appears, then *you also will appear with him in glory.*"

1 THESSALONIANS 5:23–24: "Now may the God of peace himself sanctify you completely, and may your whole spirit and soul and body be *kept blameless* at the coming of our Lord Jesus Christ. He who calls you is *faithful; he will surely do it.*"

2 TIMOTHY 4:18: "The Lord will rescue me from every evil deed and *bring me safely into his heavenly kingdom.* To him be the glory forever and ever. Amen."

HEBREWS 9:12, 15: "He entered once for all into the holy places, not by means of the blood of goats and calves but by means of his own blood, thus *securing an eternal redemption.* . . . Therefore he is the mediator of a new covenant, so that those who are called may *receive the promised eternal inheritance,* since a death has occurred that redeems them from the transgressions committed under the first covenant."

HEBREWS 10:14: "For by a single offering he has *perfected for all time* those who are being *sanctified.*"

HEBREWS 12:28: "Therefore let us be grateful for *receiving* a kingdom that *cannot be shaken,* and thus let us offer to God acceptable worship, with reverence and awe."

1 PETER 1:3–5: "Blessed be the God and Father of our Lord Jesus Christ! According to his great mercy, *he has caused us to be born again to a living hope* through the resurrection of Jesus Christ from the dead, to an inheritance that is imperishable, undefiled, and unfading, *kept in heaven for you,* who by God's power are *being guarded* through faith for a salvation ready to be revealed in the last time."

1 JOHN 2:19, 25: "They went out from us, but they were not of us; for if they had been of us, they would have *continued with us.* But they went out, that it might become plain that they all are not of us. . . . And this is *the promise* that he made to us—*eternal life.*"

1 JOHN 5:4, 11–13, 20: "For everyone who has been born of God *overcomes* the world. And this is the victory that has overcome the world—our faith. . . . And this is the testimony, that God *gave us eternal life,* and this life is in his Son. Whoever has the Son *has life;* whoever does not have the Son of God does not have life. I write these things to you who believe in the name of the Son of God that you may know that you *have eternal life.* . . . And we know that the Son of God has come and has given us understanding, so that we may know him who is true; and we are in him who is true, in his Son Jesus Christ. He is the true God and eternal life."

JUDE 1: ". . . To those who are called, beloved in God the Father and *kept* for Jesus Christ . . ."

JUDE 24–25: "Now to him who is able to *keep you from stumbling* and to present you blameless before the presence of his glory with great joy, to the only God, our Savior, through Jesus Christ our Lord, be glory, majesty, dominion, and authority, before all time and now and forever. Amen."

This brings to completion the second phase of our survey. We have by no means exhausted the biblical texts which support the five points of Calvinism. We hope, however, that enough evidence has been presented to show that these doctrines are drawn directly from the Holy Scriptures.

Part Three

THE FIVE POINTS DOCUMENTED: RECOMMENDED READING

I n this, the third and final part of our survey, we shall briefly review a number of works that have been written on behalf of Calvinism. It is our hope that your interest has been stimulated and that you will make a serious study of this system of theology.

If you make such a study, you will find that, as Packer says,

Calvinism is something much broader than the "five points" indicate. Calvinism is a whole worldview, stemming from a clear vision of God as the whole world's Maker and King. Calvinism is the consistent endeavor to acknowledge the Creator as the Lord, working all things after the counsel of His will. Calvinism is a theocentric way of thinking about all life under the direction and control of God's own Word. Calvinism, in other words, is the theology of the Bible viewed from the perspective of the Bible—the God-centred outlook which sees the Creator as the source, and means, and end, of everything that is, both in nature and in grace. Calvinism is thus theism (belief in God as the ground of all things), religion (dependence on God as the giver of all things), and evangelicalism (trust in God through Christ for all things), all in their purest and most highly developed form. And Calvinism is a unified philosophy of history which sees the whole diversity of processes and events that take place in God's world as no more, and no less, than the outworking of His great preordained plan for His creatures and His church. The five points assert no more than that God is sovereign in saving the individual, but Calvinism, as such, is concerned with the much broader assertion that He is sovereign everywhere.[1]

If, in your investigation, you probe into the history and influence of Calvinism, you will discover that its doctrines have been incorporated into the majority of the great creeds of the Protestant churches. For example, the Presbyterian and Reformed churches, the established Church of England and her daughter, the Episcopal Church of America, the free church of Holland, almost all of the churches of Scotland, and most Baptist and Congregationalist churches in both England and America possess creeds or confessions of faith which are Calvinistic in content.

Calvinism has not only been incorporated into the creeds of the majority of the evangelical Protestant churches, but has also been championed by many of the church's greatest theologians and preachers. A roll call of Calvinists, both past and present, would include such renowned leaders as Augustine, John Wycliffe, Martin Luther, John Calvin, Ulrich Zwingli, Jerome Zanchius, Heinrich Bullinger, Martin Bucer, John Owen, George Whitefield, Augustus Toplady, John Bunyan, Jonathan Edwards, John Gill, John Newton, William Carey, Charles H. Spurgeon, Charles Hodge, William Cunningham,

1. James I. Packer, "Introductory Essay," in *The Death of Death in the Death of Christ,* by John Owen (London: Banner of Truth, 1959), 5.

W. G. T. Shedd, A. H. Strong, B. B. Warfield, Abraham Kuyper, J. Gresham Machen, Cornelius Van Til, John Murray, D. Martyn Lloyd-Jones, James Montgomery Boice, Sinclair Ferguson, Iain Murray, R. C. Sproul, J. I. Packer, and John MacArthur, to name just a few.

The books and articles listed below will enable the reader to verify these claims for himself. These works set forth and defend Calvinistic theology. We do not agree with *everything* which is written in the following listings. However, it is believed that these representative works should be consulted if one is to properly understand the various shades and nuances of Calvinism.

Thousands upon thousands of works have been written on Calvinism down through the centuries. A vast number of books, articles, booklets, papers, pamphlets, scholarly essays, monographs, theses, and dissertations have been written on Calvin and Calvinism. Our bibliography will not include many of the more scholarly treatments of Calvinism. We are primarily concerned to list the works on Calvinism which are most readable and understandable. For more scholarly treatments of Calvinism, the reader is encouraged to look, for instance, to the H. Henry Meeter Center for Calvin Studies, which is located at Calvin College and Calvin Theological Seminary in Grand Rapids, Michigan. Vast holdings of scholarly works are available there for the more serious student of Calvinistic theology.

In 1963 (when the first edition of this book was published), there was no capacity for fast and easy computer searches for literature on Calvinism. But with the advent of present technology, it is easy to find books related to Calvinism (both new and used), to say nothing of Reformed theological chat rooms, websites, on-line magazines, sermons, and so much more. If one were simply to input such words and phrases as *Calvin, Calvinism, the five points of Calvinism, Reformed, Reformed theology, election,* and *predestination* in an Internet search engine, hundreds of thousands of sources of information would be available at one's fingertips. Every website catering to Reformed literature cannot be cited, but persons interested in books by John Calvin himself should consult Ages Software Inc. at P.O. Box 1926, Albany, OR 97321-0509 (541-928-8502) or visit their website at *www.ageslibrary.com*. The John Calvin Center purports to have the most complete collection of John Calvin's writings ever published (albeit in digital form). Log on to *www.john-calvin.com* for a complete listing of materials on the Genevan Reformer.

The ministry called the E4 Group offers books on CD-ROM, including many great Calvinistic authors, both past and present. You can receive their study library by accessing *www.FreeBibleSoftware.com*. You may also want to purchase a collection of Reformed books from Still Waters Revival Books in CD-ROM format. They have released an incredible array of 62 compact disks which contain over 2,000 titles of some of the best Reformation and Calvinistic books ever written. It is by far the best and widest collection of Reformed literature ever assembled. With capabilities to index and search through these classic authors, this set of CDs is a must for those who desire to read and study our Reformed theological heritage. The president of Still Waters Revival Books, Reg Barrow, is to be highly commended for his insight and perseverance in placing these books—many of them otherwise unavailable—within reach of anyone who has a computer with a CD-ROM drive. If you want more information about how to obtain these CDs, please visit their website: *www.swrb.com/Puritan/reformation-bookshelf-CDs.htm*.

Because this book is about Calvinism, rather than John Calvin himself, we have chosen not to include any of the commentaries written by Calvin. In recent years, these have been republished by Eerdmans, Baker, the Banner of Truth Trust, and others. Scholars are currently working on a completely new translation of all of Calvin's commentaries.

The material in this annotated bibliography is divided into two sections. The first section lists works which contain information relevant to the *overall Calvinistic system*. The second section lists works relating *specifically to each of the five points*. Since some of the books given in the first section contain important chapters or divisions that deal with the individual points, these works are repeated in the second section, with the pertinent divisions and pages indicated. The first time a work is listed, we have given the author's full name, the title, the publisher's name and address, the date of publication, and the number of pages. Thereafter, only the author's last name and the title of the work are repeated. In many cases, explanatory remarks have been added to show the nature of the material covered in these books and their suitability for various classes of readers. Keep in mind that a number of important books are discussed in the second section under each of the five headings which do not appear in the first section. Also keep in mind that in this fortieth-anniversary edition of this book, all of the volumes which have been written on some aspect of Calvinism during the past forty years could not possibly be included. If a particular work seemed to be indispensable, it is included in the appropriate section.

The following bibliography is intended to be a representative list of works on Calvinism. If the reader desires to find out more fully about Calvinism in particular or Reformed theology in general, we recommend securing *The History and Theology of Calvinism*, by Curt Daniel (Dallas: Scholarly Reprints, 1993). This excellent work has a recommended reading section after each chapter, and can be obtained by writing directly to the author at Reformed Bible Church, 4850 Old Jacksonville Road, Springfield, IL 62707. Although this important work is expected to be revised and then published again soon, this listing is its latest edition. There is also another excellent resource which gives an even wider bibliography on Reformed literature: *A Reader's Guide to Reformed Literature*, by Joel R. Beeke (Grand Rapids: Reformation Heritage Books, 1999), 98 pages. The same annotated bibliography is also contained in Joel R. Beeke and Sinclair Ferguson, *Reformed Confessions Harmonized* (Grand Rapids: Baker, 1999), pages 247–71.

Finally, we have eliminated some of the volumes listed in the 1963 edition because several of these works are now out of print or have been replaced by newer works. Every entry which has a publishing date after 1963, of course, has been added in this revised edition of the book.

WORKS BROADLY ON CALVINISM AND GOD'S SOVEREIGNTY

Books Dealing in Whole or in Part with Calvinism or Divine Sovereignty

à Brakel, Wilhelmus. *The Christian's Reasonable Service.* 4 vols. Reprint, Morgan, Pa.: Soli Deo Gloria, 1992, 2,524 pages.

Armstrong, John H., ed. "John Calvin." *Reformation and Revival Journal* 10, no. 4 (Fall 2001), 207 pages.

While this is a quarterly journal and not a book, it deserves to be mentioned because of its helpful, up-to-date articles on Calvin, as well as its annotated bibliography on the Reformer (pp. 149–61). Of particular note is Joel R. Beeke, "John Calvin: Teacher and Practitioner of Evangelism" (pp. 107–30).

Battles, Ford Lewis. *Analysis of the Institutes of the Christian Religion of John Calvin.* 1980. Reprint, Phillipsburg, N.J.: P&R, 2001, 421 pages.

Battles was recognized as a Calvin scholar almost without peer. He was a respected professor at Pittsburgh Theological Seminary and later at Calvin Theological Seminary before his death in 1979. He was the translator of the best edition of Calvin's *Institutes.* His classes at Pittsburgh Seminary were rewarded with a thorough study of Calvin's magnum opus from this syllabus (in outline form), which was originally published in 1980 by Baker Book House. Battles would take his students through this analytical study in a semester.

———. *Interpreting John Calvin.* Edited by Robert Benedetto. Grand Rapids: Baker, 1996, 377 pages.

Battles's articles on Calvin, which were previously published elsewhere, are reprinted here. His editor, Robert Benedetto, has also included several previously unpublished articles. This is an important volume, showing the sweep of Battles's thought on the writings of Calvin.

Beeke, Joel R. *The Quest for Full Assurance.* Carlisle, Pa.: Banner of Truth, 1999, 395 pages.

Beeke is pastor of Heritage Netherlands Reformed Congregation in Grand Rapids, Michigan, as well as professor of systematic theology and homiletics at Puritan Reformed Theological Seminary. This work is a revised and popularized version of the author's 1988 Westminster Theological Seminary dissertation. The doctrine of assurance in Calvin and his successors is treated with fullness and clarity.

Benton, John, and John Peet. *God's Riches: A Work-book on the Doctrines of Grace.* Carlisle, Pa.: Banner of Truth, 1991, 85 pages.

This is an excellent tool for group or personal Bible study. It allows a newcomer to the doctrines of grace to see how these truths come from the Bible, not simply from a system of theology.

Beza, Theodore. *The Life of John Calvin.* Durham: Evangelical Press, 1997, 144 pages.

This is the earliest biography of Calvin, finished within weeks of his death, and its author was a close associate of Calvin in Geneva. It was first published in Geneva in 1564. A revised and enlarged edition was published in 1657.

Boettner, Loraine. *The Reformed Doctrine of Predestination.* Philadelphia: Presbyterian and Reformed, 1963, 435 pages.

Of all the works on Calvinism with which we are familiar, this in our opinion is the best overall popular treatment of the subject. It is clearly written and logically arranged. Dr. Boettner has made good use of extensive quotations from a number of outstanding theological writers, both ancient and modern. These quotations not only clarify the Calvinistic position, but also show that many of the leading Christian thinkers have endorsed and defended this system of thought. After giving a brief introduction to the issues under discussion, Boettner explains and defends each of the five points at length. He then states and answers objections commonly urged against Calvinism and closes with a survey of its influence on history. We strongly recommend this work; it is one of those rare books that is profitable for both the beginner and the more advanced student. P&R Publishing has recently reissued this classic in an affordable paperback edition.

Boice, James Montgomery. *Amazing Grace.* Wheaton, Ill.: Tyndale House, 1993, 277 pages.

This is a rich study of the biblical concept of God's grace and its operation within man, by the late Dr. Boice. The book explains grace as a matter of divine prerogative.

————. *Christ's Call to Discipleship.* Chicago, Ill.: Moody Press, 1986, 170 pages.

Boice calls for a reevaluation of how the gospel is presented in this age of "easy believism." Looking through the Gospels at how Jesus summoned sinners to repentance and the necessity of following Him as Lord, this book is a needed antidote to sham conversions and false professions. It has recently been reprinted by Kregel Publications (1998, 168 pages).

————. *Two Cities, Two Loves.* Downers Grove, Ill.: InterVarsity Press, 1996, 279 pages.

Fashioned after Augustine's *City of God,* Boice calls the church to awaken to its true role in the world. As the book's dust jacket says, "Deeply biblical in its argument, thoroughly conversant with contemporary culture and practically informed by personal involvement in urban ministry, this is a book for the hour. It awakens Christians to their identity within society and their eternal destiny, and it instructs them in the one right thing to do: 'Be God's people in the midst of this world's culture.'"

————. *Whatever Happened to the Gospel of Grace?* Wheaton, Ill.: Crossway Books, 2001, 224 pages.

Concerned about evangelical drift, Boice wrote this book as his final message before succumbing to cancer. As the publisher states in the foreword, "Stated simply as his last word, Jim Boice has given us a three-fold message, calling us as Christians: 1) to repent of our worldliness; 2) to recover the great salvation doctrines of the Bible as the Reformers did five hundred years ago; and 3) to live a life transformed by the essential truths of the gospel" (p. 9). This was the essence of the life and ministry of Boice himself, and his passion to see it fulfilled in our own day comes shining through in this volume.

————, ed. *Our Sovereign God.* Grand Rapids: Baker, 1977, 175 pages.

These essays were first given as lectures at the first three conferences of the Philadelphia Conference on Reformed Theology (1974–76). The contributors are all well-known leaders within the Reformed theology movement: Boice, John Stott, Roger Nicole, Stuart Sacks, J. I. Packer, R. C. Sproul, and Ralph Keiper. Several areas of God's sovereignty and how it intersects with the Christian life and understanding are discussed, including: knowing God, praying to God, discerning the will of God, witnessing for God, God's sovereignty and grace, optimism and sovereignty, the sovereignty of God and the church, the five points of Calvinism, and God's glory in His sovereignty.

————, ed. *Our Savior God.* Grand Rapids: Baker, 1980, 189 pages.

These pages contain still more lectures given at the Philadelphia Conference on Reformed Theology from 1977 to 1979. Like the previous volume, there is much to commend in these messages, which present a Reformed understanding of man, the image of God in man, men and women, sinful man, depraved man, the unchanging Christ, the incarnation of

Christ, the Lord Christ, the work of Christ, our reconciliation to Christ, Christ's satisfaction and sacrifice, particular redemption, and the offer of Christ to the world.

Boice, James Montgomery, and Benjamin E. Sasse, eds. *Here We Stand! A Call from Confessing Evangelicals*. Grand Rapids: Baker, 1996, 207 pages.

These essays were first delivered as papers at the meeting of the Alliance of Confessing Evangelicals on April 17–20, 1996, in Cambridge, Massachusetts. They represent the concerns of some Calvinistic evangelicals that evangelicals as a whole had become worldly. Some of the more outstanding essays are David Wells, "Our Dying Culture"; R. Albert Mohler, "Contending for Truth in an Age of Anti-Truth"; and James Montgomery Boice, "Reformation in Doctrine, Worship, and Life." The Alliance of Confessing Evangelicals continues to this day.

Boice, James Montgomery, and Philip Graham Ryken. *The Doctrines of Grace*. Wheaton, Ill.: Crossway Books, 2002, 240 pages.

Dr. Boice was one of the most able defenders of the Reformed faith. Just before he died in 2000, he asked his colleague and assistant pastor for preaching, Philip Graham Ryken (who has now succeeded him as pastor of Tenth Presbyterian Church in Philadelphia), to finish the manuscript for publication. The book is a testament to Dr. Boice's effort to call the professing church to return to the doctrines of grace. Chapter 8 is especially poignant as it argues for the truest kind of Calvinism to be at work within evangelicalism.

Bonar, Horatius, and others. *The Five Points of Calvinism*. Jenkintown, Pa.: Sovereign Grace, n.d., 199 pages.

This is a collection of six articles written by Horatius Bonar, Andrew Fuller, John Calvin, John Gill, Thomas Goodwin, and Jonathan Edwards dealing with various aspects of Calvinism. These articles differ greatly in style and approach. To one seeking a unified survey of the five points or an introductory study of the system, this collection would not prove satisfactory.

But for one who is interested in some solid discussions relating to these doctrines, the work will be helpful.

Booth, Abraham. *The Reign of Grace.* 1768. Reprint, Grand Rapids: Eerdmans, 1949, 291 pages.

The theme of this work is salvation by grace. Grace is shown to reign in the sinner's election, calling, justification, sanctification, etc. This sound and stimulating book has been brought back into print by Grace Abounding Ministries. You may obtain a copy by writing to G.A.M. Printers/G.A.M. Publications, P.O. Box 25, 1102 West Church Road, Sterling, VA 22170, or by calling (703) 403–2813 or (703) 405–4121.

Bridges, Jerry. *Trusting God.* Colorado Springs: NavPress, 1988, 215 pages.

This well-written book has been used very effectively in pastoral counseling. It has excellent sections on the Christian's basis for trusting the sovereignty of God. It makes rich use of Reformed and Puritan literature.

Bunyan, John. *Pilgrim's Progress.* Carlisle, Pa.: Banner of Truth, 1982, 396 pages.

Except for the Bible, this classic is the best-selling work ever to be published in English.

Calvin, John. *Calvin's Calvinism.* Translated by Henry Beveridge. Grand Rapids: Eerdmans, 1950, 350 pages.

This book contains three treatises. The first is on the eternal predestination of God (pp. 25–186). The second is a brief reply (pp. 189–206), and the third deals with the secret providence of God (pp. 223–350). In a masterful way, Calvin probes the depths of his subject. The material is not always easy reading, but it is extremely profitable. The great Reformer faces squarely the problems involved in these doctrines and constantly turns to the Scriptures for their solutions. This work will prove especially helpful in studying the problem of evil.

————. *Day by Day with John Calvin: Selected Readings for Daily Reflection*. Peabody, Mass.: Hendrickson, 2002, 377 pages.

————. *Institutes of the Christian Religion*. Edited by John T. McNeill. Translated by Ford Lewis Battles. Library of Christian Classics, vols. 20 and 21. Philadelphia: Westminster Press, 1960, 1,734 pages.

This is generally considered the definitive edition of Calvin's *Institutes*, though it is not without its critics. There is also an abridged edition of the *Institutes*, edited by Tony Lane and Hilary Osborne (Grand Rapids: Baker, 1987), for those who would find reading the Battles edition too daunting. Michael Horton has written regarding this abridged work: "An abridged edition of any book is like walking into the middle of a movie, and more so when it is a classic. Nevertheless, Lane and Osborne have done a service for people who are taking their first steps in the wisdom and insight of Calvin" (*Putting Amazing Back into Grace* [Grand Rapids: Baker, 2002], 312). Another abridged edition of the *Institutes* is edited by Donald McKim (Louisville: Westminster/John Knox Press, 2001, 189 pages).

————. *Truth for All Time*. Carlisle, Pa.: Banner of Truth, 1998, 77 pages.

Stuart Olyott, the translator of this brief work, says in the preface: "John Calvin knew that if the biblical truths rediscovered at the Reformation were to spread throughout the world, they would have to be presented in a form which ordinary people could understand." This handy volume will be welcomed by many for its brevity and clarity. It also shows Calvin as a warmhearted shepherd, feeding not only his own flock, but the larger Reformed movement as well.

Cottret, Bernard. *Calvin: A Biography*. Grand Rapids: Eerdmans, 2000, 376 pages.

Cunningham, William. *Historical Theology*. 2 vols. 1862. Reprint, London: Banner of Truth, 1960, 1,253 pages.

Cunningham was one of Scotland's greatest theologians. He served as principal of New College, Edinburgh, from 1847 until his death in 1861. Charles Hodge regarded him as the foremost Reformed scholar of his day. *Historical Theology* is considered Cunningham's masterpiece. In vol. 2, he sets forth the historical development of Arminianism and Calvinism and shows the theological implication of each system. No serious student of theology can afford to neglect this important work. Thanks to the Banner of Truth Trust, this work has remained in print.

Custance, Arthur C. *The Sovereignty of Grace*. Phillipsburg, N.J.: Presbyterian and Reformed, 1979, 379 pages.

Daniel, Curt. *The History and Theology of Calvinism*. Dallas: Scholarly Reprints, 1993, 521 pages.

Daniel, who has also published a 900-page book on John Gill (his 1983 dissertation at the University of Edinburgh), has written one of the most helpful and readable treatments of Calvinism in print. The comments are fair and irenic, and the book attempts to cover the entire sweep of Calvinism (including much information on Puritanism and other Reformed groups, past and present). It is only available through Reformed Bible Church, 4850 Old Jacksonville Road, Springfield, IL 62707. It is worth its weight in gold!

De Greef, Wulfert. *The Writings of John Calvin*. Grand Rapids: Baker, 1993, 254 pages.

Translated from the Dutch by Lyle D. Bierma, once professor of theology at Reformed Bible College in Grand Rapids, and now at Calvin Theology Seminary, this material is intended to present Calvin's writings in a way that anyone can easily understand. This is truly a significant work.

De Kroon, Marijn. *The Honour of God and Human Salvation*. Edinburgh: T & T Clark, 2001, 256 pages.

This is an explication of Calvin's *Institutes*.

Dickinson, Jonathan. *The True Scripture Doctrine Concerning Some Important Points of Christian Faith.* Philadelphia: Presbyterian Board of Publication, 1841, 252 pages.

This valuable work was brought back into print by Sprinkle Publications in 1992. (You may obtain a copy by writing to Sprinkle Publications, P.O. Box 1094, Harrisonburg, VA 22801.) Dickinson presents five discourses on election, original sin, conversion, justification by faith, and the saint's perseverance. The work is scholarly, logically arranged, and devotional. Dickinson constantly appeals to the reader (especially in the chapter conclusions) to apply these doctrines to his life. A valuable feature of this reprint is that the publisher has added to Dickinson's work a smaller treatise entitled *The Five Points of Calvinism,* by Robert L. Dabney (1820–1898). Dabney's writing here is excellent and very readable.

Edwards, Jonathan. *The Works of Jonathan Edwards.* 2 vols. Carlisle, Pa.: Banner of Truth, 1974, 1,660 pages.

No bibliography on Calvinism would be complete without including the works of America's greatest Calvinistic theologian. Yale University Press is producing a much larger, multivolume set on the works of Edwards, which has already extended past seventeen volumes.

Gaffin, Richard. *Calvin and the Sabbath.* Fearn, U.K.: Christian Focus, 1998, 173 pages.

This book is a revised and expanded version of Gaffin's Th.M. thesis (1962). Gaffin has for many years been professor of systematic theology at Westminster Theology Seminary in Philadelphia. He concludes: "At the coming of Christ, the light in whose presence all shadows disappear, spiritual rest became a full reality; consequently, the weekly Sabbath as a type and sacrament was abrogated" (p. 142). He goes on to write: "Today the Lord's Day still serves the need it was designed to meet; in principle, however, those Christians cannot be condemned who may wish to set apart some other day or even to pattern their lives by some other arrangement than a weekly day of rest, as long as they keep in view the need for stated times of worship and meditation" (p. 143). This book both clarifies and critiques Calvin's position on the Sabbath question and does so very well.

Gerstner, John H. *The Rational Biblical Theology of Jonathan Edwards*. 3 vols. Orlando, Fla.: Ligonier Ministries, 1991, 1,960 pages.

Gerstner sets out to write the full theology (in three volumes) that Edwards himself was never able to finish.

Gill, John. *The Cause of God and Truth*. Atlanta: Turner Lassetter, 1962, 328 pages.

In part 1, Gill examines those passages most frequently appealed to by the Arminians in support of their system (sixty texts are examined). Part 2 is devoted to refuting the Arminian explanations of passages that are appealed to by Calvinists in defense of their system. These texts are classified under the heads of the doctrines contained in the five points (sixty-two passages are dealt with in this section). Part 3 is a refutation of many of the standard arguments used by Arminians in relation to the doctrines of reprobation, election, freedom of the will, the foreknowledge and providence of God, the state of the heathen, etc. Part 4 deals with the testimony of the early church fathers regarding these doctrines. Gill's exegesis and argumentation are outstanding. It is important to note, however, that Gill is considered by many to have had hyper-Calvinistic tendencies, and one would do well to read Curt Daniel's book on the theology of John Gill. In his excellent work on the history and theology of Calvinism, Daniel writes: "Dr. John Gill was the archetypal Hyper-Calvinist. Throughout his 51-year pastorate in London, he reigned as the undisputed leader among both the Baptists and the Hyper-Calvinists. No study of Hyper-Calvinism is complete without a look at Gill. Hyper-Calvinism was sometimes called 'Gillism'" (*The History and Theology of Calvinism*, 86). For more information on the theology of Gill, visit the website *www.standardbearer.org*.

Girardeau, John L. *Calvinism and Evangelical Arminianism: Compared as to Election, Reprobation, Justification, and Related Doctrines*. Columbia, S.C.: W. J. Duffie; New York: Baker and Taylor, 1890, 574 pages.

The first 177 pages deal with election and reprobation. In this section, Girardeau distinguishes sublapsarianism from supralapsarianism and insists that the former is the position held by the main body of Calvinists. For our criticism of Girardeau's view of the Fall, see our review of his book *The Will in Its Theological Relations*. On pages 178–393, Girardeau answers objections to Calvinism based on the moral attributes of God, e.g., His justice, goodness, wisdom, and veracity. Pages 394–412 deal with objections based on the moral agency of man. The remainder of the book (pp. 413–566) is devoted to the doctrine of justification. This volume contains much worthwhile material. This work has been reprinted by Sprinkle Publications (1984) and can be obtained by writing to Sprinkle Publications, P.O. Box 1094, Harrisonburg, VA 22801.

Girod, Gordon. *The Deeper Faith*. Grand Rapids: Reformed Publications, 1958, 135 pages.

Written in a clear, simple style, this book is very easy to read. The first five chapters are based on the five Canons of Dort. Chapter 6 answers some of the objections that are commonly raised against these doctrines. Chapter 7 is a reprint of the positive articles on the five points contained in these Canons. Boettner says that this work "is one of the clearest and most convincing statements of the distinguishing doctrines of the Reformed Faith that can be found anywhere." This book was reprinted by Baker Book House in 1978.

Good, Kenneth. *Are Baptists Calvinists?* 1975. Reprint, Rochester, N.Y.: Backus Books, 1988, 271 pages.

Good argues for a return of the General Association of Regular Baptists to their Calvinistic roots. An insightful look into a contemporary Calvinist-Arminian debate.

Good, Kenneth. *Are Baptists Reformed?* Lorain, Ohio: Regular Baptist Heritage Fellowship, 1986, 394 pages.

Good argues that it is appropriate for Baptists to be called Calvinists, but not necessarily Reformed. One could argue, however, that "Reformed" does not have a narrow meaning. Not all Calvinistic Baptists would agree with Good's theses, but this is still a work with which one should interact.

Hagopian, David G., ed. *Back to Basics*. Phillipsburg, N.J.: P&R, 1996, 319 pages.

In the foreword, R. C. Sproul writes: "In this most commendable work, *Back to Basics*, the authors consistently demonstrate that the supreme 'basic' or foundation of all true theology is the nature and character of God Himself. This book, both readable and instructive, is a marvelous exposition of the essence of Reformed thought. If Charles Spurgeon was correct in his assessment that Calvinism is merely a nickname for biblical Christianity, then *Back to Basics* shows that Reformed theology is the purest expression of basic Christianity. It is a clarion call to return to the foundation of faith that was laid in Christ by God our Father."

Hayden, Eric W. *Spurgeon on Revival: A Biblical and Theological Approach*. Grand Rapids: Zondervan, 1962, 144 pages.

In this work, Hayden demonstrates the practical value of Calvinistic theology by showing the results it had in Spurgeon's ministry, especially during the great revival of 1859. In chapter 5 (pp. 85–138), entitled "What Spurgeon Preached During the Revival Year," the author documents the fact that Spurgeon not only held to, but vigorously proclaimed, the five doctrines which make up the Calvinistic system. Hayden contends that if we want a revival in our day, then we should pattern our evangelism after Spurgeon's. Among other things, this would involve a return to these sound, old doctrines. Compare also the volume by Spurgeon, *Sermons on Sovereignty*, mentioned below. Another great resource for Spurgeon materials is the CD-ROM entitled *The C. H. Spurgeon Collection*, which can be obtained by contacting Ages Software Inc., P.O. Box 1926, Albany, OR 97321-0509 (541–928–8502), or by visiting *www.ageslibrary.com/spurgeon.html* for more information. See also *www.pilgrimpublications.com* for information on obtaining additional Spurgeon literature.

Helm, Paul. *Calvin and the Calvinists.* Carlisle, Pa.: Banner of Truth, 1982, 84 pages.

In his preface, Helm writes: "Recently it has come more and more to be believed that Puritan theology departed significantly from, and even opposed, the theology of John Calvin. This study rejects such a view, and does so by examining the work of one of its most recent exponents, Dr. R. T. Kendall's *Calvin and English Calvinism to 1649.* My aim is to show that Calvin and the Puritans were, theologically speaking, at one, and thus to support the truism that Calvin was a Calvinist."

Hoeksema, Homer. *The Voice of Our Fathers: An Exposition of the Canons of Dordrecht.* Grandville, Mich.: Reformed Free Publishing Association, 1981, 873 pages.

Horton, Michael. *Putting Amazing Back into Grace.* Grand Rapids: Baker, 1994, 319 pages.

Horton is professor of theology and apologetics at Westminster Theology Seminary in California. This is a good introduction to the doctrines of grace. The latest edition of this work (2002) contains the same material as the 1994 edition, adding only the Cambridge Declaration of the Alliance of Confessing Evangelicals, of which Horton is president. This declaration also appears in appendix H of this work.

Hunt, Dave, and James White. *Debating Calvinism: Five Points, Two Views.* Sisters, Oreg.: Multnomah, 2004, 427 pages.

This book grew out of James White's response to Dave Hunt's 2002 book, *What Love Is This?* (see the annotation on *The Potter's Freedom,* by James White, under "Articles in Reference Works, Systematic Theologies, Etc." below). This book has a debate format and could well go down as the most lopsided debate in church history. Once again, as in *What Love Is This?* Dave Hunt neither understands true Calvinism nor correctly represents classic Arminianism. If you want to see an excellent presentation of classic Calvinism, you will find it in James White's portion of *Debating Calvinism.*

Johnson, Terry. *When Grace Comes Home*. Fearn, U.K.: Christian Focus, 2000, 186 pages.

In one of the endorsements of this work, the late James Montgomery Boice writes: "If anyone is foolish enough to think that theology, particularly Calvinistic theology, is impractical, he needs to read this book. And even if you don't, read it anyway. . . . This [book] is exactly what the evangelical church needs, because, whether evangelicals know it or not, their future as a viable movement depends upon the rediscovery of such God-honoring theology."

Keesecker, William F., ed. *A Calvin Treasury*. 2d ed. Louisville: Westminster/John Knox Press, 1992, 206 pages.

Keesecker was the pastor of First Presbyterian Church in Oklahoma City and died in 1992. He arranges several important sections of the *Institutes* topically and provides a study guide that could be useful in a Bible study or Sunday school class.

Kelly, Douglas F. *The Emergence of Liberty in the Modern World*. Phillipsburg, N.J.: P&R, 1992, 156 pages.

The subtitle of this book is "The Influence of Calvin on Five Governments from the 16th Through 18th Centuries." Kelly chronicles Calvinism's impact on Calvin's Geneva, Hugenot France, Knox's Scotland, Puritan England, and Colonial America. Kelly is well equipped to present such a study, having translated Calvin's sermons on 2 Samuel into English and having taught systematic theology at Reformed Theological Seminary (Jackson and now Charlotte) for many years.

Kuyper, Abraham. *Lectures on Calvinism*. Grand Rapids: Eerdmans, 1931, 298 pages.

Often reprinted, Kuyper's book consists of the six Stone Lectures for 1898, which were delivered at Princeton Seminary by this former prime minister of the Netherlands. They begin with Calvinism as a life-system (i.e., as a world-and-life view) and then deal with Calvinism and religion, politics, science, art, and the future. Kuyper was a theologian of the first order, as well as a statesman; these lectures reflect the keen powers of his mind. An abbreviated edition of this work was published in 1996 as *Christianity: A Total World and Life System*, by the Plymouth Rock Foundation of Marlborough, N.H. (121 pages), with an attached study guide prepared by T. M. Moore.

————. *Particular Grace*. Grandville, Mich.: Reformed Free Publishing Association, 2001, 376 pages.

Lillback, Peter A., ed. *The Practical Calvinist: An Introduction to the Presbyterian and Reformed Heritage*. Ross-shire, Scotland: Christian Focus, 2003, 584 pages.

Here is a goldmine of theological and practical articles and essays honoring D. Clair Davis, longtime professor at Westminster Theological Seminary. This is a marvelous volume with both breadth and depth.

Lloyd-Jones, D. Martyn. *Great Doctrines of the Bible*. Wheaton, Ill.: Crossway Books, 2003, 910 pages.

Originally published by Crossway in three volumes, this important work is now published in one volume.

Machen, J. Gresham. *The Christian View of Man*. 1937. Reprint, London: Banner of Truth, 1965, 254 pages.

This is a tremendous volume on the doctrine of man by the founder of Westminster Theological Seminary in Philadelphia.

————. *God Transcendent*. Carlisle, Pa.: Banner of Truth, 1982, 206 pages.

Martin, A. N. *The Practical Implications of Calvinism*. Carlisle, Pa.: Banner of Truth, 1979, 23 pages.

This excellent lecture gives great insight into the spiritual and eternal value of Calvinism.

Meeter, H. Henry. *The Basic Ideas of Calvinism.* 6th ed., revised and expanded by Paul Marshall. Grand Rapids: Baker, 1990, 221 pages.

Meeter was for thirty years an influential Bible professor at Calvin College in Grand Rapids, before his death in 1963. His name is honored by the H. Henry Meeter Center for Calvin Studies at Calvin College/Seminary, where the finest American collection of books and materials on Calvin is housed. This book was originally published in 1939. The sixth edition contains additional chapters by Paul Marshall and covers a wide spectrum of Calvinistic ideas. These include theological ideas (the fundamental principle, the place of the Bible and faith, main tenets, etc.) and political ideas (politics and the Bible, the origin and function of the state, the form and task of government, and the relation of church and state). Louis Berkhof writes in the foreword to the second edition: "No other work in the English language offers us such a concise, and yet complete and thoroughly reliable resume of the teachings of Calvinism."

McGrath, Alister E. *A Life of John Calvin.* Cambridge, Mass.: Basil Blackwell, 1990, 332 pages.

This portrait of the life of John Calvin takes its place alongside other superior biographies of the Reformer. McGrath is generally considered to be one of the premier scholars of the Reformation and post-Reformation eras. This work also traces the influence of Calvin's thought upon European history, including modern attitudes regarding work, wealth, civil rights, capitalism, and the natural sciences.

McNeill, John T. *The History and Character of Calvinism.* New York: Oxford University Press, 1954, 466 pages.

This volume has received warm recommendations from Calvinistic writers who, nevertheless, take sharp issue with its author's theological views. It is, for the greater part, fair, factual, and objective in its presentation of Calvinism and deserves serious attention. The work is divided into four sections. The first part deals with the Zwinglian background of the Genevan Reformation (pp. 3–89). Part 2 is devoted to Calvin and the Reformation in Geneva (pp. 93–234). Part 3 deals with the spread of Calvinism (pp. 237–350). Part 4 discusses Calvinism and modern issues (pp. 353–439); this part of the work should be read with critical discernment.

Muller, Richard. *Post-Reformation Reformed Dogmatics.* 4 vols. Grand Rapids: Baker, 2003, 2,163 pages.

This long-awaited series is now complete with the publication of the last two volumes. Muller is a preeminent Calvin scholar.

Packer, J. I. *Evangelism and the Sovereignty of God.* Chicago: InterVarsity Press, 1961, 126 pages.

This is an excellent discussion of evangelism, its definition, its message, its motive, the methods and means by which it should be practiced, and its relation to the sovereignty of God in saving sinners. Packer shows that God's sovereignty and man's responsibility are taught side by side in the Bible; both are true and both must be believed and stressed if we are to do justice to the biblical message. This book is a much-needed and penetrating treatment of the subject. Because of its high quality, this book has remained in print for over forty years.

———. "Introductory Essay," in *The Death of Death in the Death of Christ,* by John Owen. London: Banner of Truth, 1959, 25 pages.

This twenty-five-page essay is a masterpiece in miniature. After briefly reviewing the origin and contents of the five points, Packer sets forth five reasons why Calvinism should not simply be equated with the five points. Packer makes some penetrating observations about the Calvinistic system, as well as the Arminian system. By all means read this essay. Regarding Owen's work, which this essay introduces, see below, under "The Nature and Extent of the Atonement." This essay has been printed separately, but it is best read as an introduction to Owen's *Death of Death.*

Palmer, Edwin H. *The Five Points of Calvinism.* Enlarged ed. Grand Rapids: Baker, 1980, 132 pages.

Palmer, known also for *The Person and Ministry of the Holy Spirit,* was formerly the executive secretary of the NIV Bible Committee, as well as the editor of *The NIV Study Bible.* This book seeks to explain, as simply and plainly as possible, both what Calvinism is and what it is not.

Parker, T. H. L. *Calvin: An Introduction to His Thought.* Louisville: Westminster/John Knox Press, 1995, 166 pages.

This is one of the best overviews of Calvin's thought in print. Parker, who has written many helpful works on Calvin, gives the reader rich and understandable explanations for Calvin's writings in the *Institutes,* including Calvin's treatments of the knowledge of God, the knowledge of Christ's role as Redeemer, the ways believers receive God's grace, both inwardly (regeneration, faith, justification, prayer, election, the final resurrection), and outwardly (the true church and its ministry, authority, sacraments, and government).

———. *Calvin's Preaching.* Louisville: Westminster/John Knox Press, 1992, 202 pages.

This is a complete rewriting of Parker's 1947 book, *The Oracles of God: An Introduction to the Preaching of John Calvin.* It is a marvelous exposition on Calvin as a preacher and teacher. B. A. Gerrish of the University of Chicago writes in his endorsement of the work: "*Calvin's Preaching* is an excellent introduction to an important but neglected side of Calvin's activity as a reformer; it is the work of a recognized authority and will appeal both to students of Calvin and to those whose responsibility it is to be servants of the word."

———. *Portrait of Calvin.* London: SCM Press, 1954, 125 pages.

This little biography of Calvin is included because of Parker's great knowledge and skill in writing. Even though Parker wrote a more full-length work on the life of Calvin (Philadelphia: Westminster, 1976), which is superior to this listing, this smaller book may help the beginner to understand Calvin before diving into the larger work.

Peterson, Robert A. *Calvin and the Atonement.* Fearn, U.K.: Christian Focus, 1999, 154 pages.

Peterson, professor of systematic theology at Covenant Theological Seminary in St. Louis, has completely revised this work that was first published in 1983, taking into account the literature published since then. This important work helps to frame Calvin's view of the Atonement (including the oft-debated issue of its extent), when so many (such as R. T. Kendall, *Calvin and English Calvinism to 1649,* 2d ed. [Carlisle, U.K.: Paternoster, 1997], and G. M. Thomas, *The Extent of the Atonement* [Carlisle, U.K.: Paternoster, 1997]) are claiming that Calvin definitely did not teach particular redemption. The reader is especially encouraged to read chapter 10 of this work in order to see the fruit of Peterson's study of Calvin's view of the extent of the Atonement.

Pink, Arthur W. *The Doctrine of Salvation.* Grand Rapids: Baker, 1975, 169 pages.

———. *Eternal Security.* Grand Rapids: Baker, 1981, 128 pages.

———. *Gleanings from the Scriptures.* Chicago, Ill.: Moody Press. 1974, 478 pages.

———. *Gleanings in the Godhead.* Chicago, Ill.: Moody Press, 1975, 247 pages.

Moody Press is to be commended for keeping this volume in print. They have been retitling and reprinting all of their A. W. Pink titles.

———. *The Sovereignty of God.* Revised editions. London: Banner of Truth, 1961, 1968, 1972, 160 pages.

This book deals with the sovereignty of God in creation, administration, salvation, and operation. Pink also develops the relationship between God's sovereignty and man's will, as well as its relation to prayer. He closes with a discussion of what our attitude should be toward this doctrine and its practical value in our lives. We have listed the revised British editions of 1961, 1968, and 1972, rather than the various American editions, because the original edition of 1918 and the revised edition of 1929 do not reflect the maturation of Pink's theology in certain key areas after the early 1930s (see Iain Murray, *The Life of Arthur W. Pink* [Carlisle, Pa.: Banner of Truth, 1981], 194–99).

Piper, John. *The Legacy of Sovereign Joy.* Wheaton, Ill.: Crossway Books, 2000, 158 pages.

Piper, pastor of Bethlehem Baptist Church in Minneapolis, Minnesota, has captured the essence of Augustine, Luther, and Calvin in this biographical work. His writing is clear and he is able to distill in these pages the triumph of God's sovereign grace in the lives of these noble Christian leaders.

Reid, W. Stanford, ed. *John Calvin: His Influence in the Western World.* Grand Rapids: Zondervan, 1982, 415 pages.

This remarkably broad array of important essays helps the reader to understand the incredible impact of Calvin's ministry on the Western world. Of special note are Robert Knudsen's essay on "Calvinism as a Cultural Force," Robert Godfrey's essay on "Calvin and Calvinism in the Netherlands," and George Marsden's essay, "America's 'Christian' Origins: Puritan New England as a Case Study." Each essay in the book should be read with care and great profit.

Reymond, Robert. *The Reformation's Conflict with Rome: Why It Must Continue.* Fearn, U.K.: Christian Focus, 2001, 155 pages.

Reymond shows why evangelicals must not unite with Roman Catholics on primary matters of the faith.

Ryken, Philip Graham. *What Is a True Calvinist?* Phillipsburg, N.J.: P&R, 2003, 32 pages.

This booklet is taken from chapter 8 of *The Doctrines of Grace: Rediscovering the Evangelical Gospel,* by Boice and Ryken (see above). It is part of a larger series of booklets published by P&R Publishing entitled *Basics of the Reformed Faith*.

Schreiner, Thomas, and Bruce Ware, eds. *The Grace of God, the Bondage of the Will*. 2 vols. Grand Rapids: Baker, 1995, 521 pages.

In 1975, Clark Pinnock, a noted Arminian, and now retired professor of theology at McMaster Divinity School in Ontario, Canada, edited a volume of essays that espoused Arminianism, entitled *Grace Unlimited* (Minneapolis: Bethany House, 1975, 264 pages). In 1989, he edited another book on Arminianism, *The Grace of God, the Will of Man* (Grand Rapids: Zondervan, 1989, 318 pages), which sought to bring it to an even wider audience. The volumes edited by Schreiner and Ware more than capably answer each of these books with a thoroughly biblical and Calvinistic response. If one wants to see the classic differences between the two rival theologies, these are the books to read. Recently, because of the continued impact of Arminianism, but also due to the influence of so-called "Openness of God" advocates, Schreiner and Ware reissued fourteen chapters out of the original two volumes under the title *Still Sovereign* (Grand Rapids: Baker, 2000, 356 pages).

Schreiner, Thomas R., and Ardel B. Caneday. *The Race Set Before Us: A Biblical Theology of Perseverance and Assurance*. Downers Grove, Ill.: InterVarsity Press, 2001, 344 pages.

Seaton, W. J. *The Five Points of Calvinism*. Edinburgh: Banner of Truth, 1970; reprinted, 2000, 24 pages.

Shedd, W. G. T. *Calvinism: Pure and Mixed*. 1893. Reprint, Carlisle, Pa.: Banner of Truth, 1986, 161 pages.

Shedd (1820–1894) was a professor at Union Theological Seminary in New York. This book is essentially a defense of the doctrinal propositions of the Westminster standards. It is a strong statement of Calvinism.

Smith, Morton H. *Studies in Southern Presbyterian Theology.* Jackson, Miss.: Presbyterian Reformation Society, 1962, 367 pages.

This volume first appeared as a doctoral dissertation under the direction of Professor G. C. Berkouwer. Its purpose is to trace the theological thought of some of the past leaders of the Southern Presbyterian Church, especially regarding the inspiration of Scripture and election. The author demonstrates that the Southern Presbyterian Church of the past was led by men who were devoted to Calvinistic theology and the inerrancy of Scripture. Among those discussed are Thornwell, Dabney, Palmer, Plumer, and Girardeau. The work contains an extensive bibliography on Southern Presbyterian theology. This important work was reissued by P&R Publishing in 1987. Readers may also be interested in a new edition of Henry Alexander White's 1911 work, *Southern Presbyterian Leaders,* reprinted by the Banner of Truth Trust in 2000. Readers may also profit greatly from Douglas Kelly's *Preachers with Power* (Carlisle, Pa.: Banner of Truth, 1992), an account of the lives and preaching of "four stalwarts of the South": Daniel Baker, James Henley Thornwell, Benjamin Morgan Palmer, and John Girardeau.

Spencer, Duane Edward. *Tulip: The Five Points of Calvinism in the Light of Scripture.* 2d ed. Grand Rapids: Baker, 1979, 93 pages.

Spencer was the pastor of Grace Orthodox Presbyterian Church in San Antonio, Texas. This new edition has a foreword by Luder G. Whitlock, recently retired president of Reformed Theological Seminary. This book succinctly describes the essence of Calvinism's five points, and does so quite well.

Sproul, R. C. *Essential Truths of the Christian Faith.* Wheaton, Ill.: Tyndale House, 1992, 302 pages.

———. *Getting the Gospel Right.* Grand Rapids: Baker, 1999, 207 pages.

Because of the great confusion created by the recent documents "Evangelicals and Catholics Together" and "The Gift of Salvation," evangelicals need help in understanding the real issues. In this important work, Sproul's surefootedness in articulating the biblical gospel leads the way.

———. *Grace Unknown: The Heart of Reformed Theology*. Grand Rapids: Baker, 1997, 230 pages.

Sproul is a master at making difficult theological subjects understandable. This is one of the best books at a popular level on Reformed theology.

Sproul, R. C., Jr. *Almighty Over All*. Grand Rapids: Baker, 1999, 184 pages.

———, ed. *After Darkness, Light*. Phillipsburg, N.J.: P&R, 2003, 214 pages.

This clearly written book brings together a number of Christian leaders such as Robert Godfrey, Sinclair Ferguson, O. Palmer Robertson, John MacArthur, and Jay Adams, in order to pay tribute to the ministry of R. C. Sproul. Ten essays cover both the so-called five *solas* of the Reformation and the five points of Calvinism. Sometimes collaborative works of this sort are uneven in style and depth, but this one is excellent throughout.

Spurgeon, Charles Haddon. *Sermons on Sovereignty*. Ashland, Ky.: Baptist Examiner Book Shop, 1959, 256 pages.

Spurgeon was probably the greatest Baptist preacher of all time. This volume contains a brief sketch of his life and a selection of eighteen sermons preached by him over a period of twenty-eight years. Each of these sermons deals with some aspect of Calvinism or the sovereignty of God. Such subjects as human inability, election, particular redemption, and providence are covered. These messages were delivered to thousands who came to hear Spurgeon preach. See the comments on *Spurgeon on Revival*, by Hayden, above. For a further reference on Spurgeon's view of Calvinism, see appendix D in this volume. For the best collection of material on Spurgeon's life and sermons, as well as related areas of interest, see the excellent website *www.spurgeon.org.*

Van Til, Cornelius. *The Case for Calvinism.* Philadelphia: Presbyterian and Reformed, 1963, 154 pages.

In 1959, Westminster Press published three volumes presenting a case for a particular theology (*The Case for a New Reformation Theology,* by William Hordern; *The Case for Theology in Liberal Perspective,* by L. Harold DeWolf; *The Case for Orthodox Theology,* by Edward J. Carnell). Van Til, longtime professor of apologetics at Westminster Theological Seminary, and the modern father of presuppositionalism, was asked to critique each of these works, providing an alternative view, that of Calvinism. Although this book is out of print, the entire collection of Van Til's works is available on a CD-ROM entitled *The Works of Cornelius Van Til,* and can be obtained at *www.bibletheology.com/products/wcvt/html.*

Wallace, Ronald S. *Calvin, Geneva and the Reformation.* Grand Rapids: Baker, 1988, 310 pages.

This is a wonderful, enriching study of Calvin as a social worker, churchman, pastor, and theologian. Wallace is a noted Calvin scholar and has produced many enlightening studies on the Genevan Reformer, and this is at the top of the list. While this edition is out of print, Wipf and Stock Publishers have recently republished it. It is available on their website, *www.wipfandstock.com,* as are many other helpful reprints.

Warburton, Ben A. *Calvinism.* Grand Rapids: Eerdmans 1955, 248 pages.

The full title of this book—*Calvinism: Its History and Basic Principles, Its Fruits and Its Future, and Its Practical Application to Life*—gives an outline of its contents. The book, written on a popular level, presents the historical background of Arminius and the Synod of Dort. Among other things, the five articles of the Synod are explained and defended. A related and fascinating book, which includes much information on the Synod of Dort, is by Thomas Scott, entitled *The Articles of the Synod of Dort* (reprint, Harrisonburg, Va.: Sprinkle, 1993).

Warfield, Benjamin Breckinridge. *Calvin and Augustine.* Philadelphia: Presbyterian and Reformed, 1956, 507 pages.

This work consists of nine articles originally written for various theological journals and encyclopedias. These studies are devoted to Calvin and Augustine and certain aspects of their thought. Directly or indirectly, a good deal of the material is related to Calvinistic theology, although only one article is on Calvinism itself. This work is a superb example of accurate scholarship, and the theology student will find the material exceedingly rich, although much of it will prove too technical for the average reader. This volume is part of a five-volume set of Warfield's works, published by P&R Publishing, as the Presbyterian and Reformed Publishing Company is now known. The original ten-volume edition of Warfield's works (Oxford University Press, 1927), was brought back into print by Baker Book House in 1991. For those who desire to read more extensively in Warfield's writings (which may be some of the richest works ever produced by an American theologian), John E. Meeter and Roger Nicole have compiled *A Bibliography of Benjamin Breckenridge Warfield: 1851–1921* (Presbyterian and Reformed, 1974, 108 pages). In addition, P&R Publishing reissued John Meeter's excellently edited two-volume edition of *Benjamin B. Warfield: Selected Shorter Writings* (originally published in 1970 and 1973) in 2001.

———. *The Plan of Salvation.* Grand Rapids: Eerdmans, 1955, 112 pages.

This small volume deals with the order of the decrees. There is an excellent chart on page 31 that summarizes the contents of the book. The vocabulary is heavy and at times the material is rather technical, which makes it somewhat difficult to read. But for those who are willing to study it, this is one of the most rewarding works ever written on the plan of salvation. Every student should read this.

Wells, David F., ed. *Reformed Theology in America.* Grand Rapids: Baker, 1997, 287 pages.

Wells, well known for his incisive critiques of modern evangelicalism, has brought together a number of excellent essayists on American Reformed theologians and movements, including Princeton theology, Dutch theology, and Southern Reformed theology. This is an outstanding book with a wealth of information and background on the shapers of Reformed theology in America.

Wells, Tom. *Faith: The Gift of God.* Carlisle, Pa.: Banner of Truth, 1983, 156 pages.

———. *God Is King!* Darlington, U.K.: Evangelical Press, 1992, 128 pages.

Wendel, François. *Calvin: Origins and Development of His Religious Thought.* Translated by Philip Mairet. Grand Rapids: Baker, 1997, 383 pages.

John T. McNeill writes: "There exists no comparable book on Calvin. Indeed, it would be difficult to point to one like it in quality on any great theologian." This Baker edition is a reprint of the 1963 English edition, which was a translation of the first French edition of 1950.

White, James R. *Drawn by the Father.* Lindenhurst, N.Y.: Reformation Press, 1999, 63 pages.

A friendly, readable study of John 6:35–45.

———. *The Sovereign Grace of God.* Lindenhurst, N.Y.: Reformation Press, 2003, 198 pages.

Zemek, George J. *A Biblical Theology of the Doctrines of Sovereign Grace.* Self-published, 2002, 277 pages.

This is a masterful exegetical treatment of the relevant passages of both the Old and the New Testaments which relate to the doctrines of grace. Dr. Zemek is the dean of the Ministry Training Center at The Bible Church of Little Rock,

Arkansas. The book can be received free of charge by writing to: B. T. D. S. G., 1615 Dorado Beach Drive, Little Rock, AR 72212–2685. Look for this volume to be published in the future by Wipf and Stock (www.wipfandstock.com).

There are a number of important books (dealing specifically with each of the five points) discussed below under "Books on the Five Points Individually." For example, Edwards's *Freedom of the Will* and Luther's *The Bondage of the Will* are listed and annotated under the heading "Human Inability and the Freedom of the Will."

Articles in Reference Works, Systematic Theologies, Etc.

The books listed under this heading contain articles or sections pertaining to Calvinism or the various doctrines related to it. By consulting the alphabetical arrangement of subjects, the table of contents, or the index of the book, one may locate material on such topics as the sovereignty of God, the decrees of God, Calvinism, original sin, depravity, election, predestination, the Atonement, satisfaction, grace, calling, regeneration, faith, perseverance, and the security of believers.

It must not be supposed that because we have not commented on many of the books listed in this section, they are of less value than the ones listed in the previous section. We have limited our remarks so as to conserve space, but each work deserves serious study.

The following works are representative of some of the most notable writings on topics related to Calvinism:

Augustine. *Saint Augustine's Anti-Pelagian Works*. Vol. 5 of *The Nicene and Post-Nicene Fathers*. Edited by Philip Schaff. Introduction by B. B. Warfield. Grand Rapids: Eerdmans, 1956, 568 pages.

This multivolume work is available on the Internet at *www.ccel.org*, the website of the Christian Classics Ethereal

Library, the largest on-line center for classic Christian literature, including the early church fathers. Their link to this work is *www.ccel.org/fathers2* and could save much bookshelf space!

Baker, Alvin. *Berkouwer's Doctrine of Election: Balance or Imbalance?* Phillipsburg, N.J.: P&R, 1981, 204 pages.

Barber, Jimmy K. *Justification: The Heart of the Gospel.* Memphis: Veritas, 1989, 256 pages.

Basinger, David, and Randall Basinger, eds. *Predestination and Free Will: Four Views of Divine Sovereignty and Human Freedom.* Downers Grove, Ill.: InterVarsity Press, 1986, 180 pages.

Bavinck, Herman. *The Doctrine of God.* Translated by William Hendriksen. Grand Rapids: Eerdmans, 1951, 407 pages.

A paperback edition was issued in 1977 by Baker Book House, as well as a hardback edition in that same year by the Banner of Truth Trust.

———. *Reformed Dogmatics: Prolegomena.* Edited by John Bolt. Translated by John Vriend. Grand Rapids, Baker, 2003, 685 pages.

This is volume 1 of Bavinck's four-volume *Dogmatics,* which will finally appear in English to many grateful readers.

Begg, Alistair. *Preaching for God's Glory.* Wheaton, Ill.: Crossway Books, 1999, 48 pages.

Berkhof, L. *Systematic Theology.* Grand Rapids: Eerdmans, 1949, 784 pages.

In 1996, Eerdmans reissued this text with Berkhof's own introduction reinserted and with a new preface by Richard A. Muller of Calvin Theology Seminary. The introductory material is 200 pages, and the remaining material is still 784 pages.

Boettner, Loraine. *The Reformed Faith.* Phillipsburg, N.J.: P&R, 1983, 28 pages.

Boice, James Montgomery. *What Makes a Church Evangelical?* Wheaton, Ill.: Crossway Books, 1999, 48 pages.

Buchanan, James. *The Doctrine of Justification.* 1867. Reprint, Carlisle, Pa.: Banner of Truth, 1961, 514 pages.

Long considered to be the classic work on the subject, this Banner of Truth edition includes an excellent introductory essay by J. I. Packer.

Cheeseman, John. *Saving Grace.* Carlisle, Pa.: Banner of Truth, 1999, 136 pages.

Originally published under a different title, this is a wonderful treatment of the doctrine of God's grace.

Dabney, R. L. *Systematic and Polemic Theology.* Richmond: Presbyterian Committee of Publication, 1927, 903 pages.

In 1985, the Banner of Truth Trust reissued this important work. Previously, in 1967, it reprinted the three-volume *Discussions: Evangelical and Theological* as *Discussions of Robert L. Dabney.*

Daniel, Curt. *Biblical Calvinism.* Self-published, n.d., 12 pages.

A brief but good introduction to the doctrines of grace.

DeWitt, John Richard. *What Is the Reformed Faith?* Carlisle, Pa.: Banner of Truth, 1981, 24 pages.

Douglas, J. D., ed. *New Bible Dictionary.* Grand Rapids: Eerdmans, 1962, 1,375 pages.

This dictionary is an excellent general resource. The best dictionary to consult on Calvinism might be *Dictionary of the Presbyterian and Reformed Tradition in America,* edited by D. G. Hart (Downers Grove, Ill.: InterVarsity Press, 1999, 286 pages). Although not a Bible dictionary *per se,* it contains a wealth of information on people, denominations, and influences from a Reformed perspective. An even wider perspective on the Reformed world is presented by *The Encyclopedia of the Reformed Faith,* edited by Donald K. McKim (Louisville: Westminster/John Knox Press, 1992). On the history and influence of Scottish Calvinism, see the *Dictionary of Scottish Church History and Theology,* edited by Nigel M. de S. Cameron (Downers Grove, Ill.: InterVarsity Press, 1993).

Edwards, Jonathan. *Justification by Faith Alone.* Morgan, Pa.: Soli Deo Gloria, 2000, 154 pages.

This reprint is an excerpt from the Hickman edition of Edwards's works (1838).

Ehrhard, Jim. *The Dangers of the Invitation System.* Kansas City: Christian Communicators Worldwide, 1999, 23 pages.

Finlayson, R. A. *Reformed Theological Writings.* Fearn, U.K.: Christian Focus, 1996, 272 pages.

Frame, John M. *The Doctrine of God.* Phillipsburg, N.J.: P&R, 2002, 864 pages.

Frame, who now teaches at Reformed Seminary in Orlando, is a leading present-day Calvinist. This volume is the second one to appear in the series A Theology of Lordship (see on volume 1 below); the third volume (*The Doctrine of the Christian Life*) is forthcoming.

————. *The Doctrine of the Knowledge of God.* Phillipsburg, N.J.: P&R, 1987, 437 pages.

This is the first volume in the series A Theology of Lordship. The previous listing is the second in this series; the third (*The Doctrine of the Christian Life*) is forthcoming. Frame is noted for his ability to take complicated theological issues and bring clarity and focus to them.

Gill, John. *A Body of Doctrinal Divinity.* Grand Rapids: Baker, n.d., 1,023 pages.

Gill's works, including this book, can be obtained at the website *www.standardbearer.org.*

Grudem, Wayne. *Systematic Theology.* 2d ed. Grand Rapids: Zondervan, 2000, 1,290 pages.

Grudem provides solid, yet readable, chapters on all areas of theology. He writes, "I hold . . . a traditional Reformed position with regard to questions of God's sovereignty and man's responsibility (chapter 16), the extent of the atonement (chapter 27), and the question of predestination (chapter 32). Consistent with the Reformed view, I hold that those who are truly born again will never lose their salvation (chapter 40)" (p. 16). Grudem has also become well known for his view on present-day prophecy in the church (a minority view within Calvinism), an extension of his overall view that all the sign gifts of the New Testament age are operative today (also a minority view in the history of Calvinism). There is a scaled-down version of this work, edited by one of his former students, and also published by Zondervan, entitled *Bible Doctrine*.

Hannah, John. *To God Be the Glory*. Wheaton, Ill.: Crossway Books, 2000, 48 pages.

Harrison, Everett F., ed. *Baker's Dictionary of Theology*. Grand Rapids: Baker, 1960, 566 pages.

Baker Book House has published a new dictionary of theology, edited by Walter Elwell of Wheaton College, entitled *Evangelical Dictionary of Theology*, 2d ed. (Grand Rapids: Baker, 2001, 1,312 pages).

Haykin, Michael A. G., ed. *A Foundation for Life*. Dundas, Ont.: Joshua Press, 2002, 140 pages.

This is a collaborative effort by several Reformed evangelicals including Jim Elliff, Jerry Marcellino, Stephen Wellum, and Fred Zaspel.

Heppe, Heinrich. *Reformed Dogmatics, Set Out and Illustrated from the Sources*. Translated by G. T. Thompson. London: George Allen and Unwin, 1950, 721 pages.

Paternoster Press in the U.K. and Baker Books in the U.S. are jointly releasing a series of reprinted works under the editorship of Richard A. Muller and others. This important work will become volume 5 in this new series.

Hodge, Archibald Alexander. *Outlines of Theology*. Grand Rapids: Eerdmans, 1959, 678 pages.

This important volume was reprinted by the Banner of Truth Trust in 1972, from the rewritten and enlarged edition of 1879. A. A. Hodge also wrote *Evangelical Theology*, which was reprinted in 1976, also by the Banner of Truth Trust. Hodge was the eldest son and successor to the great Charles Hodge at Princeton Theological Seminary.

Hodge, Charles. *Systematic Theology.* 3 vols. 1872–73. Reprint, Grand Rapids: Eerdmans, 1952, 2,260 pages.

Hodge, the most influential of the Princeton theologians of his day, has written one of the most beloved systematic theologies. This 2,000-page work is also available in an abridged edition, by Edward N. Gross, published by P&R Publishing (1997, 585 pages).

Hoekema, Anthony A. *Saved by Grace.* Grand Rapids: Eerdmans, 1989, 277 pages.

Jewett, Paul King. *Election and Predestination.* Grand Rapids: Eerdmans, 1985, 147 pages.

Johnson, Gary L. W., and R. Fowler White, eds. *Whatever Happened to the Reformation?* Phillipsburg, N.J.: P&R, 2001, 399 pages.

MacArthur, John F., Jr. *Ashamed of the Gospel.* Expanded ed. Wheaton, Ill.: Crossway Books, 1993, 266 pages.

———. *The Gospel According to the Apostles.* Dallas: Word, 2000, 272 pages.

———. *The Gospel According to Jesus.* Revised ed. Grand Rapids: Zondervan, 1994, 302 pages.

———. *The Love of God.* Dallas: Word, 1996, 251 pages.

Mack, Wayne. *To God Be the Glory: A Study in the Biblical Doctrine of Particular Redemption.* Fullerton, Calif.: Reformed Baptist Publications, n. d., 20 pages.

McDonald, H. D. *The Atonement of the Death of Christ.* Grand Rapids: Baker, 1985, 371 pages.

———. *New Testament Concept of Atonement.* Grand Rapids: Baker, 1994, 144 pages.

———. *Salvation.* Wheaton, Ill.: Crossway Books, 1982, 188 pages.

McGrath, Alister. *Iustitia Dei: A History of the Christian Doctrine of Justification.* 2d ed. New York: Cambridge, 1998, 532 pages.

Although very useful, this work is not Reformed.

McKim, Donald K. *Introducing the Reformed Faith.* Louisville: Westminster/John Knox Press, 2001, 261 pages.

McKim does not reside within the conservative Reformed movement.

Morey, Robert. *Studies in the Atonement.* Southbridge, Mass.: Crowne, 297 pages.

Morris, Leon. *The Apostolic Preaching of the Cross.* 3d ed. Grand Rapids: Eerdmans, 1965, 318 pages.

Murray, Iain H. *The Invitation System.* Carlisle, Pa.: Banner of Truth, 1967, 37 pages.

———. *Revival and Revivalism: The Making and Unmaking of American Evangelicalism 1750–1858.* Carlisle, Pa.: Banner of Truth, 1994, 455 pages.

Simply the best book written on the subject.

———. *Spurgeon v. Hyper-Calvinism.* Carlisle, Pa.: Banner of Truth, 1995, 164 pages.

An excellent presentation of the historical context of Spurgeon's battle with the hyper-Calvinism of his day.

Murray, John. *The Collected Writings of John Murray.* 4 vols. Carlisle, Pa.: Banner of Truth, 1976–1982, 1,570 pages.

The reader is encouraged especially to read "The Free Offer of the Gospel," 4:113–32. This essay was reprinted separately by the Banner of Truth Trust in 2001.

Nettles, Thomas J. *By His Grace and for His Glory: A Historical, Theological, and Practical Study of the Doctrines of Grace in Baptist Life.* 2d ed. Lake Charles, La.: Cor Meum Tibi, 2002, 442 pages.

An important work for understanding the Calvinistic roots of the Southern Baptists.

Nicole, Roger. *Our Sovereign Saviour: The Essence of the Reformed Faith.* Fearn, U.K.: Christian Focus, 2002, 184 pages.

These essays were originally prepared as messages for theological conferences. Note especially "Particular Redemption," pp. 57–73.

———. *Standing Forth: Collected Writings of Roger Nicole*. Fearn, U.K.: Christian Focus, 2002, 492 pages.

One of the best treatments of the Calvinistic view on the extent of the Atonement is "John Calvin's View of the Extent of the Atonement," pp. 283–312. It alone is worth the price of the book.

Payne, William E. *Life-Transforming Truth*. Dundas, Ont.: Joshua Press, 2001, 77 pages.

A fine introduction to the doctrines of grace.

Picirilli, Robert E. *Grace, Faith, Free Will. Contrasting Views of Salvation: Calvinism and Arminianism*. Nashville: Randall House, 2002, 245 pages.

For almost half a century Dr. Picirilli has been professor of theology and dean of the Free-Will Baptist College in Nashville, Tennessee. He presents what he terms "Reformation Arminianism." For an incisive critique of his view and this book, see Roger Nicole's review in *The Founder's Journal*, no. 52 (Spring 2003), pp. 26–29.

Piper, John. *The Justification of God: An Exegetical and Theological Study of Romans 9:1–23*. 2d ed. Grand Rapids: Baker, 1993, 245 pages.

No one who comes from the Arminian persuasion can ignore this book. In our judgment, its exegesis and logic are airtight.

Piper, John, and the pastoral team. *Tulip: What We Believe About the Five Points of Calvinism*. Minneapolis: Bethlehem Baptist Church, n.d., 33 pages.

Reisinger, Ernest C. *The Law and the Gospel*. Phillipsburg, N.J.: P&R, 1997, 196 pages.

———. *Today's Evangelism: Its Message and Methods*. Phillipsburg, N.J.: Craig Press, 1982, 163 pages.

Reisinger, Ernest C., and D. Matthew Allen. *Beyond Five Points*. Cape Coral, Fla.: Founders Press, 2002, 270 pages.

An important work by Southern Baptists on issues related to the five points of Calvinism. This is an articulate expression of the doctrines of grace and is written in a gracious spirit. See also James McGuire's valuable essay in the present book (appendix A) in this regard.

————. *A Quiet Revolution: A Chronicle of Beginnings of Reformation in the Southern Baptist Convention*. Cape Coral, Fla.: Founders Press, 2000, 107 pages.

Reymond, Robert L. *A New Systematic Theology of the Christian Faith*. 2d ed. Nashville: Thomas Nelson, 1998, 1,210 pages.

Reymond, emeritus professor of systematic theology at Knox Theological Seminary in Ft. Lauderdale, Florida, has written arguably the best Reformed systematic theology within Calvinistic circles in recent times. He interacts with current literature, yet recasts the Reformed faith from a faithful reading and interaction with the Reformers themselves. Not all from a Calvinistic perspective will agree with some of what Reymond has written, but all can agree that he attempts to base all of his systematizing upon the biblical texts themselves. His work is refreshingly exegetical, when so many other theologies—past and present—have attempted to formulate the doctrines of the Word of God from a philosophical or pragmatic basis, with a few Bible verses thrown in for good measure. Reymond is to be applauded for seeking to give the Christian community a systematic theology from the Bible's own propositions.

Ryken, Philip Graham. *Is Jesus the Only Way?* Wheaton, Ill.: Crossway Books, 1999, 48 pages.

————. *The Message of Salvation*. Downers Grove, Ill.: InterVarsity Press, 2001, 311 pages.

Sell, Alan P. F. *The Great Debate: Calvinism, Arminianism and Salvation*. Grand Rapids: Baker, 1983, 141 pages.

Shedd, William G. T. *Dogmatic Theology*. 3 vols. 1888–94. Reprint, Nashville: Thomas Nelson, 1980, 1,877 pages.

Called by Mark Noll "the greatest systematizer, after Charles Hodge, of American Calvinistic theology between the Civil

War and World War I" (cited in *Evangelical Dictionary of Theology*, ed. Walter Elwell, 2d ed. [Grand Rapids: Baker, 2001], 1098). P&R Publishing has republished Shedd's important work under the editorship of Alan Gomes.

Smith, Morton H. *The Biblical Doctrine of Predestination*. Self-published, 1995, 113 pages.

———. *Systematic Theology*. 2 vols. Greenville, S.C.: Greenville Seminary Press, 1994, 850 pages.

Smith has been a faithful servant of the Lord; he now teaches at Greenville Presbyterian Theological Seminary. He attempts to be exegetical, nontechnical, and readable. While this work has not gained recognition as a standard Reformed systematic theology, it is nevertheless a fine work of good depth.

Sproul, R. C. *The Invisible Hand*. Dallas: Word, 1996, 210 pages.

This book on the doctrine of God's providence has been reissued by P&R Publishing (2003) with indices added.

———. *Justified by Faith Alone*. Wheaton, Ill.: Crossway Books, 1999, 48 pages.

Strong, Augustus Hopkins. *Systematic Theology*. Chicago: Judson Press, 1947, 1,166 pages.

This work, by an influential Baptist theologian of a century ago, has had enduring value.

Talbot, Mark R. *The Signs of True Conversion*. Wheaton, Ill.: Crossway Books, 2000, 47 pages.

Toon, Peter. *Justification and Sanctification*. Wheaton, Ill.: Crossway Books, 1983, 162 pages.

Turretin, Francis. *Institutes of Elenctic Theology*. 3 vols. Phillipsburg, N.J.: P&R, 1992–97, 2,223 pages.

Francis Turretin (1623–1687) was an important figure in the Reformed movement, because this work heavily influenced the Princeton theologians of the nineteenth century, especially Charles Hodge. In order to understand the development of Reformed theology, especially in the seventeenth century and beyond, you must read Turretin.

Wallace, Ronald. *The Atoning Death of Christ*. Wheaton, Ill.: Crossway Books, 1981, 147 pages.

Walton, John H. *Covenant: God's Purpose/God's Plan*. Grand Rapids: Zondervan, 1994, 192 pages.

Warfield, Benjamin Breckinridge. *Biblical and Theological Studies*. Philadelphia: Presbyterian and Reformed, 1952, 580 pages.

This is part of a series of five volumes of Warfield's writings published by P&R Publishing. It contains some of the richest theological writing you will find. Such chapters as "The Biblical Doctrine of the Trinity," "Imputation," and "Predestination," along with some supplemental sermons, are wonderful examples of Calvinistic literature. Three volumes of the more basic and readable writings of Warfield have been reprinted by the Banner of Truth Trust: *Biblical Doctrines* (1929, reprinted in 1988, 665 pages), *Faith and Life* (1916, reprinted in 1974, 458 pages), and *The Saviour of the World* (1916, reprinted in 1991, 270 pages).

White, James R. *The Potter's Freedom: A Defense of the Reformation and a Rebuttal of Norman Geisler's* Chosen But Free. Amityville: Calvary Press, 2000, 343 pages.

White is to be thanked for carefully, fairly, and meticulously refuting Geisler's disturbing and misleading book, *Chosen but Free: A Balanced View of Divine Election*, 2d ed. (Minneapolis: Bethany House, 2001, 283 pages). In the preface to the book, Phillip R. Johnson, executive director of Grace to You (the media ministry of John MacArthur), writes of Geisler's book, "Unfortunately, *Chosen But Free* is a disappointment. More than a mere letdown, actually. It is a stunningly inept treatment of the subject it undertakes" (p. 11). Geisler responds to White in the second edition of the book, and White has a detailed response to Geisler at *www.aomin.org/CBFRep2.html*. White has also answered the most egregious misrepresentation of Calvinism in print today, Dave Hunt's *What Love Is This?* (Sisters, Oreg.: Loyal, 2002, 436 pages). See also James White's website, *www.aomin.org*, and the listing of his debate with Hunt, at Hunt and White, *Debating Calvinism,* above, under "Books Dealing in Whole or in Part with Calvinism or Divine Sovereignty."

Information Concerning Creeds and Confessions

Below are listed the official confessions of faith of the majority of the major evangelical Protestant churches of the world. The fact that these confessions are Calvinistic in content testifies to the tremendous influence that Calvinism has exerted upon history. A number of other Calvinistic confessions could have been included, but it seemed best to confine the list to those confessions which have enjoyed an official capacity or (as in the case of the Baptists and the Congregationalists) have received the widest recognition among the churches. None of these confessions has been officially revised so as to exclude Calvinism, nor officially repudiated because of it. Of the Church of England, Lord Brougham said, "It has a Romish ritual, a Calvinistic creed, and an Arminian clergy." Since his time, more Protestant groups than wish to admit it have found themselves in the embarrassing position of possessing a Calvinistic confession and at the same time being dominated by ministers who believe and preach Arminianism while professing to be loyal to the historic doctrines of their churches.

For an excellent study of the creeds, consult Philip Schaff's three-volume work, *The Creeds of Christendom* (New York: Harper and Brothers, 1919). Volume 1 gives a history of the creeds, volume 2 is devoted to the Greek and Latin creeds, and volume 3 contains the texts of all the major evangelical creeds. Baker Book House reprinted this three-volume set in 1983 from the 1931 Harper & Row edition. This work is now accessible on the Internet through *www.ccel.org* (Christian Classics Ethereal Library). The specific link on their website to *The Creeds of Christendom* is *www.ccel.org/s/schaff/creeds2/.*

The other books given in this section are devoted to the study of particular creeds. If you wish to read each of these church documents and their historical contexts in book form and not simply from your computer, please refer to the following sources:

Beeke, Joel R., and Sinclair Ferguson. *Reformed Confessions Harmonized.* Grand Rapids: Baker, 1999, 271 pages.

Bettenson, Henry, and Chris Mauder. *Documents of the Christian Church.* 3d ed. New York: Oxford University Press, 1999, 463 pages.

Campbell, Ted A. *Christian Confessions: An Introduction.* Louisville: Westminster/John Knox Press, 1996, 336 pages.

Cochrane, Arthur C., ed. *Reformed Confessions of the Sixteenth Century.* Louisville: Westminster/John Knox Press, 2003, 336 pages.

Ecumenical Creeds and Reformed Confessions. Grand Rapids: Faith Alive Christian Resources, Christian Reformed Church, 1988, 149 pages.

Hall, David W., and Joseph H. Hall, eds. *Paradigms in Polity: Classic Readings in Reformed and Presbyterian Church Government.* Grand Rapids: Eerdmans, 1994, 621 pages.

This may be the most complete listing of important Presbyterian and Reformed literature on church government.

Hoezee, Scott. *Speaking As One: A Look at the Ecumenical Creeds.* Grand Rapids: CRC Publications and Eerdmans, 1997, 61 pages.

Leith, John H. *Creeds of the Churches.* 3d ed. Louisville: Westminster/John Knox Press, 1982, 736 pages.

McKim, Donald K. *Theological Turning Points.* Louisville: Westminster/John Knox Press, 1988, 211 pages.

Noll, Mark A. *Turning Points: Decisive Moments in the History of Christianity.* 2d ed. Grand Rapids: Baker, 2000, 352 pages.

Orr, James. *Progress of Dogma.* 1901. Reprint, Old Tappan, N.J.: Revell, n.d., 365 pages.

Rohls, Jan. *Reformed Confessions*. Louisville: Westminster/John Knox Press, 1998, 311 pages.

Smith, Morton. *Harmony of the Westminster Confession and Catechisms*. Greenville, S.C: Southern Presbyterian Press, 1990, 154 pages.

Williamson, G. I., ed. *The Heidelberg Catechism: A Study Guide*. Phillipsburg, N.J.: P&R, 1993, 241 pages.

Working, Randal. *From Rebellion to Redemption: A Year of Reflections on the Heidelberg Catechism*. Colorado Springs: Navpress, 2001, 317 pages.

The Major Confessions of the Reformed or Calvinistic Churches

The Second Helvetic Confession, A.D. 1564. For the sections relating to Calvinistic doctrines, see Chapters VI, VII, IX, X, XIV, and XVI.

This confession was adopted by the Reformed churches in Switzerland, Poland, Hungary, Scotland, and France.

The Thirty-nine Articles of the Church of England, A.D. 1562. See Articles IX, X, XI, and XVII.

This document is the doctrinal standard of the Episcopal churches in England, Scotland, and America. The Episcopal Church of America made some slight alterations, but these did not affect the Calvinistic character of the document.

The Belgic Confession, A.D. 1561. See Articles XIII, XIV, XV, XXI, XXII, and XXIII.

This confession, along with the positive articles of the Canons of Dort and the Heidelberg Catechism, is the official standard of the French and Dutch Reformed churches, as well as the Reformed Church of America.

Ursinus, Zacharias. *Commentary on the Heidelberg Catechism*. Grand Rapids: Eerdmans, 1954, 659 pages.

This has been reprinted by P&R Publishing (n.d.).

The Canons of the Synod of Dort, A.D. 1619. See all five chapters.

The positive articles are given in Gordon Girod's book, *The Deeper Faith*. See also *The Articles of the Synod of Dort*, by Thomas Scott (reprint, Harrisonburg, Va.: Sprinkle, 1993, 371 pages).

The Westminster Confession, A.D. 1646. See Chapters III, V, VI, VII, IX, X, XIV, XV, and XVII.

This, the most famous of all the Reformed confessions, along with the Larger and Shorter Catechisms, forms the common doctrinal standard of all Presbyterian churches of English and Scottish derivation. A. A. Hodge observes, "It is also of all Creeds the one most highly approved by all the bodies of Congregationalists in England and America." Over sixty leading scholars met in 1,163 sessions during a five-and-one-half-year period in order to draw up this Confession along with the two Catechisms and other documents.

Boston, Thomas. *Commentary on the Shorter Catechism*. 2 vols. Reprint, Edmonton: Still Waters Revival Books, 1993, 1,335 pages.

Carson, John L., and David W. Hall., eds. *To Glorify and Enjoy God: A Commemoration of the 350th Anniversary of the Westminster Assembly*. Carlisle, Pa.: Banner of Truth, 1994, 338 pages.

Clark, Gordon H. *What Presbyterians Believe*. Philadelphia: Presbyterian and Reformed, 1956, 130 pages.

This is a fine exposition of the Westminster Confession. Dr. Clark was not only a brilliant student in the field of theology and philosophy, but also an unusually gifted writer, who had the rare talent of making his subject clear and interesting. This work is written on a popular level; do not fail to read it.

Gerstner, John, Douglas Kelly, and Philip Rollinson. *The Westminster Confession of Faith: A Guide and Commentary*. Signal Mountain, Tenn.: Summertown Texts, 1992, 202 pages.

Green, J. B. *A Harmony of the Westminster Standards*. Richmond: John Knox Press, 1951, 231 pages.

See the harmonies listed above.

Hodge, A. A. *The Confession of Faith*. Carlisle, Pa.: Banner of Truth, 1958, 430 pages.

Professor F. L. Patton of Princeton Seminary said, "This book provides probably the finest concise exposition of the greatest systematic Confession of Faith in the English Language." Hodge, here as elsewhere, demonstrates his ability as a thinker and writer. By all means consult this book. It is still in print.

Meade, Starr. *Training Hearts/Teaching Minds*. Phillipsburg, N.J.: P&R, 2000, 349 pages.

Nettles, Tom J. *Teaching Truth, Training Hearts*. Amityville, N.Y.: Calvary Press, 1998, 256 pages.

This study of the various historical catechisms used in Baptist life is a tremendous resource.

Reid, James. *Memoirs of the Westminster Divines*. Carlisle, Pa.: Banner of Truth, 1982, 390 pages.

Shaw, Robert. *An Exposition of the Westminster Confession of Faith*. Fearn, U.K.: Christian Focus, 1973, 335 pages.

Smith, Paul. *The Westminster Confession: Enjoying God Forever*. Chicago: Moody Press, 1998, 237 pages.

Van Dyken, Donald. *Rediscovering Catechism*. Phillipsburg, N.J.: P&R, 2000, 146 pages.

Vos, Johannes G. *The Westminster Larger Catechism: A Commentary*. Edited by G. I. Williamson. Phillipsburg, N.J.: P&R, 2002, 614 pages.

Westminster Confession of Faith. Glasgow: Free Presbyterian Publications, 1994, 438 pages.

Williamson, G. I. *The Westminster Confession of Faith*. Phillipsburg, N.J.: P&R, 1964, 309 pages (plus two work books).

The Savoy Declaration, A.D. 1658. See Chapters III, V, VI, VII, IX, X, XIV, XV, and XVII.

Schaff says of the creeds or declarations of faith which have been approved by the Congregational churches in England and America: "They agree substantially with the Westminster Confession, or the Calvinistic system of doctrine, but differ from Presbyterianism by rejecting the legislative and judicial authority of presbyteries and synods, and by maintaining the independence of the local churches" (1:829). Of all the Congregational creeds, the Savoy Declaration of 1658 is perhaps the most important. Schaff observes that it "is the work of a committee, consisting of Drs. Goodwin, Owen, Nye, Bridge, Caryl, and Greenhill, who had been members of the Westminster Assembly, with the exception of Dr. Owen. It contains a lengthy Preface (fourteen pages), the Westminster Confession of Faith with sundry changes (twenty-two pages), and a Platform of Church Polity (five pages)" (1:832). Because of the close identity between the Savoy Declaration and the Westminster Confession, the commentaries on the latter listed above will serve as excellent guides in the study of the Declaration.

The (Second) London Confession, A.D. 1689. See Chapters III, V, VI, VII, IX, X, XIV, XV, and XVII.

This historic English Baptist confession (drawn up in 1677) was adopted in America by the Philadelphia Baptist Association in 1742 with two articles added. In this country, it has ever since been known as the Philadelphia Confession. It is, as Schaff observes, "simply the Baptist recension of the Westminster Confession . . . with very few verbal alterations, except in the doctrine of the Church and the Sacraments" (1:885). The Baptists gave two reasons for following the Westminster Confession so closely: first, they wanted to emphasize the agreement between the two groups, and second, they had "no itch to clog religion with new words." This confession has exerted greater influence and received wider recognition among the Baptists of England and America than any other statement of doctrine.

Because of the close identity between the two, the commentaries on the Westminster Confession listed above will also serve as excellent guides in the study of the London Confession. One other commentary, however, is specifically an exposition of the London Confession of 1689: Sam Waldron, *A Modern Exposition of the 1689 Baptist Confession of Faith*, 2d ed. (Durham: Evangelical Press, 1995, 490 pages). See also a facsimile edition of the so-called 1689 Baptist Confession, *A Confession of Faith: The London Baptist Confession of 1689* (Auburn, Mass.: Baptist & Reformed Press, 2000, 142 pages). There is also an important Baptist version of the Shorter Catechism available: *The Shorter Catechism: A Modest Revision for Baptists Today* (Grand Rapids: Truth for Eternity Ministries, 1991, 38 pages).

BOOKS ON THE FIVE POINTS INDIVIDUALLY

Some of the books listed above under "Books Dealing in Whole or in Part with Calvinism or Divine Sovereignty" contain chapters or divisions that deal significantly with the individual points of Calvinism, and so they are repeated in this section of the bibliography with the appropriate divisions and pages indicated. Because of a lack of space, we will not refer to similar materials listed above under "Articles in Reference Works, Systematic Theologies, Etc." and "Information Concerning Creeds and Confessions." However, they should be given special attention in the study of each of the five points.

Human Inability and the Freedom of the Will

Boettner, Loraine. *The Reformed Doctrine of Predestination.* Chap. 10, pp. 61–82.

Boston, Thomas. *Human Nature in Its Fourfold State.* 1720. Reprint, Jenkintown, Pa.: Sovereign Grace, 1957, 360 pages.

This is written in the style of the Puritans and is not an easy book to read, but it contains some worthwhile material. Pages 23–92 deal with human depravity and pages 118–30 with human inability. This book was reprinted by the Banner of Truth Trust in 1964 and is still available today. For an account of Thomas Boston himself, see Philip Graham Ryken, *Thomas Boston as Preacher of the Fourfold State* (Carlisle, U.K.: Paternoster Press, 1999, 357 pages). This work is the author's slightly revised doctoral dissertation at Oxford University.

Carson, D. A. *Divine Sovereignty and Human Responsibility: Biblical Perspectives in Tension.* Grand Rapids: Baker, 1994, 271 pages.

Carson, one of the most astute theologians of our day, is research professor of New Testament at Trinity Evangelical Divinity School in Deerfield, Illinois. His view of these twin truths, which is called compatibilism, seeks to be faithful to the text of Scripture. This book was originally the substance of Carson's doctoral dissertation at Cambridge University in 1975, and was reprinted in 2002 by Wipf and Stock Publishers.

Clark, Gordon H. *Religion, Reason and Revelation.* Philadelphia: Presbyterian and Reformed, 1961, 241 pages.

Part 5 of this book deals with the problem of "God and Evil" (pp. 194–241). There is an excellent discussion of free will throughout this section. Clark's arguments are devastating to the Arminian position.

Cunningham, William. *Historical Theology.* Vol. 2, pp. 333–46 and pp. 496–639.

Edwards, Jonathan. *Freedom of the Will.* Edited by Paul Ramsey. New Haven: Yale University Press, 1957, 494 pages.

A classic! Ramsey says, "This book alone is sufficient to establish its author as the greatest philosopher-theologian yet to grace the American scene." Edwards's purpose is to show that the Arminian view of the freedom of the will is both unreasonable and unscriptural. Ramsey continues: "Edwards' argument in this treatise rests upon two pillars: the proof from biblical revelation and the proof from reason." Although first published in 1754, the arguments set forth in this work have never been answered by the Arminians. It requires hard study, but no serious student can afford to neglect it. Yale University Press's multivolume edition of Edwards's work is still in progress.

Gill, John. *The Cause of God and Truth.* Part 2, chap. 5, pp. 122–30, and part 3, chap. 5, pp. 183–98.

Girardeau, John L. *The Will in Its Theological Relations.* Columbia, S.C.: W. J. Duffie; New York: Baker and Taylor, 1891, 497 pages.

This is a heavy, technical effort to explain the nature of the freedom of the will. The major part of the work centers around the freedom of Adam's will before the Fall. The author contends that Edwards and Calvin did not hold identical views with regard to the nature of the liberty of the will, and he makes a fair case for saying that he is in agreement with Calvin on this matter. However, after establishing this point, Girardeau then argues that the Fall was avoidable and contingent and not efficiently decreed by God. Here he admits that he must disagree with Calvin, who taught the freedom of Adam's will, but at the same time held that Adam's fall was decreed and therefore unavoidable. In insisting on the avoidability of the Fall, Girardeau parts company with mainline Calvinism. We feel that his arguments in support of this position are based on philosophical speculation, rather than biblical evidence. The work is presently out of print.

Girod, Gordon. *The Deeper Faith.* Chap. 2, pp. 46–60.

Luther, Martin. *The Bondage of the Will.* Translated by J. I. Packer and O. R. Johnston. Westwood, N.J.: Revell, 1957, 320 pages.

Luther considered this his most significant contribution to the study of theology. As the translators of this edition state, it is "one of the enduring monuments of evangelical doctrine;

a masterpiece in the realm of polemics, dogmatics and exegesis." Warfield said of it, "It is . . . in a true sense the manifesto of the Reformation." This new translation by Packer and Johnston, with its forty-eight page "Historical and Theological Introduction," greatly enhances its value. As the translators state, "It was man's total inability to save himself, and the sovereignty of Divine grace in his salvation, that Luther was affirming when he denied 'free-will.' . . . The deepest truth about him [fallen man] is that his arbitrium, his power and exercise of choice, is enslaved—to sin and Satan; and his natural condition is one of total inability to merit anything other than wrath and damnation" (pp. 48, 50–51). This is one of the great classics of Calvinistic literature and merits serious study.

Machen, J. Gresham. *What Is Faith?* 1925. Reprint, Carlisle, Pa.: Banner of Truth, 1991, 262 pages.

Machen left Princeton Seminary in 1929 because of its liberalism and was the leading founder of Westminster Theology Seminary in Philadelphia. This is an important and readable book on the Reformed doctrine of faith.

Sproul, R. C. *Faith Alone*. Grand Rapids: Baker, 1995, 221 pages.

Sproul, possibly more than anyone else in our generation, has awakened American evangelicals to the Reformed faith. In this book, he defends the Reformation doctrine of *sola fide*, especially against the recent attacks by those who desire to see the merger of Catholics and evangelicals.

———. *Willing to Believe*. Grand Rapids: Baker, 1997, 221 pages.

An excellent treatment of the freedom of the will.

Spurgeon, C. H. *Sermons on Sovereignty*. Pp. 121–33.

This is a sermon on John 6:44. For more of Spurgeon's sermons, go to *www.spurgeon.org*.

Warburton, B. A. *Calvinism*. Chap. 7, pp. 126–48.

Wells, Tom. *Faith: The Gift of God*. Carlisle, Pa.: Banner of Truth, 1983, 156 pages.

Wells is a good writer who captures the essence of the doctrine of faith.

Also consult the works listed above under "Articles in Reference Works, Systematic Theologies, Etc."

Election and Predestination

Baugh, S. M. "The Meaning of Foreknowledge." In *Still Sovereign*, edited by Schreiner and Ware. Chap. 7, pp. 183–200.

Berkouwer, G. C. *Divine Election*. Translated by Hugo Bekker. Grand Rapids: Eerdmans, 1960, 336 pages.

The theological student should not neglect this monumental work; it reflects the wide reading and penetrating thought of its author, who was professor of systematic theology at the Free University in Amsterdam. This is the seventh volume of Berkouwer's series entitled Studies in Dogmatics. For some pertinent observations concerning this work, see Gordon H. Clark's remarks in *Religion, Reason and Revelation*, pp. 233–41.

Bianchi, Joseph. *God Chose to Save: Why Man Cannot and Will Not Be Saved Apart from Election*. Amityville, N.Y.: Calvary Press, 2001, 91 pages.

Boettner, Loraine. *The Reformed Doctrine of Predestination*. Chap. 11, pp. 83–149.

Booth, Abraham. *The Reign of Grace*. Chap. 2, pp. 53–97.

Clark, Gordon. *Predestination*. Phillipsburg, N.J.: Presbyterian and Reformed, 1987, 215 pages.

Dr. Clark, the late philosopher and theologian, wrote two works, *Biblical Predestination* (1969) and *Predestination in the Old Testament* (1978), which were posthumously combined into this 1987 edition.

Cunningham, William. *Historical Theology*. Vol. 2, pp. 416–90.

Custance, Arthur C. *The Sovereignty of Grace*. Phillipsburg, N.J.: Presbyterian and Reformed, 1979, 398 pages.

According to the publishers, "Custance gives clear, solid definitions of the five points of Calvinism. With compelling logic he points out the inconsistencies in the Arminian position (among others) and the undeniable necessity of the Calvinistic view."

Gill, John. *The Cause of God and Truth*. Part 2, chap. 1, pp. 71–78, and chap. 2, pp. 78–94; part 3, chap. 1, pp. 149–58, and chap. 2, pp. 158–68.

Girod, Gordon. *The Deeper Faith*. Chap. 1, pp. 13–28.

Klooster, Fred. *Calvin's Doctrine of Predestination*. Grand Rapids: Calvin Theological Seminary, 1961, 77 pages.

In this study, Klooster gives an excellent analysis of Calvin's doctrine of double predestination. He carefully documents the fact that Calvin held to the equal ultimacy of both election and reprobation. This monograph deserves the attention of all who desire to understand the great Reformer's position, as well as those who wish to sharpen their own thinking in this area. Besides being well documented, it contains a helpful bibliography.

Love, Christopher. *A Treatise of Effectual Calling and Election*. Morgan, Pa.: Soli Deo Gloria, 1998, 298 pages.

Love was one of the most beloved Puritans, who was killed for his faith. This classic Puritan treatise explains effectual calling and election.

Murray, John. *Calvin on Scripture and Divine Sovereignty*. Grand Rapids: Baker, 1960, 71 pages.

This small volume contains three lectures, the last of which (16 pages in length) is devoted to Calvin's doctrine of God's sovereignty in election and reprobation, as well as in His providential control of all events, both good and evil. This is a superb treatment of the subject and well documented. These essays can also be read in *The Collected Writings of John Murray*, vol. 4, *Studies in Theology*, as chaps. 10 ("Calvin's Doctrine of Scripture," pp. 158–75) and 11 ("Calvin on the

Authority of Scripture," pp. 176–90). See also chap. 12, "Calvin on the Sovereignty of God" (pp. 191–204).

Ortland, Raymond C. "The Sovereignty of God: Case Studies in the Old Testament." In *Still Sovereign,* edited by Schreiner and Ware. Chap. 1, pp. 25–46.

Packer, J. I. "The Love of God: Universal and Particular." In *Still Sovereign,* edited by Schreiner and Ware. Chap. 11, pp. 277–92.

Pink, A. W. *The Doctrines of Election and Justification.* Grand Rapids: Baker, 1974, 252 pages.

Piper, John. "Are There Two Wills in God?" In *Still Sovereign,* edited by Schreiner and Ware. Chap. 5, pp. 107–31.

This same essay is found in the appendix to Piper's *The Pleasures of God,* rev. ed. (Sisters, Oreg.: Multnomah, 2000), pp. 313–40.

Schreiner, Thomas R. "Does Romans 9 Teach Individual Election unto Salvation?" In *Still Sovereign,* edited by Schreiner and Ware. Chap. 4, pp. 89–106.

Sproul, R. C. *Chosen by God.* Wheaton, Ill.: Tyndale House, 1986, 213 pages.

The best book currently in print on this subject.

———. *Loved By God.* Nashville: Word, 2001, 213 pages.

Sproul helps believers understand the different kinds of God's love, including His general love for mankind and His special, electing love for believers. There is much comfort here, as well as much instruction.

———. *Saved from What?* Wheaton, Ill.: Crossway Books, 2002, 128 pages.

In this short book, Sproul teaches us (among other things) that believers are saved from the wrath of God, an important doctrine in Reformed theology.

Spurgeon, C. H. *Sermons on Sovereignty.* Pp. 51–67, 69–93.

Here are sermons on 2 Thessalonians 2:13–14 and 1 Thessalonians 1:4–6.

Storms, C. Samuel. *Chosen for Life*. Grand Rapids: Baker, 1987, 142 pages.

This book and Sproul's *Chosen by God* are easily the best popular treatments of the doctrine of election.

Thornwell, James H. *Election and Reprobation*. 1840. Reprint, Jackson, Miss.: Presbyterian Reformation Society, 1961, 97 pages.

This book has also been published in paperback by Presbyterian and Reformed Publishing Company. The author begins by giving a clear statement of the doctrines of election and reprobation as set forth in the Westminster standards (pp. 5–8). He then shows that these doctrines are vindicated by the Word of God (pp. 8–44). On pages 44–87, he deals with various objections. Thornwell closes by drawing some inferences from these doctrines (pp. 87–97). This work is characterized by clarity, directness, and, what is more important, sound biblical exegesis. It is regrettable that a table of contents and an index of the biblical texts dealt with were not included in this edition. We highly recommend this work.

Warburton, B. A. *Calvinism*. Chap. 5, pp. 80–106.

Westblade, Donald J. "Divine Election in the Pauline Epistles." In *Still Sovereign*, edited by Schreiner and Ware. Chap. 3, pp. 63–87.

Yarbrough, Robert W. "Divine Election in the Gospel of John." In *Still Sovereign*, edited by Schreiner and Ware. Chap. 2, pp. 47–62.

Zanchius, Jerome. *Absolute Predestination*. Jenkintown, Pa.: Sovereign Grace, n.d., 150 pages.

This book was written during the sixteenth century in Latin and translated into English and augmented by Augustus Toplady. The work consists of preliminary observations on the divine attributes and five chapters dealing with definitions of terms, predestination at large, election in particular, reprobation, and the duty of openly preaching these doctrines. It is regrettable that Toplady's preface has not been included in this edition. Due to its stiff style and formal argumentation, this book is difficult to read, but it will prove of value to the diligent student. It has also been reprinted by Baker House Book.

Consult the works listed above under "Articles in Reference Works, Systematic Theologies, Etc."

The Nature and Extent of the Atonement

One should not attempt to settle the question of the extent or intended application of Christ's atoning work until he first considers the broader question of the nature or purpose of the Atonement. Before asking the profound question "For whom did Christ die?" one should first ask the more fundamental question "Why did Christ die?" Or, to state it more pointedly, "What was accomplished by His death?" The works by Crawford, Hodge, and Smeaton, listed below, are especially recommended for the general study of Christ's redeeming work. Owen's book will prove to be of particular value to those who will devote the time and effort required to read it.

Berkhof, Louis. *Vicarious Atonement Through Christ*. Grand Rapids: Eerdmans, 1936, 184 pages.

This is a brief survey of the doctrine of Christ's substitutionary atonement. It is well written and easy to read. The last two sections (pp. 151–78) deal with the particularized design of the Atonement.

Boettner, Loraine. *The Reformed Doctrine of Predestination*. Chap. 12, pp. 150–61.

Crawford, Thomas J. *The Doctrine of the Holy Scriptures Respecting the Atonement*. Grand Rapids: Baker, 1954, 538 pages.

Crawford first sets forth the doctrine of the New Testament respecting the Atonement (pp. 3–202). He then confirms the

New Testament doctrine by appealing to the teaching contained in the Old Testament (pp. 203–84). Next he reviews the various theories respecting the suffering of Christ which have been substituted for the biblical doctrine (pp. 284–401), as well as the objections which have been made to the scriptural doctrine (pp. 403–89). This is an excellent work, well outlined and thoroughly indexed. Every student's library should include this volume. On the definite design of Christ's saving work, see pp. 122, 148–57, 196–202, and note G, pp. 510–16.

Cunningham, William. *Historical Theology.* Vol. 2, pp. 237–370.

Gill, John. *The Cause of God and Truth.* Part 2, chap. 2, pp. 98–104; part 3, chap. 2, pp. 163–78.

Girod, Gordon. *The Deeper Faith.* Chap. 2, pp. 29–45.

Hodge, Archibald Alexander. *The Atonement.* Grand Rapids: Eerdmans, 1953, 440 pages.

Whereas Crawford's work, listed above, and Smeaton's two volumes, given below, use the "inductive" method in the study of the Atonement, Hodge chose the "dogmatic" approach. His work is divided into two parts. Part 1 deals with the nature of the Atonement (pp. 13–346). In this section, Hodge carefully defines the doctrine and the major terms to be used in its study, after which he sets out to systematically establish it upon biblical grounds. Part 2 is devoted to the design or intended application of the Atonement (pp. 347–429). This section contains a superb explanation and defense of the doctrine of limited atonement. By all means study this work! There is a good reprint edition of this work, with an appendix by Curtis I. Crenshaw on the problem passages regarding the extent of the Atonement. This work was reprinted by Footstool Publishers in 1987, but is unfortunately out of print today.

Kuiper, R. B. *For Whom Did Christ Die?* Grand Rapids: Eerdmans, 1959, 104 pages.

This book is "A Study of the Divine Design of the Atonement." It deals with the unscriptural views of unrestricted universalism, Arminian universalism, and Barthian universalism.

The scriptural view is divided into two sections: scriptural particularism and scriptural universalism. The former deals with "special grace," and the latter with "common grace." This is a good work which deserves attention. It was reprinted by Baker Book House in 1982 and should be brought back into print.

Murray, John. *Redemption—Accomplished and Applied.* Grand Rapids: Eerdmans, 1955, 236 pages.

Part 1 of this book deals with the necessity, nature, perfection, and extent of the Atonement; part 2 discusses its application through effectual calling, regeneration, faith and repentance, justification, etc. This is a very fine treatment of the subject. Professor Murray was one of the giants of the Reformed world and deserves to be read continually.

Owen, John. *The Death of Death in the Death of Christ.* London: Banner of Truth, 1959, 312 pages.

In the opening words of the "Introductory Essay," J. I. Packer states that this "is a polemic work, designed to show, among other things, that the doctrine of universal redemption is unscriptural and destructive of the gospel." It was first published in 1648. The work is divided into four books. Books 1 and 2 survey the biblical account of redemption with a view to determining its intended and accomplished end. Book 3 contains sixteen arguments against the "general ransom" idea. Book 4 refutes the exegetical and theological arguments for universal redemption which Owen had encountered. This is the most thorough defense of the doctrine of limited atonement ever written. Packer's analysis of Owen's work (pp. 26–31) will prove to be of untold value in its study. His introduction to this new edition is worth the price of the book. See our comments on Packer's "Introductory Essay" above, under "Books Dealing in Whole or in Part with Calvinism or Divine Sovereignty."

Packer, J. I. "What Did the Cross Achieve?" In *Collected Shorter Writings of J. I. Packer.* 4 vols. Carlisle, U.K.: Paternoster Press, 1988–89. Vol. 1, pp. 85–123.

Packer deals with the logic of penal substitution.

Pink, Arthur W. *The Satisfaction of Christ.* Swengel, Pa.: Bible Truth Depot, 1955, 313 pages.

This book contains twenty-four chapters dealing with the doctrine of the Atonement on a popular level. Chapters 19 and 20 (pp. 240–65) discuss the extent of the Atonement. We cannot always agree with Pink's exegesis (e.g., he is given to excessive typology, and at times he rests arguments upon texts that are improperly translated or are taken out of context), but in spite of these occasional flaws, his writings contain much that is sound and edifying. This was later reprinted as *The Atonement* (Swengel, Pa.: Reiner, n.d.).

Rainbow, Jonathan. *The Will of God and the Cross.* Allison Park, Pa.: Pickwick Press, 1990, 206 pages.

Smeaton, George. *The Apostles' Doctrine of the Atonement.* Grand Rapids: Zondervan, 1957, 548 pages.

In this work, Smeaton expounds the doctrine of the Atonement by appealing to the teachings of the apostles. In the work which immediately follows, he treats the same subject, but expounds the teachings of Christ. The two volumes together deal with all of the significant passages in the New Testament that reveal the doctrine of the Atonement. Both works are well outlined and well indexed. At the end of this volume, there is a 66-page historical sketch of the doctrine, which explains the views of the Atonement held by such men as Augustine, Calvin, Arminius, Amyraut, etc. Wilbur Smith says of Smeaton that he "was in his day considered the outstanding Calvinistic theologian of Scotland." This volume and the one listed below will prove to be invaluable aids in the study of this important subject. Do not neglect them. They have been brought back into print by the Banner of Truth Trust (1991).

————. *The Doctrine of the Atonement as Taught by Christ Himself*. Grand Rapids: Zondervan, 1953, 502 pages.

See the comments above on Smeaton's *The Apostles' Doctrine of the Atonement*. The Banner of Truth Trust reprinted this volume as *Christ's Doctrine of the Atonement* (1991).

Spurgeon, C. H. *Sermons on Sovereignty*. Pp. 81–93, 95–105.

Here are sermons on Matthew 20:28 and Psalm 130:9.

Warburton, B. A. *Calvinism*. Chap. 6, pp. 107–25.

Wells, Tom. *A Price for a People*. Carlisle, Pa.: Banner of Truth, 1993, 168 pages.

The most readable resource now available, this more than adequately articulates the "limited atonement" view. Wells is to be commended for his biblical perspective. If one compares his book with *The Death Christ Died: A Biblical Case for Unlimited Atonement*, by Robert P. Lightner, one can see how unconvincing Lightner is and can easily note how Wells interprets the Scripture passages properly.

Consult the works listed above under "Articles in Reference Works, Systematic Theologies, Etc."

Efficacious Grace

Since the doctrine of efficacious grace is so vitally connected with the doctrine of the Holy Spirit and His work, we suggest that they be studied in conjunction with one another. The books below by Owen, Kuyper, Smeaton, and Winslow will prove invaluable in the study of the overall work of the Spirit, as well as in the study of His special work of effectually drawing the elect to Christ.

Belcher, Richard P. *A Journey in Grace*. Southbridge, Mass.: Crowne, 1990, 154 pages.

This is a provocative and well-written novel which seeks to show the power of the doctrines of grace. The main character of the novel, a young pastor, cannot rest until he settles his mind on the beautiful doctrines known as Calvinism. The book has become something of a classic.

―――. *A Journey in Salvation.* Columbia, S.C.: Richbarry Press, 2001, 201 pages.

This is a continuation of *A Journey in Grace* (see above). In a very interesting manner, Belcher deals with the whole subject of salvation—sin, conviction, repentance, faith, regeneration, etc. These novels are excellent because they are so true to life.

Boettner, Loraine. *The Reformed Doctrine of Predestination.* Chap. 13, pp. 162–81.

Coles, Elisha. *A Practical Discourse of God's Sovereignty.* 1673. Reprint, London: Thomas Tegg, 1845. Pp. 193–259.

Cunningham, William. *Historical Theology.* Vol. 1, pp. 346–55; vol. 2, pp. 394–416.

George, Timothy. *Amazing Grace.* Nashville: LifeWay Press, 2000, 126 pages.

George, a Reformed Southern Baptist, is dean of Beeson Divinity School in Birmingham, Alabama.

Gill, John. *The Cause of God and Truth.* Part 2, chap. 4, pp. 105–21; part 3, chap. 4, pp. 178–83.

Girod, Gordon. *The Deeper Faith.* Chap. 4, pp. 61–75.

Kuiper, Herman. *By Grace Alone.* Grand Rapids: Eerdmans, 1955, 165 pages.

This is a study of the *ordo salutis* (order of salvation). It deals with the application of Christ's redeeming work to sinners. Such subjects as calling, regeneration, faith and conversion, justification, sanctification, preservation, and glorification are admirably covered. It is well written and logically arranged, but somewhat technical at points. This is a good treatment of an important subject.

Kuyper, Abraham. *The Work of the Holy Spirit.* Grand Rapids: Eerdmans, 1941, 664 pages.

This work consists of three volumes in one. The first volume deals with the work of the Holy Spirit in the church as a whole; the second and third volumes are devoted to the Holy Spirit's work in the individual. Warfield said of this book, "It brings together the material belonging to this great topic with a systematizing genius that is very rare." There is no doubt that this is one of the most important studies ever written on this profound subject. In relation to the doctrine of efficacious grace, note especially the material contained in vol. 2, pp. 203–427.

Murray, John. *Redemption—Accomplished and Applied.* Part 2, chaps. 1–4, pp. 97–143.

Owen, John. *The Holy Spirit, His Gifts and Power.* Edited by George Buirder. Grand Rapids: Kregel, 1954, 356 pages.

This classic work on the Holy Spirit covers such topics as His name, nature, personality, dispensations, operations, and effects. John Owen was probably the most renowned of all the Puritan writers, and this is considered by some to be his masterpiece. For over 250 years, it has received the highest recognition. Abraham Kuyper, who himself produced a monumental work on this subject, said of Owen's work that it is the "most widely known and still unsurpassed." The situation has not changed during the many years that have elapsed since Kuyper made this evaluation. In connection with the doctrine of efficacious grace, see book 3, pp. 119–218.

Palmer, Edwin H. *The Holy Spirit.* Grand Rapids: Baker, 1958, 174 pages.

This book will prove especially helpful to those who are just beginning a study of the Holy Spirit and His work. It is written in a clear, simple style and is well outlined. In connection with the efficacious work of the Spirit, see chap. 3, pp. 29–39; chap. 5, pp. 53–61; chap. 7, pp. 77–86; and chap. 14, pp. 165–74.

Smeaton, George. *The Doctrine of the Holy Spirit.* 2d ed. 1889. Reprint, London: Banner of Truth, 1974, 418 pages.

We have already had occasion to refer to Smeaton's reputation as a theologian and scholar (under "The Nature and Extent of the Atonement"). This work on the Holy Spirit is of the same high quality as his two volumes on the Atonement. Caspar W. Hodge of Princeton recommended Smeaton's book on the Holy Spirit as the best on the subject. Lecture 4, entitled "The Spirit's Regenerating Work on the Individual" (pp. 175–220), deals with the subject of efficacious grace. At the end of the book, Smeaton gives an excellent "Historical Survey of the Doctrine of the Holy Spirit" (pp. 291–414). Pages 327–84 are devoted to the history of views on the work of the Spirit; Smeaton surveys the different positions held by the major theologians and confessions of faith in relation to the efficacious call of the Spirit, as well as briefly reviewing many of the books previously written on the subject. By all means consult this work!

Spurgeon, C. H. *Sermons on Sovereignty.* Pp. 135–46.

Here is a sermon on Genesis 12:5.

Suggs, Terrell D. *My Journey in Grace.* Rev. ed. Self-published, 1998, 178 pages.

This is an account of one who made a pilgrimage from Arminianism to Calvinism. The book may be obtained by writing to Terrell Suggs, P.O. Box 129, Union, MS 39365, or by calling First Baptist Church at 601–774–8144.

Warburton, B. A. *Calvinism.* Chap. 8, pp. 149–68.

Ware, Bruce. "Effectual Calling and Grace." In *Still Sovereign,* ed. Schreiner and Ware. Chap. 8, pp. 203–27.

Winslow, Octavius. *The Work of the Holy Spirit.* 1843. Reprint, London: Banner of Truth, 1961, 223 pages.

The author exhibits a clear insight into the work of the Holy Spirit as well as a deep regard for the person of the Spirit as a member of the Godhead. The work is fairly comprehensive without being technical. Chapters 2 and 3 (pp. 31–86) discuss the Spirit's work with regard to efficacious grace (chap. 2, before conversion; chap. 3, after conversion).

Consult the works listed above under "Articles in Reference Works, Systematic Theologies, Etc."

The Perseverance of the Saints

Berkouwer, G. C. *Faith and Perseverance.* Translated by Robert D. Knudsen. Grand Rapids: Eerdmans, 1958, 256 pages.

This is a penetrating treatment of the doctrine of the perseverance of the saints and of its place in the history of the church. This doctrine is examined against the backdrop of the Reformed standards (in chap. 2) and the three major controversies which have arisen over the subject of perseverance (in chap. 3)—namely, the controversies between the Reformed or Calvinistic theologians and (1) the Remonstrants (the Arminian party of Holland), (2) the Roman Catholics, and (3) the Lutherans. The problem of perseverance as it relates to admonition, prayer, and temptation is discussed in chaps. 4, 5, and 6, respectively. Berkouwer concludes in chaps. 7 and 8 by showing the consolation and reality of perseverance. This valuable contribution throws much light on this blessed doctrine. Although the book may be difficult in places for the beginning student, the effort spent reading it will be well worth it.

Boettner, Loraine. *The Reformed Doctrine of Predestination.* Chap. 14, pp. 182–200.

Carson, D. A. "Reflections on Assurance." In *Still Sovereign,* ed. Schreiner and Ware. Chap. 10, pp. 247–76.

Coles, Elisha. *A Practical Discourse of God's Sovereignty.* Pp. 259–328.

Cunningham, William. *Historical Theology.* Vol. 1, pp. 355–58; vol. 2, pp. 490–501.

Gill, John. *The Cause of God and Truth.* Part 2, chap. 6, pp. 131–49; part 3, chap. 6, pp. 198–202.

Girod, Gordon. *The Deeper Faith.* Chap. 5, pp. 76–90.

Grudem, Wayne. "Perseverance of the Saints: A Case Study from the Warning Passages in Hebrews." In *Still Sovereign,* ed. Schreiner and Ware. Chap. 6, pp. 133–82.

Kuiper, Herman. *By Grace Alone.* Chap. 7, pp. 138–47.

Murray, John. *Redemption—Accomplished and Applied.* Part 2, chap. 8, pp. 189–98.

Pinson, J. Matthew, ed. *Four Views on Eternal Security.* Grand Rapids: Zondervan, 2002, 302 pages.

Michael S. Horton takes the classical Calvinistic position in this work.

Spurgeon, C. H. *Sermons on Sovereignty,* pp. 201–14.

Here is a sermon on Job 17:9.

Warburton, B. A. *Calvinism.* Chap. 9, pp. 169–88.

Consult the works listed above under "Articles in Reference Works, Systematic Theologies, Etc."

May God grant each of us the desire to *study,* the wisdom to *understand,* and the courage to *witness* to the truth of His Holy Word.

AFTERWORD

I am thankful for this timely revision of a wonderful classic that has already been an immense blessing to countless thousands. Notwithstanding its success over the years, the only question that *ultimately* matters about the "five points of Calvinism" is whether these doctrines are biblical. This book has demonstrated (conclusively, in my judgment) that the "five points" are nothing more or less than what the Bible teaches. The doctrines of grace and divine sovereignty are the very lifeblood of the full and free salvation promised in the gospel.

Today Calvinism is being subjected to constant attack. Several recent, popular, published critiques have tried to discredit John Calvin the man, or they have unfairly blamed Calvinism for the dubious politics of the Reformation era. But the *doctrines* of a Calvinistic soteriology must stand or fall by the test of Scripture, period.

Scripture speaks with absolute, unmistakable clarity on these vital issues: (1) Sinners are utterly helpless to redeem themselves or to contribute anything meritorious toward their own salvation (Rom. 8:7–8). (2) God is sovereign in the exercise of His saving will (Eph. 1:4–5). (3) Christ died as a substitute who bore the full weight of God's wrath on behalf of His people, and His atoning work alone is efficacious for their salvation (Isa. 53:5). (4) God's saving purpose cannot be thwarted (John 6:37), meaning none of Christ's true sheep will ever be lost (John 10:27–29). That is because (5) God assures the perseverance of His elect (Jude 24; Phil. 1:6; 1 Peter 1:5).

Those *are* the five points of Calvinism. I believe them not because of their historical pedigree, but because that is what *Scripture* teaches.

John F. MacArthur Jr.

Appendix A

A KINDER, GENTLER CALVINISM

JAMES N. MCGUIRE[1]

I think I heard a snort from someone who read this title just now. The mood of many in the Reformed camp is anything but kinder and gentler as they wrestle with the seeming mudslide of lukewarm evangelicalism which, they contend, has lost the holiness of God in a man-centered gospel. Our evangelical churches, they say, are overrun with preachers and parishioners who think the acronym **TULIP** (**t**otal depravity, **u**nconditional election, **l**imited atonement, **i**rresistible grace, **p**erseverance of the saints) is a colorful bulb grown by the Dutch. What we need,

1. James N. McGuire is senior pastor of Ward Evangelical Presbyterian Church in Northville, Michigan. This article is from *RTS Reformed Quarterly*, Summer 2000, 14–16. Used by permission of Reformed Theological Seminary. All Bible quotations are taken from the HOLY BIBLE, NEW INTERNATIONAL VERSION®. NIV®. Copyright © 1973, 1978, 1984 by International Bible Society. Used by permission of Zondervan Publishing House. All rights reserved.

they insist, is a lean, mean Calvin machine, barring no holds and taking no prisoners. Kinder and gentler should be saved for the clean-up operation after a new Reformation has occurred.

I marvel at that spirit—perhaps because I once participated in it. Being ready to give a reason for the hope that is within one can quickly become justification for swinging one's theological machete at the slightest sniff of any teaching that gives unconverted man the power to choose God. When I was young, some of my Calvinist colleagues landed in quiet churches that quickly became noisy battlegrounds, reputedly over theology. Unfortunately, some of my friends were turned out of those churches after relatively short stays, but they left feeling vindicated by their ouster. They seemed to believe that their dismissals were a sign that they were faithful to the truth— they were being banished by the heretics.

But the reason for their meltdowns wasn't really over protecting the truth. It seems in most cases—maybe in all—that the churches were looking for pastors whose theology made them love the truth enough to love the theological sinners who comprised the congregation. Diatribes about the depravity of man and the wrath of God were not the apex of biblical theology or good pastoral practice. They still aren't.

I consider myself blessed to have been confronted early on in my first pastorate. An elder commented to me, after what I thought was a particularly good sermon on sin, "Son, don't you know any good news?" He made me mad. He made me real mad. Mumbling to myself for weeks thereafter, I privately reviewed my sermons. He was right. The love of God shed abroad in Jesus Christ was in short supply. I was unwittingly dispensing total depravity without much amazing grace. I needed new models, someone theologically correct, unyielding of the truth, yet full of the Good News. I didn't have to look far.

With my attitude adjustment, I saw the Lord Jesus and the apostles teaching vital truth without compromise, but practicing the touch of love. That's why sinners listened. That's why you listen. There really is good news. The great sovereign God has so loved the world that He gave His one and only Son, that whosoever believes in Him should not perish but have eternal life. Our job is to go into the highways and byways and compel sinners to come in faith to Jesus, knowing that as many as are ordained for eternal life will come.

And they respond to the simple telling of the Good News about Jesus. This means that you can start with any of the petals of TULIP and lead directly to Jesus crucified for sinners, even real sinners with whom you are speaking face-to-face. This means if your TULIP doesn't lead directly to Jesus crucified for sinners, you missed the point.

I recently heard a Presbyterian preacher's approach to evangelism heavily criticized because he didn't begin with the law, but instead with the great love of God. I reflected that Charles Spurgeon had taught that honey attracts more flies than vinegar. Surely a faithful Calvinist doesn't have to open every evangelism effort with the wrath of God revealed from heaven. A kinder lead-in like "Heaven is a free gift" seems faithful to Scripture, too. A faithful presentation of Christ Jesus crucified can even begin with, "I see that in every way you are very religious. For as I walked around and looked carefully at your objects of worship, I even found an altar with this inscription: TO AN UNKNOWN GOD. Now what you worship as something unknown I am going to proclaim to you" (Acts 17:22–23).

Obviously, the Bad News about God's wrath is what makes the Good News about Jesus good. But I am finding many people who are afraid to tell people that Christ came into the world to save sinners, like the sinner to whom they are speaking face-to-face. They don't want to risk offending the sovereignty of God by telling men who are dead in their sins that dead men are commanded everywhere to repent and believe the Good News.

But they are forgetting a most important point: it is by the preaching of the Good News about Jesus that dead men come to life. It is by the face-to-face pressing of the claims of Christ to men who are dead in sins that the power of the Gospel to save is unleashed. Furthermore, telling men and women, boys and girls, that they are personally responsible to receive Jesus as Lord and trust in Him alone for their salvation must be done because God has ordained that in begging (2 Cor. 5:20) men and women to be reconciled to God through the death of His Son, faith is created in them by the Holy Spirit.

A man distressed by my allegiance to Reformed theology recently gave me a book titled *The Other Side of Calvinism*, a misguided nuclear attack on Calvinistic understanding and practice of theology. Vance passionately writes,

> Nothing will deaden a church or put a young man out of the ministry any more than an adherence to Calvinism. Nothing will foster pride and indifference as will an affection for Calvinism. Nothing will destroy holiness and spirituality as an attachment to Calvinism. There is no greater violator of every hermeneutical, contextual, analytical, and exegetical interpretation of Scripture than Calvinism.[2]

Again he writes, "The doctrines of Calvinism will deaden and kill anything: prayer, faith, zeal, holiness."[3] The entire book is a bitter tirade that should be read by all good Calvinists. He moves far beyond intellectual debate with brothers in the Lord. He's downright nasty. But it makes me ask, "What has been this man's experience with Calvinists that evokes the scathing hostility oozing from this book?"

What disturbs me most is not that he accuses Reformed people of being mean-spirited, heretical dispensers of unholy, devilish lies. What disturbs me most is not that Reformed theologians are accused of sick interpretation of Scripture and, therefore, are false witnesses of God. *What disturbs me most is*

2. Laurence M. Vance, *The Other Side of Calvinism* (Pensacola, Fla.: Vance, 1991), viii.
3. Ibid., 15.

*that he never accuses Calvinists of being great lovers of sinners.
Is there evidence to support such an accusation if someone were
bold enough to make it?*

You may say, "Telling them the Truth is the highest form
of love," and I will agree, but add, "Beloved, let us not love in
word only, but in word and in deed." *How* you tell the truth and
how you *practice* the truth make the difference. Deeds of real
love accompanying vital evangelism are often woefully miss-
ing from Reformed students of the Bible. Kinder, gentler Calvinism driven by demonstrative love seems to be a rare commod-
ity. It ought not to be. Calvinism, above other understandings
of the Bible, rests on the only true foundation for preaching
about the loving God who has sovereignly guaranteed the success of the Gospel.

The observation made of the early church was "Behold
how they love one another." John, the apostle of love, gives clear
criteria for determining true disciples of Jesus, finally boiling
it down to 1 John 3:23, "And this is his command: to believe in
the name of his Son, Jesus Christ, and to love one another as
he commanded us." Surely John missed a good opportunity to
state clearly and succinctly the five points of Calvinism as the
criteria of true discipleship!

Even Paul's letter to the Romans, the master systematic
presentation of election and predestination, calling, regeneration, conversion, justification, adoption, sanctification, and glorification of believers, folds the practical outcome of God's revelation into the immutable truths that "love is the fulfillment
of the law" (Rom. 13:10) and "clothe yourselves with the Lord
Jesus Christ" (13:14). Who should be surprised? Correct theology, believed correctly, always leads to the sanctification of
the believer, which, simply put, is the practice of love. We are
never more like God than when we love. Does your Calvinism
show itself in love for God and love for man? Has it freed you
to love sinners?

It is so much easier to be lost in the beauty, the faithfulness, the cohesiveness, the clarity of sound Reformed theology

than to be lost in the practice of love, which is, after all, the great aim of orthodox theology. Galatians 5:6b says, *"The only thing that counts is faith expressing itself through love."* This is a stunning statement. Yes, we must earnestly contend for the faith that was once and for all entrusted to the saints. But *to contend* is quite different from *to be contentious,* which Webster's dictionary defines as "exhibiting an often perverse and wearisome tendency to quarrels and disputes." The only thing that counts is faith expressing itself through love.

The Reformers personally paid a great price to rediscover the foundations of the faith once and for all delivered to the saints, and we have an obligation to preserve it and pass it on intact. But passing it on requires more than sterile repetition of Calvinism's five points, the Westminster Confession of Faith, or the Heidelberg Catechism. This precious faith must also find loving expression simultaneously in the free offer of the Gospel (sufficient for the world, efficient for the elect) and in care for the poor, the crippled, the lame, the blind, the victims of war and disease, widows, orphans, and others. Lovers of Reformed theology must be lovers of fallen men, women, and children. The main issue is not the content of Calvinism, but the attitude and practice of its messengers. We need a kinder, gentler Calvinism because truth fueled by love is the most liberating force known to man.

Appendix B

PERSEVERANCE AND PRESERVATION

The fifth point of Calvinism has been variously named "the perseverance of the saints," "the security of the believer," "once saved, always saved," and "the preservation of the saints." Regardless of what it is called, the doctrine teaches that *the true child of God* can never fall from grace. Through faith he is justified, and God will keep him safe and secure in Christ. As we stated previously in this book, "Many who profess to believe fall away, but they do not fall from grace, for they were never in grace. True believers do fall into temptations, and they do commit grievous sins, but these sins do not cause them to lose their salvation or separate them from Christ."[1]

In our earlier discussion of the perseverance of the saints, our primary emphasis was actually on the preservation of the saints. Almost all of the biblical references cited had to do with *God's* activity in maintaining the security of the believer and thus with His giving them an eternal salvation. God keeps His true children safe through various means. They have been chosen before the foundation of the world (Eph. 1:4) and foreordained

1. See above, pp. 64–65.

to be the recipients of God's love. In time they are justified, and their sins can never be charged against them. They are kept safe through the means that God uses, such as the inner work of the Spirit, prayer, scriptural warnings and encouragements, the fellowship of other believers, the discipline of the church, and, even at times, the discipline of his child by God, the wise and loving Father. God will never allow them to stray permanently away from the love of Christ (Rom. 8:28–39). Through His sovereign power and plan, God brings a people together through Christ. Election, foreordination, justification, adoption, and glorification for the true child of God are wrought by God Himself, and He alone should receive the glory for the absolute security of the believer.

Yet, there is in Scripture another side of this beautiful doctrine. Whereas we previously emphasized the *preservation* of the saints, we must also emphasize the *perseverance* of the saints in faith and holiness.[2] Too many people have been led to think that if they have ever made a profession of faith, or ever prayed a "sinner's prayer," or were baptized and joined a church, they can rely on their having been "once saved and always saved." Insufficient emphasis is given to God's requirement that *we must persevere to the end* in a life that seeks after holiness.

We are convinced that there will be many who think that heaven is certain and will realize too late that their sense of security in Christ was actually a false hope. While they acknowledged Christ as their savior, their lives did not reflect a genuine relationship with Him, and consequently they were still dead in their sins. There was no perseverance, no running of the race to the end, only a mere profession made years earlier.

One could almost speak of the six points of Calvinism, the *fifth* point being the *preservation* of the saints and the *sixth* point

2. W. E. Vine defines the Greek verb translated "persevere" as "continue steadfastly" (*An Expository Dictionary of New Testament Words* [Westwood, N.J.: Revell, 1959], 87). A. S. Wood defines it as "continue unswervingly" ("Perseverance," in *The New Bible Dictionary*, ed. J. D. Douglas [Grand Rapids: Eerdmans, 1962], 969).

being the *perseverance* of the saints. The Bible repeatedly emphasizes both sides of this wonderful doctrine. This is one of those doctrines that we classify as an *antinomy* (containing two teachings which appear contradictory to the human mind, but which in God's mind are not in tension).[3] Other examples of antinomies are God's sovereignty in salvation and yet man's responsibility to respond in faith; the fact that God is three, yet one; and the truth that Christ was fully God, but also fully human. Our minds are limited, and to us these truths are irreconcilable, but to God there is no problem. Both are true, though we cannot fathom how that can be. And the same is true with regard to preservation and perseverance. God preserves us, beyond any doubt. Yet we have a responsibility to persevere in the faith to the end (striving after holiness),[4] and if we do not hold out, we have no basis for assurance that God is preserving us. This doctrine has been well summarized in these words: "Faith alone saves, but the faith that saves is never alone." A. N. Martin asks and answers the right question: "Do I confess that I am being preserved by God's keeping power? Then his preserving must be coming to light in my persevering. The only proof I have that he preserves me is that by his grace, I am enabled to persevere."[5]

With a minimum of comment, we list the following verses that emphasize the *perseverance of the saints*. We hope that by doing so, we will strike the proper balance between the preservation of the saints and the perseverance of the saints. This is not an exhaustive list, but merely a sample of the New Testament teaching on the believer's perseverance.[6]

3. See J. I. Packer, *Evangelism and the Sovereignty of God* (Downers Grove, Ill.: InterVarsity Press, 1961), for an excellent discussion of antinomies.

4. See 1 Thess. 4:7; Titus 2:14; Heb. 12:14.

5. A. N. Martin, *The Practical Implications of Calvinism* (Carlisle, Pa.: Banner of Truth, 1979), 18.

6. All biblical quotations in this section are from the Holy Bible, New International Version®. NIV®. Copyright © 1973, 1978, 1984 by International Bible Society. Used by permission of Zondervan Publishing House. All rights reserved.

MATTHEW 10:22: "All men will hate you because of me, but he who *stands firm to the end* will be saved."

MATTHEW 24:12–13: "Because of the increase of wickedness, the love of most will grow cold, but he who *stands firm to the end* will be saved."

LUKE 8:15: "But the seed on good soil stands for those with a noble and good heart, who hear the word, retain it, and by *persevering* produce a crop."

LUKE 22:31–32: "Simon, Simon, Satan has asked to sift you as wheat. But I have prayed for you, Simon, that your *faith may not fail.*"

JOHN 15:5–6, 8–10: "I am the vine; you are the branches. *If a man remains in me* and I in him, he will bear much fruit; apart from me you can do nothing. If anyone *does not remain in me,* he is like a branch that is thrown away and withers; such branches are picked up, thrown into the fire and burned. . . . This is to my Father's glory, that you bear much fruit, *showing* yourselves to be my disciples. As the Father has loved me, so have I loved you. Now *remain in my love. If you obey my commands,* you will remain in my love, just as I have obeyed my Father's commands and remain in his love."

ACTS 13:43: "When the congregation was dismissed, many of the Jews and devout converts to Judaism followed Paul and Barnabas, who talked with them and urged them *to continue in the grace of God.*"

ACTS 14:21–22: "They preached the good news in that city and won a large number of disciples. Then they returned to Lystra, Iconium and Antioch, strengthening the disciples and encouraging them *to remain true to the faith.*"

1 CORINTHIANS 15:58: "Therefore, my dear brothers, *stand firm*. Let nothing move you. Always give yourselves fully to the work of the Lord, because you know that your labor in the Lord is not in vain."

1 CORINTHIANS 16:13–14: "Be on your guard; *stand firm in the faith*; be men of courage; be strong. Do everything in love."

2 CORINTHIANS 13:5: *"Examine yourselves* to see whether you are in the faith; *test yourselves."*

GALATIANS 6:9: "Let us not become weary in doing good, for at the proper time we will reap a harvest *if we do not give up."*

PHILIPPIANS 2:12–13: "Therefore, my dear friends, as you have always obeyed . . . *continue to work out your salvation* with fear and trembling, for it is God who works in you to will and to act according to his good purpose."

PHILIPPIANS 3:12–14: "Not that I have already obtained all this [see verses 8–11], or have already been made perfect, but *I press on* to take hold of that for which Christ Jesus took hold of me. . . . Forgetting what is behind and straining toward what is ahead, *I press on* toward the goal to win the prize for which God has called me heavenward in Christ Jesus."

COLOSSIANS 1:21–23: "Once you were alienated from God and were enemies in your minds because of your evil behavior. But now he has reconciled you by Christ's physical body through death to present you holy in his sight, without blemish and free from accusation—*if you continue in your faith*, established and firm, *not moved* from the hope held out in the gospel."

1 TIMOTHY 4:15–16: "Be *diligent* in these matters [Paul's pastoral instructions to Timothy]; give yourself wholly to them, so that everyone may see your progress. Watch your life and doctrine closely. *Persevere in them,* because if you do, you will save both yourself and your hearers."

HEBREWS 3:12–14: "See to it, brothers, that none of you has a sinful, unbelieving heart that turns away from the living God. But encourage one another daily, as long as it is called Today, so that none of you may be hardened by sin's deceitfulness. We have come to share in Christ *if we hold firmly till the end* the confidence we had at first."

HEBREWS 10:23, 36, 39: "Let us hold unswervingly to the hope we profess, for he who promised is faithful. . . . You need *to persevere* so that when you have done the will of God, you will receive what he has promised. . . . But we are not of those who shrink back and are destroyed, but of those who believe and are saved."[7]

HEBREWS 12:1–3: "Therefore, since we are surrounded by such a great cloud of witnesses, let us throw off everything that hinders and the sin that so easily entangles, and let us *run with perseverance* the race marked out for us. Let us fix our eyes on Jesus, the author and perfecter of our faith, who for the joy set before him endured the cross, scorning its shame, and sat down at the right hand of the throne of God. Consider him who endured such opposition from sinful men, so that you *will not grow weary and lose heart.*"

JAMES 1:12: "Blessed is the man who *perseveres under trial,* because when he has stood the test, he will receive the

---

7. For brief but excellent comments on these verses, see the section on "Perseverance" in Jerry Bridges, *Trusting God* (Colorado Springs: NavPress, 1988), 184–87.

crown of life that God has promised to those who love him."

2 PETER 1:10–11: "Therefore, my brothers, be all the more eager to *make your calling and election sure*. For if you do these things, you will *never fall*, and you will receive a rich welcome into the eternal kingdom of our Lord and Savior Jesus Christ."

1 JOHN 2:3–6: "We know that we have come to know him *if we obey his commands*. The man who says, 'I know him,' but *does not do* what he commands is a liar, and the truth is not in him. But if anyone *obeys his word*, God's love is truly made complete in him. *This is how we know* we are in him: Whoever claims to live in him must *walk as Jesus did*."

1 JOHN 2:19: "They went out from us, but they did not really belong to us. For if they had belonged to us, *they would have remained with us;* but their going showed that none of them belonged to us."

1 JOHN 2:28: "And now, dear children, *continue in him,* so that when he appears we may be confident and unashamed before him at his coming."

JUDE 20–21: "But you, dear friends, *build yourselves up in your most holy faith* and pray in the Holy Spirit. *Keep yourselves in God's love* as you wait for the mercy of our Lord Jesus Christ *to bring you to eternal life*."

Additional passages that speak of various aspects of perseverance are:

MATTHEW 7:24–27 (It is not those who merely hear the word, but those who persevere in practicing it, who will enter the kingdom of heaven.)

MATTHEW 13:8, 18–23 (It is not those who merely hear the word and even rejoice for a time, but those who produce a crop, who will be accepted by God. To produce a crop requires perseverance.)

MATTHEW 25:14–30 (God expects us to continue steadfastly in putting our talents to work; otherwise, there will be a terribly sad accounting at the end of the age.)

LUKE 9:57–62 (There is no hope for the man who puts his hand to the spiritual plow and who does not persevere, but turns back.)

LUKE 12:35–48 (We must be ready for the master's return at all times—which requires that we continue unswervingly in our service.)

1 CORINTHIANS 9:24–27 (It is those who persevere in the race who win the prize.)

1 CORINTHIANS 10:1–13 (We must stand firm, persevering in holiness.)

GALATIANS 1:6–9; 5:1–9 (There has to be a perseverance in—not a turning away from—the true gospel.)[8]

HEBREWS 2:1–3 (There must be a perseverance in the true gospel of Christ and no drifting away, in order to insure our salvation.)

---

8. John MacArthur is certainly correct when he says, "Perseverance in believing the truth always accompanies genuine conversion." See the note on 1 Timothy 4:16 in *The MacArthur Study Bible,* p. 1868. See also John Piper, *Brothers, We Are Not Professionals* (Nashville: Broadman and Holman, 2002), 105–11 (chap. 15, "Brothers, Save the Saints"); Thomas R. Schreiner and Ardel B. Caneday, *The Race Set Before Us: A Biblical Theology of Perseverance and Assurance* (Downers Grove, Ill.: InterVarsity Press, 2001).

HEBREWS 5:11–6:8 (Those who do not persevere in the truth of the gospel and who fall away from it will not be restored.)

HEBREWS 10:26–31 (Those who do not persevere in the gospel after having received knowledge of the truth will not be saved.)

HEBREWS 13:15–21 (A persevering life of sacrificial praise and obedience is required of God's people.)

JAMES 2:14–26 (A mere intellectual assent is insufficient; perseverance in our works must prove that our faith is genuine.)

2 PETER 2:17–22 (To not persevere and to turn back to the corruption of the world is to destroy our souls.)

1 JOHN 3:16–24 (To know that we belong to the truth requires us to continue steadfast in our obedience to the Lord and in our practice of love to our brothers.)

1 JOHN 5:18 (In order to know that we have been born of God, we must persevere in our attempts to avoid sin.)

2 JOHN 9 (Anyone who does not persevere in the teaching of Christ does not have God.)

REVELATION 2 AND 3 (Christ, speaking to the seven churches, *commends* the perseverance of the churches in Ephesus [2:2–3], Pergamum [2:13], Thyatira [2:19], and Philadelphia [3:8, 10–11]. He *urges* perseverance in the churches of Smyrna [2:10] and Sardis [3:2–3]. And he *warns* the Laodicean church because of their lack of persevering in the faith [3:16]. In each case, he promises good things to him "who overcomes" [see 2:7, 11, 17, 26; 3:5, 12–13, 21].)

REVELATION 14:12 (Because of the evil coming into the world, God's people must persevere in keeping His commandments and remain faithful [persevere] in Christ.)

Appendix C

THE MEANING OF "FOREKNEW" IN ROMANS 8:29

"For those whom he foreknew he also predestined to be conformed to the image of his Son, in order that he might be the firstborn among many brothers. And those whom he predestined he also called, and those whom he called he also justified, and those whom he justified he also glorified."
—Romans 8:29–30

Broadly speaking, there have been two general views as to the meaning and use of the word "foreknew" in Romans 8:29. One class of commentators (the Arminians) maintain that Paul is saying that God predestined to salvation those whom He *foreknew* would respond to His offer of grace (i.e., those whom He saw would of their own free will repent of their sins and believe the gospel). Godet, in commenting on Romans 8:29, asks the question, "In what respect did God thus *foreknow* them?" and answers that they were "foreknown as sure to fulfill the conditions of salvation, viz. *faith;* so: foreknown as His

157

by faith."[1] The word "foreknew" is thus understood by the Arminians to mean that God knew beforehand which sinners would believe, etc., and on the basis of this knowledge He predestined them unto salvation.

The other class of commentators (the Calvinists) reject the above view on two grounds. First, because the Arminians' interpretation is not in keeping with the meaning of Paul's language, and second, because it is out of harmony with the system of doctrine taught in the rest of the Scriptures. Calvinists contend that the passage teaches that God set His heart upon (i.e., foreknew) certain individuals; these He predestined or marked out to be saved. Notice that the text does *not* say that God *knew something about* particular individuals (that they would do this or that), but that God *knew the individuals themselves:* those *whom He knew* He predestined to be made like Christ. The word "foreknew" as used here is thus understood to be equivalent to "foreloved"—those who were the objects of God's love He marked out for salvation.

The questions raised by the two opposing interpretations are these: Did God look down through time and see that certain individuals would believe and thus predestine them unto salvation on the basis of this foreseen faith? Or did God set His heart on certain individuals and because of His love for them predestine that they should be called and given faith in Christ by the Holy Spirit and thus be saved? In other words, is the individual's faith the *cause* or the *result* of God's predestination?

"KNOW" AND "FOREKNOW"

God has always possessed perfect knowledge of all creatures and of all events. There has never been a time when anything past, present, or future was not fully known to Him. But

---

1. Frederic Godet, *Commentary on the Epistle to the Romans* (Grand Rapids: Zondervan, 1956), 325. Italics are his.

it is not His knowledge of future events (of what people would do, etc.) which is referred to in Romans 8:29–30, for Paul clearly states that those whom He *foreknew* He predestined, He called, He justified, etc. Since all men are *not* predestined, called, and justified, it follows that all men were *not foreknown* by God in the sense spoken of in verse 29.

It is for this reason that Arminians are forced to add some qualifying notion. They read into the passage some idea not contained in the language itself, such as that those whom He foreknew *would believe, etc.*, He predestined, called, and justified. But according to the biblical usage of the words "know," "knew," and "foreknew," there is not the least need to make such an addition, and since it is unnecessary, it is improper. When the Bible speaks of God knowing particular individuals, it often means that He has special regard for them, that they are the objects of His affection and concern. For example, in Amos 3:2 God, speaking to Israel, says, "You only have I known of all the families of the earth; therefore I will punish you for all your iniquities." The Lord knew *about* all the families of the earth, but He knew Israel in a special way. They were His chosen people, upon whom He had set His heart. See Deuteronomy 7:7–8; 10:15. Because Israel was His in a special sense, He chastised them (cf. Heb. 12:5–6). God, speaking to Jeremiah, said, "Before I formed you in the womb I knew you" (Jer. 1:5). The meaning here is not that God knew *about* Jeremiah, but that He had special regard for the prophet before He formed him in his mother's womb. Jesus also used the word "knew" in the sense of personal, intimate awareness. "On that day many will say to me, 'Lord, Lord, did we not prophesy in your name, and cast out demons in your name, and do many mighty works in your name?' And then will I declare to them, 'I never knew you; depart from me, you workers of lawlessness'" (Matt. 7:22–23). Our Lord cannot be understood here as saying, "I knew nothing about you," for it is quite evident that He knew all too much about them—their evil character and evil works; hence, His meaning must be, "I never knew you intimately or personally,

I never regarded you as the objects of my favor or love." Paul uses the word in the same way in 1 Corinthians 8:3, "But if anyone loves God, he is *known* by God," and also 2 Timothy 2:19, "The Lord knows those who are his." The Lord knows *about* all men, but He only *knows* those "who love God . . . who are called according to his purpose" (Rom. 8:28)—*those who are His!*

Murray's argument in favor of this meaning of "foreknew" is very good:

> It should be observed that the text says *"whom* he foreknew"; *whom* is the object of the verb and there is no qualifying addition. This, of itself, shows that, unless there is some other compelling reason, the expression "whom he foreknew" contains within itself the differentiation which is presupposed. If the apostle had in mind some "qualifying adjunct" it would have been simple to supply it. Since he adds none we are forced to inquire if the actual terms he uses can express the differentiation implied. The usage of Scripture provides an affirmative answer. Although the term "foreknew" is used seldom in the New Testament, it is altogether indefensible to ignore the meaning so frequently given to the word "know" in the usage of Scripture; "foreknow" merely adds the thought of "beforehand" to the word "know." Many times in Scripture "know" has a pregnant meaning which goes beyond that of mere cognition. It is used in a sense practically synonymous with "love," to set regard upon, to know with peculiar interest, delight, affection, and action (*cf.* Gen. 18:19; Exod. 2:25; Psalm 1:6; 144:3; Jer. 1:5; Amos 3:2; Hosea 13:6; Matt. 7:23; I Cor. 8:3; Gal. 4:9; II Tim. 2:19; I John 3:1). There is no reason why this import of the word "know" should not be applied to "foreknow" in this passage, as also in 11:2 where it also occurs in the same kind of construction and where the thought of election is patently present (*cf.* 11:5, 6). When this import is appreciated, then

there is no reason for adding any qualifying notion and "whom he foreknew" is seen to contain within itself the differentiating element required. It means "whom he set regard upon" or "whom he knew from eternity with distinguishing affection and delight" and is virtually equivalent to "whom he foreloved." This interpretation, furthermore, is in agreement with the efficient and determining action which is so conspicuous in every other link of the chain—it is God who predestinates, it is God who calls, it is God who justifies, and it is he who glorifies. Foresight of faith would be out of accord with the determinative action which is predicated of God in these other instances and would constitute a weakening of the total emphasis at the point where we should least expect it. . . . It is not the foresight of difference but the foreknowledge that makes difference to exist, not a foresight that recognizes existence but the foreknowledge that determines existence. It is a sovereign distinguishing love.[2]

Hodge observes that

as *to know* is often *to approve* and *love,* it may express the idea of peculiar affection in this case; or it may mean *to select* or *determine upon.* . . . The usage of the word is favourable to either modification of this general idea of *preferring.* "The people which he foreknew," *i.e.,* loved or selected, Rom. xi. 2; "Who verily was foreordained (Gr. *foreknown*), *i.e., fixed upon, chosen* before the foundation of the world," 1 Peter i. 20; 2 Tim. ii. 19; John x. 14, 15; see also Acts ii. 23; 1 Peter i. 2. The idea, therefore, obviously is, that those whom God peculiarly loved, and by thus loving, distinguished or selected from the

2. John Murray, *The Epistle to the Romans,* 2 vols. (Grand Rapids: Eerdmans, 1959, 1965), 1:316–18. Italics are his.

rest of mankind; or to express both ideas in one word, those whom he *elected* he predestined, etc.[3]

Although God knew *about* all men before the world began, He did not *know* all men in the sense that the Bible sometimes uses the word "know," i.e., with intimate personal awareness and love. It is in this latter sense that God fore*knew* those whom He predestined, called, and justified, as outlined in Romans 8:29–30!

NOT FORESIGHT OF FAITH OR GOOD WORKS

As was pointed out above, it is unnecessary and therefore indefensible to add any qualifying notion, such as faith, to the verb "foreknew" in Romans 8:29. The Arminians make this addition, not because the language requires it, but because their theological system requires it—they do it to escape the doctrines of unconditional predestination and election. They *read* the notion of foreseen faith *into* the verse and then appeal to it in an effort to prove that predestination was based on foreseen events. Thus, particular individuals are said to be saved, not because *God willed* that they should be saved (for He willed the salvation of everyone), but because *they themselves willed* to be saved. Hence, salvation is made to depend ultimately on the individual's will, not on the sovereign will of almighty God. Faith is understood to be man's gift to God, not God's gift to man.

Haldane, comparing Scripture with Scripture, clearly shows that the foreknowledge mentioned in Romans 8:29 cannot have reference to foreseen faith, good works, or the sinner's response to God's call:

3. Charles Hodge, *Commentary on the Epistle to the Romans*, rev. ed. (reprint, Grand Rapids: Eerdmans, 1947), 283–84. Italics are his.

Faith cannot be the cause of foreknowledge, because foreknowledge is before predestination, and faith is the effect of predestination. "As many as were ordained to eternal life believed," Acts xiii. 48. Neither can it be meant of the foreknowledge of good works, because these are the effects of predestination. "We are His workmanship, created in Christ Jesus unto good works; which God hath before ordained (or before prepared) that we should walk in them," Eph. ii. 10. Neither can it be meant of foreknowledge of our concurrence with the external call, because our effectual calling depends not upon that concurrence, but upon God's purpose and grace, given us in Christ Jesus before the world began, 2 Tim. i. 9. By this foreknowledge, then, is meant, as has been observed, the love of God towards those whom he predestinates to be saved through Jesus Christ. All the called of God are foreknown by Him,—that is, they are the objects of His eternal love, and their calling comes from this free love. "I have loved thee with an everlasting love; therefore with loving-kindness I have drawn thee," Jer. xxxi. 3.[4]

Murray, in rejecting the view that "foreknew" in Romans 8:29 refers to the foresight of faith, is certainly correct in stating,

It needs to be emphasized that the rejection of this interpretation is not dictated by a predestinarian interest. Even if it were granted that "foreknew" means the foresight of faith, the biblical doctrine of sovereign election is not thereby eliminated or disproven. For it is certainly true that God foresees faith; he foresees all that comes to pass. The question would then simply be: whence proceeds this faith which God foresees? And

---

4. Robert Haldane, *Exposition of the Epistle to the Romans* (London: Banner of Truth, 1960), 397.

the only biblical answer is that the faith which God foresees is the faith he himself creates (*cf.* John 3:3–8; 6:44,
45, 65; Eph. 2:8; Phil. 1:29; II Pet. 1:1). Hence his eternal foresight of faith is preconditioned by his decree to
generate this faith in those whom he foresees as believing, and we are thrown back upon the differentiation
which proceeds from God's own eternal and sovereign
election to faith and its consequents. The interest, therefore, is simply one of interpretation as it should be
applied to this passage. On exegetical grounds we shall
have to reject the view that "foreknew" refers to the
foresight of faith.[5]

"FOREKNOW" IN SEVERAL TRANSLATIONS

The Greek words literally translated "foreknow"
(*proginōskō*) and "foreknowledge" (*prognōsis*) occur seven times
in the Greek New Testament. Twice the verb refers to previous
knowledge on the part of *man:* in Acts 26:5 to the Jews' previous knowledge of Paul, and in 2 Peter 3:17 to the Christians'
previous knowledge (having been forewarned) of scoffers who
would come in the last days. Five times reference is made to
God's foreknowledge: three times as a verb (Rom. 8:29; 11:2;
1 Peter 1:20) and twice as a noun (Acts 2:23; 1 Peter 1:2). The
following quotations show how various translations have
attempted to convey in English the biblical connotations of the
word when used in reference to God's foreknowledge. In each
quotation, the English word or phrase which corresponds to
the Greek word "foreknew" is italicized, so that the reader may
see at a glance how the translators have rendered it. These various renderings certainly show, in the opinion of these translators, that when used in the New Testament with reference to

5. Murray, *The Epistle to the Romans,* 1:316.

God's foreknowledge, the word connotes more than simple knowledge of future events.[6]

Moffatt's Translation[7]

ROMANS 8:29: "For he decreed of old that those whom he *predestined* should share the likeness of his Son."

ROMANS 11:2: "God has not repudiated his People, his *predestined* People!"

1 PETER 1:2: ". . . whom God the Father has *predestined* and chosen . . ."

1 PETER 1:20: "He was *predestined* before the foundation of the world."

ACTS 2:23: ". . . this Jesus, betrayed in the *predestined course* of God's deliberate purpose . . ."

Goodspeed's Translation[8]

ROMANS 8:29: "For those whom he *had marked out from the first* he predestined to be made like his Son."

ROMANS 11:2: "God has not repudiated his people, which he *had marked out from the first.*"

6. See Caspar Wistar Hodge, "Foreknow," in *The International Standard Bible Encyclopaedia*, ed. James Orr (Grand Rapids: Eerdmans, 1939), 2:1128–31, and Loraine Boettner, "Foreknowledge," in *Baker's Dictionary of Theology* (Grand Rapids: Baker, 1960), 225. See also William Cunningham, *Historical Theology* (1862; reprint, London: Banner of Truth, 1960), 2:441–49. Cf. J. I. Packer, "Predestination," in *The New Bible Dictionary* (Grand Rapids: Eerdmans, 1962), 1024–26.

7. *A New Translation of the Bible,* trans. James Moffatt (New York: Harper & Brothers, 1935).

8. *The New Testament: An American Translation,* trans. by Edgar J. Goodspeed (Chicago: University of Chicago Press, 1923).

1 PETER 1:2: ". . . whom God the Father has chosen and *predestined* . . ."

1 PETER 1:20: ". . . who was *predestined* for this before the foundation of the world . . ."

ACTS 2:23: "But you, by the fixed purpose and *intention* of God, handed him over to wicked men."

Wuest's Expanded Translation[9]

ROMANS 8:29: "Because, those whom He *foreordained* He also marked out beforehand."

ROMANS 11:2: "God did not repudiate His people whom He *foreordained*."

1 PETER 1:2: ". . . chosen-out ones, this choice having been determined by the *foreordination* of God the Father . . ."

1 PETER 1:20: ". . . who indeed was *foreordained* before the foundation of the universe was laid . . ."

ACTS 2:23: ". . . this One, having been delivered up by the counsel of God which [in the council held by the Trinity] had decided upon His destiny, even by the *foreordination* of God *which is that act fixing his destiny.*"

Phillips's New Testament[10]

ROMANS 11:2: "It is unthinkable that God should have repudiated his own people, the people *whose destiny he himself appointed.*"

9. Kenneth S. Wuest, *Wuest's Expanded Translation of the Greek New Testament,* 3 vols. (Grand Rapids: Eerdmans, 1956–59).
10. *The New Testament in Modern English,* trans. J. B. Phillips (New York: Macmillan, 1958).

1 PETER 1:2: ". . . whom God the Father *knew* and chose long ago to be made holy by his Spirit . . ."

1 PETER 1:20: "It is true that God *chose* him to fulfill his part before the world was founded."

The Amplified Bible[11]

ROMANS 8:29: "For those whom He *foreknew—of whom he was aware . . .*"

ROMANS 11:2: "No, God has not rejected and disowned His people [whose destiny] He had *marked out* and *appointed and foreknown from the beginning.*"

Williams's New Testament[12]

ROMANS 8:29: "For those *on whom he set his heart beforehand* He marked off as His own to be made like His Son." (Williams gives the following footnote: "Lit., fore-knew but in Septuagint used as translated.")

ROMANS 11:2: "No, God has not disowned His people, *on whom he set his heart beforehand.*"

1 PETER 1:20: ". . . who was *foreordained . . .*"

The New English Bible[13]

ROMANS 8:29: "For God *knew his own before even they were,* and also ordained that they should be shaped to the likeness of his Son."

11. *The Amplified Bible,* trans. Frances E. Siewert (Grand Rapids: Zondervan, 1965).

12. *The New Testament: A Translation in the Language of the People,* trans. Charles B. Williams (Chicago: Moody Press, 1937).

13. The New English Bible: New Testament, trans. under the supervision of the Joint Committee on the New Translation of the Bible (New York: Oxford University Press, 1961).

ROMANS 11:2: "No! God has not rejected the people which he *acknowledged of old as his own.*"

1 PETER 1:2: ". . . chosen of old *in the purpose* of God the Father . . ."

1 PETER 1:20: "He was *predestined* before the foundation of the world."

ACTS 2:23: "When he had been given to you, by the deliberate will and *plan* of God, you used heathen men to crucify and kill him."

CONCLUSION

As was stated at the outset, Calvinists reject the Arminian interpretation of Romans 8:29 on two grounds: (1) because it is not in keeping with the meaning of Paul's language, and (2) because it is out of harmony with the system of doctrine taught in the rest of the Scriptures. This appendix has been devoted to demonstrating the validity of the first objection. Part 2 of this work dealt with the latter objection.

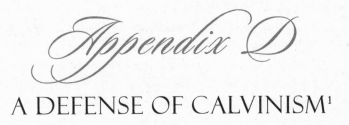

A DEFENSE OF CALVINISM[1]

CHARLES H. SPURGEON

The old truth that Calvin preached, that Augustine
preached, that Paul preached, is the truth that I must
preach today, or else be false to my conscience and my
God. I cannot shape the truth; I know of no such thing as
paring off the rough edges of a doctrine. John Knox's
gospel is my gospel. That which thundered through
Scotland must thunder through England again.

It is a great thing to begin the Christian life by believing good
solid doctrine. Some people have received twenty different
"gospels" in as many years; how many more they will accept

1. From *C. H. Spurgeon, Autobiography:* Vol. 1, *The Early Years: 1834–1859.*
Edinburgh: Banner of Truth, 1962, pp. 163–75.

before they get to their journey's end, it would be difficult to predict. I thank God that He early taught me *the* gospel, and I have been so perfectly satisfied with it, that I do not want to know any other. Constant change of creed is sure loss. If a tree has to be taken up two or three times a year, you will not need to build a very large loft in which to store the apples. When people are always shifting their doctrinal principles, they are not likely to bring forth much fruit to the glory of God. It is good for young believers to begin with a firm hold upon those great fundamental doctrines which the Lord has taught in His Word. Why, if I believed what some preach about the temporary, trumpery salvation which only lasts for a time, I would scarcely be at all grateful for it; but when I know that those whom God saves He saves with an everlasting salvation, when I know that He gives to them an everlasting righteousness, when I know that He settles them on an everlasting foundation of everlasting love, and that He will bring them to His everlasting kingdom, oh, then I do wonder, and I am astonished that such a blessing as this should ever have been given to me!

> Pause, my soul! adore, and wonder!
> Ask, "Oh, why such love to me?"
> Grace hath put me in the number
> Of the Saviour's family:
> Hallelujah!
> Thanks, eternal thanks, to Thee!

I suppose there are some persons whose minds naturally incline towards the doctrine of free will. I can only say that mine inclines as naturally towards the doctrines of sovereign grace. Sometimes, when I see some of the worst characters in the street, I feel as if my heart must burst forth in tears of gratitude that God has never let me act as they have done! I have thought, if God had left me alone, and had not touched me by His grace, what a great sinner I should have been! I should have run to the utmost lengths of sin, dived into the very depths of evil, nor should I have stopped at any vice or folly, if God had not restrained me. I feel that I should have been a very king of sinners, if God had let me alone. I cannot understand the reason why I am saved, except upon the ground that God would have it so. I cannot, if I look ever so earnestly, discover any kind of reason in myself why I should be a partaker of divine grace. If I am not at this moment without Christ, it is only because Christ Jesus would have His will with me, and that will was that I should be with Him where He is, and should share His glory. I can put the crown nowhere but upon the head of Him whose mighty grace has saved me from going down into the pit. Looking back on my past life, I can see that the dawning of it all was of God; of God effectively. I took no torch with which to light the sun, but the sun enlightened me. I did not commence my spiritual life—no, I rather kicked, and struggled against the things of the Spirit: when He drew me, for a time I did not run after Him: there was a natural hatred in my soul of everything holy and good. Wooings were lost upon me— warnings were cast to the wind—thunders were despised; and as for the whispers of His love, they were rejected as being less than nothing and vanity. But, sure I am, I can say now, speaking on behalf of myself, "He only is my salvation." It was He who turned my heart, and brought me down on my knees before Him. I can in very deed say with Doddridge and Toplady—

> Grace taught my soul to pray,
> And made my eyes o'erflow;

and coming to this moment, I can add—

> 'Tis grace *has* kept me to this day,
> And will not let me go.

Well can I remember the manner in which I learned the doctrines of grace in a single instant. Born, as all of us are by nature, an Arminian, I still believed the old things I had heard continually from the pulpit, and did not see the grace of God. When I was coming to Christ, I thought I was doing it all myself, and though I sought the Lord earnestly, I had no idea the Lord was seeking me. I do not think the young convert is at first aware of this. I can recall the very day and hour when first I received those truths in my own soul—when they were, as John Bunyan says, burnt into my heart as with a hot iron, and I can recollect how I felt that I had grown on a sudden from a babe into a man—that I had made progress in scriptural knowledge, through having found, once for all, the clue to the truth of God. One weeknight, when I was sitting in the house of God, I was not thinking much about the preacher's sermon, for I did not believe it. The thought struck me, *How did you come to be a Christian?* I sought the Lord. *But how did you come to seek the Lord?* The truth flashed across my mind in a moment—I should not have sought Him unless there had been some previous influence in my mind to *make me* seek Him. I prayed, thought I, but then I asked myself, *How came I to pray?* I was induced to pray by reading the Scriptures. *How came I to read the Scriptures?* I did read them, but what led me to do so? Then, in a moment, I saw that God was at the bottom of it all, and that He was the Author of my faith, and so the whole doctrine of grace opened up to me, and from that doctrine I have not departed to this day, and I desire to make this my constant confession, "I ascribe my change wholly to God."

I once attended a service where the text happened to be, *"He* shall choose our inheritance for us," and the good man who occupied the pulpit was more than a little of an Arminian. Therefore, when he commenced, he said, "This passage refers entirely to our temporal inheritance, it has nothing whatever to do with our everlasting destiny, for," said he, "we do not want Christ to choose for us in the matter of heaven or hell. It is so plain and easy, that every man who has a grain of common sense will choose heaven, and any person would know better than to choose hell. We have no need of any superior intelligence, or any greater Being, to choose heaven or hell for us. It is left to our own free will, and we have enough wisdom given us, sufficiently correct means to judge for ourselves," and therefore, as he very logically inferred, there was no necessity for Jesus Christ, or anyone, to make a choice for us. We could choose the inheritance for ourselves without any assistance. "Ah!" I thought, "but, my good brother, it may be very true that we *could*, but I think we should want something more than common sense before we *should* choose aright."

First, let me ask, must we not all of us admit an overruling Providence, and the appointment of Jehovah's hand, as to the means whereby we came into this world? Those men who think that, afterwards, we are left to our own free will to choose this one or the other to direct our steps, must admit that our entrance into the world was not of our own will, but that God had then to choose for us. What circumstances were those in our power which led us to elect certain persons to be our parents? Had we anything to do with it? Did not God Himself appoint our parents, native place, and friends? Could He not have caused me to be . . . brought forth by a filthy mother who would nurse me . . . and teach me to bow down to pagan gods, quite as easily as to have given me a pious mother, who would each morning and night bend her knee in prayer on my behalf? Or, might He not, if He had pleased, have given me some profligate to have been my parent, from whose lips I might have early heard fearful, filthy, and obscene language? Might He not have placed me where I should have had a drunken father, who would have immured me in a very dungeon of ignorance, and brought me up in the chains of crime? Was it not God's Providence that I had so happy a lot, that both my parents were His children, and endeavoured to train me up in the fear of the Lord?

John Newton used to tell a whimsical story, and laugh at it, too, of a good woman who said, in order to prove the doctrine of election, "Ah! sir, the Lord must have loved me before I was born, or else He would not have seen anything in me to love afterwards." I am sure it is true in my case; I believe the doctrine of election, because I am quite certain that, if God had not chosen me, I should never have chosen Him; and I am sure He chose me before I was born, or else He never would have chosen me afterwards; and He must have elected me for reasons unknown to me, for I never could find any reason in myself why He should have looked upon me with special love. So I am forced to accept that great biblical doctrine. I recollect an Arminian brother telling me that he had read the Scriptures through a score or more times, and could never find the doctrine of election in them. He added that he was sure he would have done so if it had been there, for he read the Word on his knees. I said to him, "I think you read the Bible in a very uncomfortable posture, and if you had read it in your easy chair, you would have been more likely to understand it. Pray, by all means, and the more, the better, but it is a piece of superstition to think there is anything in the posture in which a man puts himself for reading: and as to reading through the Bible twenty times without having found anything about the doctrine of election, the wonder is that you found anything at all: you must have galloped through it at such a rate that you were not likely to have any intelligible idea of the meaning of the Scriptures."

If it would be marvelous to see one river leap up from the earth full grown, what would it be to gaze upon a vast spring from which all the rivers of the earth should at once come bubbling up, a million of them born at a birth? What a vision would it be! Who can conceive it? And yet the love of God is that fountain, from which all the rivers of mercy, which have ever gladdened our race—all the rivers of grace in time, and of glory hereafter—take their rise. My soul, stand thou at that sacred fountainhead, and adore and magnify, for ever and ever God, even our Father, who hath loved us! In the very beginning, when this great universe lay in the mind of God, like unborn forests in the acorn cup; long ere the echoes awoke the solitudes; before the mountains were brought forth; and long ere the light flashed through the sky, God loved His chosen creatures. Before there was any created being—when the ether was not fanned by an angel's wing, when space itself had not an existence, when there was nothing save God alone—even then, in that loneliness of Deity, and in that deep quiet and profundity, His bowels moved with love for His chosen. Their names were written on His heart, and then were they dear to His soul. Jesus loved His people before the foundation of the world—even from eternity! And when He called me by His grace, He said to me, "I have loved *thee* with an everlasting love: therefore with loving-kindness have I drawn thee."

Then, in the fullness of time, He purchased me with His blood; He let His heart run out in one deep gaping wound for me, long ere I loved Him. Yea, when He first came to me, did I not spurn Him? When He knocked at the door, and asked for entrance, did I not drive Him away, and do despite to His grace? Ah, I can remember that I full often did so until, at last, by the power of His effectual grace, He said, "I must, I will come in," and then He turned my heart, and made me love Him. But even till now I should have resisted Him, had it not been for His grace. Well, then since He purchased me when I was dead in sins, does it not follow, as a consequence necessary and logical, that He must have loved me first? Did my Saviour die for me because I believed on Him? No; I was not then in existence; I had then no being. Could the Saviour, therefore, have died because I had faith, when I myself was not yet born? Could that have been possible? Could that have been the origin of the Saviour's love towards me? Oh! No, my Saviour died for me long before I believed. "But," says someone, "He foresaw that you would have faith; and, therefore, He loved you." What did He foresee about my faith? Did He foresee that I should get that faith myself, and that I should believe on Him of myself? No, Christ could not foresee that, because no Christian man will ever say that faith came of itself without the gift and without the working of the Holy Spirit. I have met with a great many believers, and talked with them about this matter; but I never knew one who could put his hand on his heart and say, "I believed in Jesus without the assistance of the Holy Spirit."

I am bound to the doctrine of the depravity of the human heart because I find myself depraved in heart, and have daily proofs that in my flesh there dwelleth no good thing. If God enters into covenant with unfallen man, man is so insignificant a creature that it must be an act of gracious condescension on the Lord's part; but if God enters into covenant with *sinful* man, he is then so offensive a creature that it must be, on God's part, an act of pure, free, rich, sovereign grace. When the Lord entered into covenant with me, I am sure that it was all of grace, nothing else but grace. When I remember what a den of unclean beasts and birds my heart was, and how strong was my unrenewed will, how obstinate and rebellious against the sovereignty of the divine rule, I always feel inclined to take the very lowest room in my Father's house, and when I enter heaven, it will be to go among the less than the least of all saints, and with the chief of sinners.

The late lamented Mr. Denham has put, at the foot of his portrait, a most admirable text, "Salvation is of the Lord." That is just an epitome of Calvinism; it is the sum and substance of it. If anyone should ask me what I mean by a Calvinist, I should reply, "He is one who says, *Salvation is of the Lord.*" I cannot find in Scripture any other doctrine than this. It is the essence of the Bible. "He *only* is my rock and my salvation." Tell me anything contrary to this truth, and it will be a heresy; tell me a heresy, and I shall find its essence here, that it has departed from this great, this fundamental, this rock-truth, "God is my rock and my salvation." What is the heresy of Rome, but the addition of something to the perfect merits of Jesus Christ— the bringing in of the works of the flesh, to assist in our justification? And what is the heresy of Arminianism, but the addition of something to the work of the Redeemer? Every heresy, if brought to the touchstone, will discover itself here. I have my own private opinion that there is no such thing as preaching Christ and Him crucified, unless we preach what nowadays is called Calvinism. It is a nickname to call it Calvinism; Calvinism is the gospel, and nothing else. I do not believe we can preach the gospel, if we do not preach justification by faith, without works; nor unless we preach the sovereignty of God in His dispensation of grace; nor unless we exalt the electing, unchangeable, eternal, immutable, conquering love of Jehovah; nor do I think we can preach the gospel, unless we base it upon the special and particular redemption of His elect and chosen people which Christ wrought out upon the cross; nor can I comprehend a gospel which lets saints fall away after they are called, and suffers the children of God to be burned in the fires of damnation after having once believed in Jesus. Such a gospel I abhor.

> If ever it should come to pass,
> That sheep of Christ might fall away,
> My fickle, feeble soul, alas!
> Would fall a thousand times a day.

If one dear saint of God had perished, so might all; if one of the covenant ones be lost, so may all be; and then there is no gospel promise true, but the Bible is a lie, and there is nothing in it worth my acceptance. I will be an infidel at once when I can believe that a saint of God can ever fall finally. If God hath loved me once, then He will love me forever. God has a master mind; He arranged everything in His gigantic intellect long before He did it; and once having settled it, He never alters it. "This shall be done," saith He, and the iron hand of destiny marks it down, and it is brought to pass. "This is My purpose," and it stands, nor can earth or hell alter it. "This is My decree," saith He, "promulgate it, ye holy angels; rend it down from the gate of heaven, ye devils, if ye can; but ye cannot alter the decree, it shall stand for ever." God altereth not His plans; why should He? He is almighty, and therefore can perform His pleasure. Why should He? He is the All-wise, and therefore cannot have planned wrongly. Why should He? He is the everlasting God, and therefore cannot die before His plan is accomplished. Why should He change? Ye worthless atoms of earth, ephemera of a day, ye creeping insects upon this bay leaf of existence, ye may change *your* plans, but He shall never, never change His. Has He told me that His plan is to save me? If so, I am forever safe.

> My name from the palms of His hands
> Eternity will not erase;
> Impress'd on His heart it remains,
> In marks of indelible grace.

I do not know how some people, who believe that a Christian can fall from grace, manage to be happy. It must be a very commendable thing in them to be able to get through a day without despair. If I did not believe the doctrine of the final perseverance of the saints, I think I should be of all men the most miserable, because I should lack any ground of comfort. I could not say, whatever state of heart I came into, that I should be like a wellspring of water, whose stream fails not; I should rather have to take the comparison of an intermittent spring, that might stop on a sudden, or a reservoir, which I had no reason to expect would always be full. I believe that the happiest of Christians and the truest of Christians are those who never dare to doubt God, but who take His Word simply as it stands, and believe it, and ask no questions, just feeling assured that if God has said it, it will be so. I bear my willing testimony that I have no reason, nor even the shadow of a reason, to doubt my Lord, and I challenge heaven, and earth, and hell, to bring any proof that God is untrue. From the depths of hell I call the fiends, and from this earth I call the tried and afflicted believers, and to heaven I appeal, and challenge the long experience of the blood-washed host, and there is not to be found in the three realms a single person who can bear witness to one fact which can disprove the faithfulness of God, or weaken His claim to be trusted by His servants. There are many things that may or may not happen, but this I know *shall* happen—

> He *shall* present my soul,
> Unblemish'd and complete,
> Before the glory of His face,
> With joys divinely great.

All the purposes of man have been defeated, but not the purposes of God. The promises of man may be broken—many of them are made to be broken—but the promises of God shall all be fulfilled. He is a promise maker, but He never was a promise breaker; He is a promise-keeping God, and every one of His people shall prove it to be so. This is my grateful, personal confidence: "The Lord *will* perfect that which concerneth *me*"—unworthy *me*, lost and ruined *me*. He will yet save me; and—

> I, among the blood-wash'd throng,
> Shall wave the palm, and wear the crown,
> And shout loud victory.

I go to a land which the plough of earth hath never upturned, where it is greener than earth's best pastures and richer than her most abundant harvests ever saw. I go to a building of more gorgeous architecture than man hath ever builded; it is not of mortal design; it is "a building of God, a house not made with hands, eternal in the heavens." All I shall know and enjoy in heaven, will be given to me by the Lord, and I shall say, when at last I appear before Him—

> Grace all the work shall crown
> Through everlasting days;
> It lays in heaven the topmost stone,
> And well deserves the praise.

I know there are some who think it necessary to their system of theology to limit the merit of the blood of Jesus: if my theological system needed such a limitation, I would cast it to the winds. I cannot, I dare not allow the thought to find a lodging in my mind, it seems so near akin to blasphemy. In Christ's finished work I see an ocean of merit; my plummet finds no bottom, my eye discovers no shore. There must be sufficient efficacy in the blood of Christ, if God had so willed it, to have saved not only all in this world, but all in ten thousand worlds, had they transgressed their Maker's law. Once admit infinity into the matter, and limit is out of the question. Having a divine person for an offering, it is not consistent to conceive of limited value; *bound* and *measure* are terms inapplicable to the divine sacrifice. The intent of the divine purpose fixes the *application* of the infinite offering, but does not change it into a finite work. Think of the numbers upon whom God has bestowed His grace already. Think of the countless hosts in heaven: if thou wert introduced there today, thou wouldst find it as easy to tell the stars, or the sands of the sea, as to count the multitudes that are before the throne even now. They have come from the East, and from the West, from the North, and from the South, and they are sitting down with Abraham, and with Isaac, and with Jacob in the kingdom of God; and beside those in heaven, think of the saved ones on earth. Blessed be God, His elect on earth are to be counted by millions, I believe, and the days are coming, brighter days than these, when there shall be multitudes upon multitudes brought to know the Saviour and to rejoice in Him. The Father's love is not for a few only, but for an exceeding great company. "A great multitude, which no man could number," will be found in heaven. A man can reckon up to very high figures; set to work your Newtons, your mightiest calculators, and they can count great numbers, but God and God alone can tell the multitude of His redeemed. I believe there will be more in heaven than in hell. If anyone asks me why I think so, I answer, because Christ, in everything, is to "have the preeminence," and I cannot conceive how He could have the preeminence if there are to be more in the dominions of Satan than in paradise. Moreover, I have never read that there is to be in hell a great multitude, which no man could number. I rejoice to know that the souls of all infants, as soon as they die, speed their way to paradise. Think what a multitude there is of them! Then there are already in heaven unnumbered myriads of the spirits of just men made perfect—the redeemed of all nations, and kindreds, and people, and tongues up till now; and there are better times coming, when the religion of Christ shall be universal, when—

He shall reign from pole to pole,
With illimitable sway;

when whole kingdoms shall bow down before Him, and nations shall be born in a day, and in the thousand years of the great millennial state there will be enough saved to make up all the deficiencies of the thousands of years that have gone before. Christ shall be Master everywhere, and His praise shall be sounded in every land. Christ shall have the preeminence at last; His train shall be far larger than that which shall attend the chariot of the grim monarch of hell.

Some persons love the doctrine of universal atonement because they say, "It is so beautiful. It is a lovely idea that Christ should have died for all men; it commends itself," they say, "to the instincts of humanity; there is something in it full of joy and beauty." I admit there is, but beauty may be often associated with falsehood. There is much which I might admire in the theory of universal redemption, but I will just show what the supposition necessarily involves. If Christ on His cross intended to save every man, then He intended to save those who were lost before He died. If the doctrine be true, that He died for all men, then He died for some who were in hell before He came into this world, for doubtless there were even then myriads there who had been cast away because of their sins. Once again, if it was Christ's intention to save all men, how deplorably has He been disappointed, for we have His own testimony that there is a lake which burneth with fire and brimstone, and into that pit of woe have been cast some of the very persons who, according to the theory of universal redemption, were bought with His blood. That seems to me a conception a thousand times more repulsive than any of those consequences which are said to be associated with the Calvinistic and Christian doctrine of special and particular redemption. To think that my Saviour died for men who were or are in hell, seems a supposition too horrible for me to entertain. To imagine for a moment that He was the substitute for all the sons of men, and that God, having first punished the substitute, afterwards punished the sinners themselves, seems to conflict with all my ideas of divine justice. That Christ should offer an atonement and satisfaction for the sins of all men, and that afterwards some of those very men should be punished for the sins for which Christ had already atoned, appears to me to be the most monstrous iniquity that could ever have been imputed to Saturn, to Janus, to the goddess of the Thugs, or to the most diabolical heathen deities. God forbid that we should ever think thus of Jehovah, the just and wise and good!

There is no soul living who holds more firmly to the doctrines of grace than I do, and if any man asks me whether I am ashamed to be called a Calvinist, I answer—I wish to be called nothing but a Christian; but if you ask me, do I hold the doctrinal views which were held by John Calvin, I reply, I do in the main hold them, and rejoice to avow it. But far be it from me even to imagine that Zion contains none but Calvinistic Christians within her walls, or that there are none saved who do not hold our views. Most atrocious things have been spoken about the character and spiritual condition of John Wesley, the modern prince of Arminians. I can only say concerning him that, while I detest many of the doctrines which he preached, yet for the man himself I have a reverence second to no Wesleyan; and if there were wanted two apostles to be added to the number of the twelve, I do not believe that there could be found two men more fit to be so added than George Whitefield and John Wesley. The character of John Wesley stands beyond all imputation for self-sacrifice, zeal, holiness, and communion with God; he lived far above the ordinary level of common Christians, and was one "of whom the world was not worthy." I believe there are multitudes of men who cannot see these truths, or, at least, cannot see them in the way in which we put them, who nevertheless have received Christ as their Saviour, and are as dear to the heart of the God of grace as the soundest Calvinist in or out of heaven.

I do not think I differ from any of my hyper-Calvinistic brethren in what I do believe, but I differ from them in what they do not believe. I do not hold any less than they do, but I hold a little more, and, I think, a little more of the truth revealed in the Scriptures. Not only are there a few cardinal doctrines, by which we can steer our ship north, south, east, or west, but as we study the Word, we shall begin to learn something about the northwest and northeast, and all else that lies between the four cardinal points. The system of truth revealed in the Scriptures is not simply one straight line, but two; and no man will ever get a right view of the gospel until he knows how to look at the two lines at once. For instance, I read in one book of the Bible, "The Spirit and the bride say, Come. And let him that heareth say, Come. And let him that is athirst come. And whosoever will, let him take the water of life freely." Yet I am taught, in another part of the same inspired Word, that "it is not of him that willeth, nor of him that runneth, but of God that sheweth mercy." I see, in one place, God in providence presiding over all, and yet I see, and I cannot help seeing, that man acts as he pleases, and that God has left his actions, in a great measure, to his own free will. Now, if I were to declare that man was so free to act that there was no control of God over his actions, I should be driven very near to atheism; and if, on the other hand, I should declare that God so overrules all things that man is not free enough to be responsible, I should be driven at once into antinomianism or fatalism. That God predestines, and yet that man is responsible, are two facts that few can see clearly. They are believed to be inconsistent and contradictory to each other. If, then, I find taught in one part of the Bible that everything is foreordained, *that is true;* and if I find, in another Scripture, that man is responsible for all his actions, *that is true;* and it is only my folly that leads me to imagine that these two truths can ever contradict each other. I do not believe they can ever be welded into one upon any earthly anvil, but they certainly shall be one in eternity. They are two lines that are so nearly parallel, that the human mind which pursues them farthest will never discover that they converge, but they do converge, and they will meet somewhere in eternity, close to the throne of God, whence all truth doth spring.

It is often said that the doctrines we believe have a tendency to lead us to sin. I have heard it asserted most positively, that those high doctrines which we love, and which we find in the Scriptures, are licentious ones. I do not know who will have the hardihood to make that assertion, when they consider that the holiest of men have been believers in them. I ask the man who dares to say that Calvinism is a licentious religion, what he thinks of the character of Augustine, or Calvin, or Whitefield, who in successive ages were the great exponents of the system of grace; or what will he say of the Puritans, whose works are full of them? Had a man been an Arminian in those days, he would have been accounted the vilest heretic breathing, but now *we* are looked upon as the heretics, and they as the orthodox. *We* have gone back to the old school; *we* can trace our descent from the apostles. It is that vein of free grace, running through the sermonizing of Baptists, which has saved us as a denomination. Were it not for that, we should not stand where we are today. We can run a golden line up to Jesus Christ Himself, through a holy succession of mighty fathers, who all held these glorious truths; and we can ask concerning them, "Where will you find holier and better men in the world?" No doctrine is so calculated to preserve a man from sin as the doctrine of the grace of God. Those who have called it "a licentious doctrine" did not know anything at all about it. Poor ignorant things, they little knew that their own vile stuff was the most licentious doctrine under heaven. If they knew the grace of God in truth, they would soon see that there was no preservative from lying like a knowledge that we are elect of God from the foundation of the world. There is nothing like a belief in my eternal perseverance, and the immutability of my Father's affection, which can keep me near to Him from a motive of simple gratitude. Nothing makes a man so virtuous as belief of the truth. A lying doctrine will soon beget a lying practice. A man cannot have an erroneous belief without by-and-by having an erroneous life. I believe the one thing naturally begets the other. Of all men, those have the most disinterested piety, the sublimest reverence, the most ardent devotion, who believe that they are saved by grace, without works, through faith, and that not of themselves, it is the gift of God. Christians should take heed and see that it always is so, lest by any means Christ should be crucified afresh and put to an open shame.

Appendix E

THE PRACTICAL APPLICATIONS OF CALVINISM[1]

CURT DANIEL

Earlier in this series we discussed the practical implications of the doctrine of election. We will not repeat here what we said there. The applications are the same, but here we will look at several which pertain to all five of the points of Calvinism and to the sovereignty of God in general.

It would, however, be appropriate to repeat one thing from our earlier discussion. It is this: doctrine comes first, then practice (see 2 Tim. 3:16–17). Thus far we have examined the his-

---

1. From Curt Daniel, *The History and Theology of Calvinism* (Dallas: Scholarly Reprints, 1993), 465–70. Copies may be obtained from the author at Reformed Bible Church, 4850 Old Jacksonville Road, Springfield, IL 62707. All Scripture quotations are taken from the New American Standard Bible®. © Copyright The Lockman Foundation 1960, 1962, 1963, 1968, 1971, 1972, 1973, 1975, 1977, 1995. Used by permission.

tory and theology of Calvinism. Now we must look at how to live what we have learned. However, these studies are primarily doctrinal, not practical; therefore, we will not go into the same length or depth. Lastly, since this is a series on Calvinism, we will concentrate on how the biblical truths known as Calvinism are to be put into practice. We will not, for example, explore practicalities of those doctrines which Calvinists share with non-Calvinists.

A REFORMED WORLDVIEW

Christians need to have a biblical worldview, or what is called in German a *Weltanschauung* ("world and life system"). This is especially true with Calvinist Christians. No practical philosophy is complete unless it has a general blueprint. Is there, then, a distinctively Reformed worldview?

Yes, there is. The subject has been discussed off and on among Calvinist theologians, and the most mature contributions to the subject have been made by those of the school of Abraham Kuyper. Kuyper, you may recall, was the leading Reformed theologian and preacher from about 1880 to 1920 in the Netherlands. Much of his work has been translated into English, and far more remains in Dutch. Perhaps his major contribution to Calvinist theology has been his constructing a distinctively Calvinist worldview. His views are best summed up in his handy little *Lectures on Calvinism*. Note, for example, the titles of those lectures: "Calvinism a Life-system," "Calvinism and Religion," "Calvinism and Politics," "Calvinism and Science," "Calvinism and Art," and "Calvinism and the Future."

Kuyper was certainly a theological genius. But he was not abstract and theoretical; he put his views into practice. In this he serves as a good example. He did not only lecture and write on these subjects; he also worked toward their implementation in his own life, and in the life of his church and society. You may recall that his influence spread so far that he became prime minister of Holland.

Basically, a Calvinist worldview first sees things as they are from the perspective of God, who is sovereign. Calvinists, then, see that God is ultimately in charge of the universe. This is God's universe. It does not belong to a god called Chance. Nor does it belong to sinful man. Man is only the appointed caretaker of part of the universe. This does not mean that the sovereign God has relinquished all involvement in His creation. No, of course not; otherwise we are in the darkness of Deism. God rules His universe through providence.

One of the means of providence that Kuyper especially investigated was common grace. Because of God's general love and gifts to all men as His creatures, there resides in the universe a frame of reference for carrying out the cultural mandate of Genesis 1:28. Man, though totally depraved, is still to subdue the earth and use it to God's glory. Fallen man, however, is incapable of doing so properly. Sure, common grace keeps the machinery working, but only special grace can guide it to its proper end. Christians are the elect, who have received special grace. They therefore have the added edge in carrying out the cultural mandate in spheres such as science, art, and politics.

Christians should use the gifts of common grace under the guidance of special grace to use creation to the glory of God. In practice, this means that Christians should bear Christian witness in the arts, for instance, by employing biblical principles of art. Such as? Well, true art must glorify God, not man. It must not tempt man or blaspheme God. Sheer realism is not enough. Realist art must be painted with biblical paintbrushes; otherwise, it is not reality as God sees it.

As should already be obvious, the one controlling principle in this worldview is that everything in life is to be done with a view to the glory of God. If one is a scientist, then let him be a godly scientist. That means more than simply praying before he enters the laboratory or saying a few things about Christ to his coworkers at lunch. No, it is far more. Non-Calvinists can do as much. We need to show by our words and works that we look at things from God's perspective. Now apply this to the sovereignty of God. Why does one plus one equal two? The Calvinist says it is because the sovereign God made it so. What keeps the laws of physics regular so that we can live and think and operate in this universe? Because the sovereign God is a God of order, not of chance or chaos. Sinful man, not God, is the spring of chaos. One more useful principle: though the Bible is primarily a textbook on spiritual matters, this does not mean that it has nothing at all to say about scientific matters. In fact, the Calvinist will argue that biblical principles of science take precedence over the so-called scientific method, that is, empirical experimentation. Van Til, following Kuyper, was especially fond of developing this. You may remember that Satan first tempted Eve by saying that empirical experimentation took precedence over special revelation, and that to live in this world she must prove the facts to be true by empirically experimenting with the data available to her. Or, in more familiar terminology, Satan said that God had lied and that she should eat the forbidden fruit and find out for herself the facts outside of God's Word. Thus, Calvinism stresses that even science is subject to the Bible, even as general revelation is subject to the confirmation of special revelation and not human experience. Why? Because God is God and is to be trusted as our sovereign.

This Calvinist principle applies to all other spheres of society in a truly Christian worldview. Take work as another example. What does the Bible say about labor, and specifically what do Calvinist Christians say and do? Well, there was a well-developed work ethic long before Kuyper, and it had many hallmarks of a Calvinist methodology. It generally goes by the title of the Protestant work ethic (also called the Puritan work ethic, for the Puritans developed and practiced it more consistently than their non-Reformed Protestant brethren). This ethic was formed not only as the biblical alternative to the Roman Catholic work ethic, but as a rejection of all non-Christian work principles. In place of merely secular work principles, the early

Calvinists put biblical principles. This had drastic ramifications on labor in sixteenth-century Europe and thereafter.

This had, of course, been well known among those who adhered to it, such as the Pilgrim Fathers in America. Skeptics poured scorn on it. They still do. One non-Calvinist who had a more favorable appreciation of it wrote an epochal study early in the twentieth century which caught the attention of non-Christian sociologists and historians. In *The Protestant Ethic and the Spirit of Capitalism,* Max Weber showed that more than anything else, it was the theological worldview of Calvinism that created the system of capitalism, or free enterprise. This nonfeudal economic system was not only different from non-Christian systems, but also different from Roman Catholic and non-Reformed Protestant theories. Its abuses are not due to the errors of the system, but to misunderstandings of the theory or misapplications of the principles it espouses.

What are these principles? Without going into all of them, there was one vital one that seemed to stand out. The Calvinists taught that the carpenter in his shop is every much a priest unto God as the minister in the pulpit. The preacher is obviously ordained of God, and is to proclaim special revelation to the world. But the Christian in the shop is also a priest. He exercises that priesthood in several ways, such as faith in Christ through the gospel, the true partaking of the Lord's Supper, and worship of the sovereign God. But there is more. God ordained that man use creation to glorify God, and in so doing act as a priest in the realm of work. Work is not just a curse of Genesis 3; work was commanded of Adam in Genesis 1:28. The Fall did not annul that.

How, then, does redeemed man exercise this priesthood in the workplace? By employing biblical principles of work. By so doing, he brings all things into submission to God and thereby furthers the glory of God. Again, this is far more than simply saying that we glorify God at work when we pray silently while turning the lathe or when we refrain from arguing with our fellow worker. No, the Calvinist worldview says that God is glorified by principles of work that follow the Word of God. The Calvinist Christian, more than any other, knows that good work glorifies God. Hence, over the factories and schools and art studies should be written the words "Soli Deo Gloria"—to God alone be the glory. But, and this is crucial, those words are not to be written merely with ink or paint, but with the living witness of Christians who live in the world by the principles of the sovereign God.

PITFALLS PECULIAR TO CALVINISTS

Calvinists are not to be so heavenly minded that they are of no earthly good. They are to be heavenly minded, to be sure. But there are several pitfalls to which Calvinists are prone. These prevent them from glorifying God in the world.

One of them is pride. Of course, where is the Calvinist that admits it? I am not speaking of pride in general, for non-Calvinists have that affliction as well. Rather, I am talking about Calvinist pride, or pride in being a Calvinist. This rank disease has several symptoms. One of them is personal pride. After all, one reasons, am I not one of the elect? Did not God choose me and not the reprobate? Original sin takes over and further spreads the lie that one must have been special for God to choose him. But this is all wrong. It is evidence that the Calvinist is still imperfect in his experience. A believer who makes sure of his election (2 Peter 1:10) has no reason to boast. He is one of the elect, but not one of the elite. He was not chosen because he was special. God is the special one, not him. He was chosen out of sheer grace, and therefore cannot boast. If Ephesians 2:8–9 leaves us no room for boasting because of salvation by grace, then Ephesians 1:4–6 leaves us no room for boasting because of election by grace. Paul says, "What do you have that you did not receive? And if you did receive it, why do you boast as if you had not received it?" (1 Cor. 4:7). Therefore, "let him who boasts, boast in the Lord" (1 Cor. 1:31). To God alone be the glory, fellow Calvinist!

This TULIP-flavored pride takes other forms as well. One is that Calvinists too frequently look down their noses at their non-Reformed brothers in Christ. We place ourselves above them. We are the elite; we know more about the deep mysteries than they do. What good men we are. All such attitudes are proud. Then this shows in the way we too often disparage those brethren with whom we have the most serious disagreements. In a word, some Calvinists go too far in their animosity to Arminians. Note that I did not say "animosity to Arminianism," for error cannot be hated too much. But Calvinists are not to hate Arminians, nor are we to be obsessed with an anti-Arminian inquisition. We chuckle to hear about the Puritan farmer who lost his temper with his mule, and called him an Arminian because that was the worst thing he could think of. But this is serious. Learn the lesson of Whitefield's great love for Wesley the Arminian. When asked if he would see Mr. Wesley in heaven, Whitefield reportedly replied that he would not. Wesley, he said, would be so much closer to the throne of Christ than himself that he would not be able to see him. Though the exact theology of this may not be precisely correct, the sentiments are on target. One need not be a Calvinist to be saved, and many Arminians outshine us in holiness.

The Calvinist should always see himself as a Christian first and only secondly as a Calvinist. We ridicule the Roman Catholic who sees himself as a Catholic first and a Christian second, but are not Calvinists prone to this as well? One way in which this evil disease crops up is in the "Calvinist second blessing." It is ironic that Calvinists usually denounce all theologies that promote a "second blessing," such as Pentecostalism. But we are too often guilty of it when we speak more of our coming to know the doctrines of grace than our coming to know Christ in salvation. We get more excited when we tell people how the grand truths of election and sovereign grace opened our eyes and we have never been the same. Some Calvinists describe it in almost mystical terms. But this ought never to outshine our personal testimonies of conversion. We should always be more moved to speak of how the Savior saved us from sin by sovereign grace than we are to describe how He later explained sovereign grace to us. Such a "second blessing" panders to pride and looks disparagingly on those "poor souls" who have not been so enlightened. Away with such a thing! We need no Reformed Gnosticism.

Then there is the pitfall of Calvinist intellectualism. Too often we Calvinists spend more time discussing the doctrines of grace than living the grace of the doctrines. We have already shown how this is done in the area of evangelism. To be more precise, Calvinists sometimes mistake knowledge for spirituality, as if one could somehow gauge spiritual growth by how much one knows about the finer points of Calvinism, such as the order of the decrees. But knowledge alone puffs up (1 Cor. 8:1). Unless our Calvinism is put into practice, then even Reformed theology becomes staid and proud.

This in turn is related to another pitfall, that of Reformed apathy and lethargy. This is seen, for example, in the reluctance to evangelize because, "After all, God has His elect out there and He will call them to Himself in due time." It is also seen in the overemphasis on the secret will to the detriment of the revealed will of God. When a Calvinist is more interested in election than in practical living, then it will show up in a low level of personal spirituality. The sad thing is that he does not realize it.

Similarly, some use the doctrines of grace to excuse their laziness. This is a kind of antinomianism that masquerades as Reformed faith. Trusting in God is meant to be active, not passive. Some Calvinists somehow have the erroneous notion that the pinnacle of spirituality is to be achieved by passively resigning themselves to what God is doing. As we shall see later, Christians are to submit; but an impersonal apathy is Stoicism, not Christianity.

And this leads to the almost obsessive antiemotionalism found in some Reformed quarters. Granted, emotionalism is wrong, but that does not mean that emotions do not have any place in the life of the Calvinist Christian. Admit it, brethren; have you not heard the accusation that Calvinists are personally cold and unapproachable, even distant? Sometimes they call us "the frozen chosen." Well, many are cold, but few are frozen. In any case, he who says he knows what grace is should show in his heart and life the warmth of grace.

Another odd pitfall that characterizes some Calvinists is chronic introspection. Now, I do not mean normal self-examination (2 Cor. 13:5). I mean the sort that goes too far. This sort seems to glory in introspection without the proper results. What do I mean? True self-examination should lead to renewed faith and love and obedience. False introspection leads to more introspection, and actually less faith. It produces more doubt, not faith. For example, some worry that they might not be among the elect. But this does not lead them to put faith in Christ. If that is the result, then it is not true self-examination.

This is often seen especially among hyper-Calvinists, which is another pitfall which we need to beware of. Arminians are not prone to the disease of hyper-Calvinism. Let us beware that we do not overreact against Arminianism and back into hyper-Calvinism. That syndrome occurs when the Calvinist overemphasizes the secret will of God over the revealed will, and places more importance on the sovereignty of God than on the responsibility of man. The results are not only theologically imbalanced, but also practically stagnating. Be careful.

THE TRULY REFORMED ATTITUDES

Instead of succumbing to these pitfalls, Calvinists should strive to use their knowledge of the doctrines of grace to develop certain attitudes. The first of these is humility. When the Calvinist understands the doctrine of total depravity, it smites his pride and brings him down to his knees. He abhors himself. The same is true with the wellspring of Calvinism, the sovereignty of God. A. W. Pink well wrote, "A true recognition of God's sovereignty humbles us as nothing does or can humble, and brings the heart into lowly submission before God, causing us to relinquish our own self-will and making us delight in the perception and performance of the divine will."

Thus humbled, the Calvinist will truly submit to God. This is not Stoic apathy, the sort that says, "Whatever will be, will be." No. True submission says, "It is the LORD; let Him do what seems good to Him" (1 Sam. 3:18; cf. 2 Sam. 15:26). It does not gripe; it submits without argument. After all, do we Calvinists not say that the sovereignty of God means that God does whatever He pleases (Ps. 115:3)? This is not a grudging submission, either, but a joyful submission to the One who knows more than we do and cares for us more than we can imagine. It is not a Stoic resignation to the inevitable. It is childlike trust in a loving heavenly Father, not resignation to blind fate.

And then there is the comfort of Calvinism. It is far better than the anxiety of Arminianism. This affects two things. First, afflictions. The Calvinist realizes that even his problems were predestined by God. But if the God who foreordained the afflictions is also the God who elected us to glory, then we are assured and comforted in the knowledge that "God causes all things to work together for good to those who love God, to those who are called according to His purpose" (Rom. 8:28). This lovely verse sparkles with comfort, but without an appreciation of the sovereignty of God it is nothing. Moreover, even those afflictions are blessings in disguise. As Arthur Custance wrote, "Now surely, one of the most comforting things about any faith in the absolute sovereignty of the grace of God ought to be the assurance we derive from that faith that God is still on the throne even in our most dismal defeats and that the clouds we so much dread are waiting to pour only showers of blessing on our head."

We see this everywhere in the Bible. Look at Joseph, who knew the sovereignty of God centuries before Augustine or

Calvin. His brothers sold him into slavery. But he had the faith to read the providence of that affliction. Later when he met those same brothers in Egypt, he told them, "It was not you who sent me here, but God. . . . You meant evil against me, but God meant it for good" (Gen. 45:8; 50:20).

The Calvinist is persuaded that if God elected him, then God will see him through to the end, in spite of all obstacles. Even his own sins cannot hinder him anymore. This is the perseverance of the saints. The Calvinist knows that he will make it to heaven. He need not worry as the Arminian does. He can rest assured in the promises of God. He can do more than rest, too. He can have bold confidence. How? It works like this. We know that we are eternally loved by God's sovereign grace. This produces security. And that security in turn produces confidence. Who is more confident than the one who knows that, no matter what else happens to him, he is still loved by God? And who is more secure than such a one? What security, then, is afforded by this Calvinism. As Toplady wrote, the saints in heaven are happier, but not more secure, than the saints on earth. Therefore, we know that we shall persevere to the end. What hope! What encouragement!

What should be our attitude toward God in light of His sovereign grace? Three in particular are most important, and without all three our Calvinism is worthless. First, there is thankfulness. He who knows his depravity is humbled, and such a humbled one should sing the loudest thanksgiving to God for electing him. Fellow Calvinist, have you ever taken time to thank God for choosing you?

Second, love. We should love Him because He first loved us (1 John 4:19). Our non-Calvinist brethren admit as much, but with our appreciation of the eternality of that unconditional, sovereign grace, we should have even greater love for Christ. Fellow Calvinist, do you love your Christ, who chose you to be His bride?

Third, worship. Too often Calvinists worship less than other saints, which is pitiable in light of our recognition of the doctrines of grace. Our Calvinism should move us to greater praise, and when Calvinism is properly grasped, then it shall move us to greater worship. If it does not, then one has not really grasped these truths at all. One way in which we worship God is by magnifying His wisdom. He understands the paradox of divine sovereignty and human responsibility, when we do not, and for that we should give Him great praise. Calvinists can and should worship Him for His awesome sovereignty, infinite power, and overwhelming grace. Fellow Calvinist, do you really worship God?

This, then, is the summary of the practical applications of Calvinism: "Whatever you do, do all to the glory of God" (1 Cor. 10:31). Soli Deo Gloria!

Appendix F

THE PRACTICAL IMPORTANCE
OF THE DOCTRINE
[OF PREDESTINATION][1]

LORAINE BOETTNER

INFLUENCE OF THE DOCTRINE IN DAILY LIVING

This is not a cold, barren, speculative theory, not an unnatural system of strange doctrines, such as many people are inclined to believe, but a most warm and living, a most vital and important, account of God's relations with men. It is a system of great practical truths, which are designed and adapted, under the influence of the Holy Spirit, to mold the affections

1. From Loraine Boettner, *The Reformed Doctrine of Predestination* (1932; reprint, Philadelphia: Presbyterian and Reformed, 1965), 327–32. His Bible quotations come from the American Standard Version (1901).

of the heart and to give right direction to the conduct. Calvin's own testimony in this respect is: "I would, in the first place, entreat my readers carefully to bear in memory the admonition which I offer; that this great subject is not, as many imagine, a mere thorny and noisy disputation, nor a speculation which wearies the minds of men without any profit; but a solid discussion eminently adapted to the service of the godly, because it builds us up soundly in the faith, trains us to humility, and lifts us up into an admiration of the unbounded goodness of God toward us, while it elevates us to praise this goodness in our highest strains. For there is not a more effectual means of building up faith than the giving [of] our open ears to the election of God, which the Holy Spirit seals upon our heart while we hear, showing us that it stands in the eternal and immutable goodwill of God towards us; and that, therefore, it cannot be moved or altered by any storms of the world, by any assaults of Satan, by any changes, by any fluctuations or weaknesses of the flesh. For our salvation is then sure to us, when we find the cause of it in the breast of God."[2] These, we think, are true words and much needed today.

The Christian who has this doctrine in his heart knows that he is following a heaven-directed course; that his course has been foreordained for him personally; and that it is a good course. He does not yet understand all of the details, but even amid adversities he can look forward confident of the future, knowing that his eternal destiny is fixed and forever blessed, and that nothing can possibly rob him of this priceless treasure. He realizes that after he has finished the course here, he shall look back over it and see that every single event in it was designed of God for a particular purpose, and that he will be thankful for having been led through those particular experiences. Once convinced of these truths, he knows that the day is surely coming when to all those who grieve or persecute him

2. John Calvin, *Calvin's Calvinism*, trans. Henry Cole (1856; reprint, London: Sovereign Grace Union, 1927), 29.

he shall be able to say, as did Joseph to his brothers, "As for you, ye meant evil against me, but God meant it for good." This exalted conception of God as high and lifted up, yet personally concerned with even the smallest events, leaves no place for what men commonly call chance, or luck, or fortune. When a person sees himself as one of the Lord's chosen and knows that every one of his acts has an eternal significance, he realizes more clearly how serious life is, and he is fired with a new determination to make his life count for great things.

A SOURCE OF SECURITY AND COURAGE

"It is the doctrine of a particular providence," says Rice, "that gives to the righteous a feeling of security in the midst of danger; that gives them assurance that the path of duty is the path of safety and of prosperity; and that encourages them to the practice of virtue, even when it exposes them to the greatest reproach and persecution. How often, when clouds and darkness seem to gather over them, do they rejoice in the assurance given by their Saviour, 'I will never leave thee, nor forsake thee.'"[3] The sense of security which this doctrine gives to the struggling saint results from the assurance that he is not committed to his own power, or rather weakness, but into the sure hands of the almighty Father—that over him is the banner of love and underneath are the everlasting arms. He realizes that even the devil and wicked men, regardless of whatever tumults they may cause, are not only restrained of God, but are compelled to do His pleasure. Elisha, lonely and forgotten, counted those who were with him more than those who were against him, because he saw the chariots and horsemen of the Lord moving in the clouds. The disciples, knowing that their names were written in heaven, were prepared to endure persecutions,

3. N. L. Rice, *God Sovereign and Man Free* (Philadelphia: Presbyterian Board of Publication, 1850), 46.

and on one occasion we read that, after being beaten and reviled, "they therefore departed from the presence of the council, rejoicing that they were counted worthy to suffer dishonor for the Name," Acts 5:41.

"The godly consideration of predestination, and our election in Christ," says the seventeenth article in the creed of the Church of England, "is full of sweet, pleasant, and unspeakable comfort to godly persons." Paul's injunction was, "In nothing be anxious." And it is only when we know that God actually rules from the throne of the universe, and that He has ordained us to be his loved ones, that we can have that inward peace in our hearts.

Dr. Clarence E. Macartney, in a sermon on predestination, said: "The misfortunes and adversities of life, so called, assume a different color when we look at them through this glass. It is sad to hear people trying to live over their lives again and saying to themselves: 'If I had chosen a different profession,' 'If I had taken a different turning of the road,' 'If I had married another person.' All this is weak and un-Christian. The web of destiny we have woven, in a sense, with our own hands, and yet God had His part in it. It is God's part in it, and not our part, that gives us faith and hope." And Blaise Pascal, in a wonderful letter written to a bereaved friend, instead of repeating the ordinary platitudes of consolation, comforted him with the doctrine of predestination, saying: "If we regard this event, not as an effect of chance, not as a fatal necessity of nature, but as a result inevitable, just, holy, of a decree of His Providence, conceived from all eternity, to be executed in such a year, day, hour, and such a place and manner, we shall adore in humble silence the impenetrable loftiness of His secrets; we shall venerate the sanctity of His decrees; we shall bless the acts of His providence; and uniting our will with that of God Himself, we shall wish with Him, in Him and for Him, the thing that He has willed in us and for us for all eternity."

Since the true Calvinist sees God's hand and wise purpose in everything, he knows that even his sufferings, sorrows, per-

secutions, defeats, etc., are not the results of chance or acci-
dent, but that they have been foreseen and foreappointed, and
that they are chastisements or disciplines designed for his own
good. He realizes that God will not needlessly afflict His people; that in the divine plan these are all ordered in number,
weight, and measure; and that they shall not continue a
moment longer than God sees necessary. In sorrow his heart
instinctively clings to this faith, feeling that for reasons wise
and gracious, though unknown, the affliction was sent. However keenly afflictions may at first wound, a little reasoned
thought quickly brings him to himself again, and the sorrows
and tribulations, in great measure, become pointless.

And in accordance with this the Scriptures say: "To them
that love God all things work together for good," Rom. 8:28.
"My son, regard not lightly the chastening of the Lord, nor faint
when thou art reproved of him; for whom the Lord loveth he
chasteneth, and scourgeth every son whom he receiveth," Heb.
12:5, 6. "It is Jehovah: let him do what seemeth him good,"
1 Sam. 3:18. "For I reckon that the sufferings of this present
time are not worthy to be compared with the glory which shall
be revealed to us-ward," Rom. 8:18. "Blessed are ye when men
shall reproach you, and persecute you, and say all manner of
evil against you falsely, for my sake. Rejoice, and be exceeding
glad: for great is your reward in heaven: for so persecuted they
the prophets that were before you," Matt. 5:11, 12. "If we endure
[suffer with Him], we shall also reign with him," 2 Tim. 2:12.
"Jehovah gave, and Jehovah hath taken away; blessed be the
name of Jehovah," Job 1:21. When someone slanders us, we
shall at least not be so angry if we remember with David that
"Jehovah hath bidden him" curse, 2 Sam. 16:11.

Our predestination is our one sure guarantee of salvation.
Other things may give us comfort, but only this can give us certainty. It makes the gospel to be what the word really means,
"Good News." Any other system which holds that Christ's sacrifice did not actually save anyone, but that it merely made salvation possible for all if they would comply with certain terms,

reduces it to good advice; and any system which carries with it only a "chance" for salvation, also carries with it, of logical necessity, a "chance" to be lost. And what a difference it makes to fallen man as to whether the gospel is good news or good advice! The world is full of good advice; even the books of heathen philosophers contained much of it; but the gospel alone contains for man the good news that God has redeemed him.

This system, logical and severe though it may be, does not make one sad and silent, but courageous and active. Knowing himself to be immortal until his work is done, courage is a natural result. Smith's estimate of the Calvinist is expressed in the following words: "His feet plucked from the horrible pit and planted on the Eternal Rock, his heart thrilled with an adoring gratitude, his soul conscious of a Divine love that will never forsake him and a Divine energy that in him and through him is working out eternal purposes of good, he is girded with invincible strength. In a nobler sense than Napoleon ever dreamed, he knows himself to be a 'man of destiny.'" And again he says, "Calvinism is at once the most satisfying and the most stimulating of creeds."[4]

Yet along with these motives for courage are to be found others which keep the person properly humble and grateful. In the present stage of the world, he sees himself as a brand plucked from the burning. Knowing himself to have been saved, not by any merit or wisdom of his own, but only by God's grace and mercy, he is deeply conscious of his dependence on God, and has the greatest incentive to right living. All in all, no surer way will be found to fill the mind at one time with reverence, humility, patience, and gratitude than to have it thoroughly saturated with this doctrine of predestination.

4. Egbert Watson Smith, *The Creed of Presbyterians* (New York: Baker and Taylor, 1901), 53, 94.

Appendix G

CALVINISM AND ARMINIANISM BEFORE AND AFTER: A BRIEF HISTORICAL SKETCH[1]

S. LANCE QUINN

The subject of theology has taken a real beating of late. Those who have come to question the relevance of theology in general do so for a number of reasons. For instance, they say that theology is boring, or too complicated, or over their head, or divisive, or impractical and unrelated to their life. But theology—rightly defined and understood as the

---

1. Even though some of the historical details in this appendix have already been given elsewhere in this work, it will be helpful in this updated edition to survey the leading strains of Calvinism and Arminianism, both past and present. All Bible quotations are taken from the New American Standard Bible®. Copyright © 1960, 1962, 1963, 1968, 1971, 1972, 1973, 1975, 1977, 1995 by The Lockman Foundation. Used by permission.

study of God—is the most important subject in all of life to master! Admittedly, theology sometimes has been taught in a boring way, or has been made unnecessarily complicated, or seems to be beyond the grasp of the average Christian, or has divided believers, or has been applied wrongly (or not at all). But it does not have to be this way! Theology, rightly studied, provides the key to all right thinking and right living. R. C. Sproul has well written:

> Every Christian is a theologian. We are always engaged in the activity of learning about the things of God. We are not all theologians in the professional or academic sense, but theologians we are, for better or worse. The "for worse" is no small matter. Second Peter warns that heresies are destructive to the people of God and are blasphemies committed against God. They are destructive because theology touches every dimension of our lives.
>
> The Bible declares that as a man thinks in his heart, so is he. . . . Those ideas that do grasp us in our innermost parts, are the ideas that shape our lives. We are what we think. When, however, our thoughts are corrupted, our lives follow suit.
>
> We all know that people can recite the creeds flawlessly and make A's in theology courses while living godless lives. We can affirm a sound theology and live an unsound life. Sound theology is not enough to live a godly life. But it is still a requisite for godly living. How can we do the truth without first understanding what the truth is?
>
> No Christian can avoid theology. Every Christian has a theology. The issue, then, is not, do we want to have a theology? That's a given. The real issue is, do we have a *sound* theology? Do we embrace true or false doctrine?[2]

2. R. C. Sproul, *Essential Truths of the Christian Faith* (Wheaton, Ill.: Tyndale House, 1992), vii.

How we understand the sovereignty of God in the salvation of man has eternal, life-and-death consequences. In order to help us understand this vital matter, this appendix will briefly sketch how leading theologians, both past and present, have understood it.

THE THEOLOGY OF GOD AND MAN THROUGH THE LENS OF HISTORY

Two critical areas of theology—indeed, the most important areas—are the doctrines of God and man, and how a man is to be right with God (salvation). The study of the transaction between God and man can prove to be most interesting. It can also prove critically helpful in the overall study of theology. Throughout history, the doctrine of justification (how a man is to be right with God) has been vigorously debated. Earle Cairns succinctly states the fundamental question: "Was man to be saved by divine power only, or was there a place in the process of salvation for human will?"[3]

Each successive epoch shows a classic battle between those who are *theocentric* in their soteriology (basing salvation entirely on the work of God) and those who are *anthropocentric* (basing salvation, in a greater or lesser degree, on man's work). We shall see that history recycles these two approaches. They could be rightly labeled *the religion of divine accomplishment* (that God alone saves) and *the religion of human achievement* (that man cooperates with God in salvation). The following study is designed to show the historical progression of the understanding of God and salvation, as seen especially through the church's principal combatants.

3. Earle E. Cairns, *Christianity Through the Centuries,* 3d ed. (Grand Rapids: Zondervan, 1996), 131.

Augustine and Pelagius

In 386, a young teacher of rhetoric from North Africa made
a discovery that would shape the development of Christianity
in the Western world. At age 32, Aurelius Augustine was ago-
nizing over the question of human nature and the destiny of
man. One day, he kept hearing children sing *Tolle, lege, tolle,
lege* ("Take up and read, take up and read") as they played. He
found the nearest book (the letter of Paul to the Romans), which
he picked up and began reading at Romans 13:13–14: "Let us
behave properly as in the day, not in carousing and drunken-
ness, not in sexual promiscuity and sensuality, not in strife and
jealousy. But put on the Lord Jesus Christ, and make no provision for the flesh in regard to its lusts." As he would later say
about that day, "A light of certainty entered my heart, and every
shadow of doubt vanished."[4] This portion of Scripture was especially convicting to Augustine because he had been living a profligate life. His father was a heathen, but his mother, Monica,
was a vibrant believer, who had been praying fervently for her
son and his spiritual condition. Augustine had been sent to
Carthage, the capital of North Africa, to study, and it was there
that he fell into serious sin, even fathering an illegitimate son,
Adeodatus. He found that he was unable to control his passions
and was tormented by immense guilt and total helplessness.
He realized that by his own initiative he was completely unable
to respond to God. On the day of his conversion, Augustine
knew that his heart had been regenerated by the Holy Spirit,
and he repented of his sin. He began to grow in his relationship with God and ultimately perceived his calling to pastoral
ministry. Augustine studied for the ministry and was later
named bishop (pastor) of Hippo (in what is today Algeria) in
395. Because of his enormous influence, Augustine was called
"the second founder of the Christian faith" (as by Jerome).

4. See Peter Brown, *Augustine of Hippo: A Biography* (Berkeley: University of California Press, 1967), 101–14, for details of Augustine's conversion.

Earlier in church history (but not excluding subsequent times), the main controversies within the Christian church were largely about the nature of the person of Christ. Cairns aptly writes:

> The heresies and controversies . . . were problems mainly in the Eastern wing of the church. Theology and Christology were not grave problems in the West where such leaders as Tertullian had led the church to the orthodox view of the relationship of Christ to the Father and of His two natures to each other. The Western church was not as concerned with speculative meta-physical theology as the more rationalistic Greek thinkers of the Eastern church were. Instead, the thinkers of the church in the West were concerned with more practical problems. This distinction becomes quite clear to any student of ancient history. The Greek mind made its contribution in the field of thought, whereas the more practical Roman mind was more concerned with matters of practice in the church.[5]

In the latter half of the fourth century and the early part of the fifth, the controversy over the doctrine of justification came to the forefront. The questions plaguing Augustine in his struggle against sin allowed the controversy over how a man is to be right with God to become known throughout Christendom. A raging debate was to begin with those who disagreed with Augustine's views on sin and grace.

In the early part of the fifth century, Pelagius (360–420), a British layman living in Rome, was distressed at the low morality of professing Christians in that city. Pelagius became aware of Augustine's views and began to take issue with his views of human inability and human dependence upon divine grace, arguing that they denied human responsibility and the need to exert

5. Cairns, *Christianity Through the Centuries*, 131.

strenuous effort to become right with God. In reaction to Augustine, Pelagius taught the following regarding God and man:

(1) *The Freedom of the Will.* According to Pelagius, the will of man is completely unaffected by sin. This was the cornerstone of his theology. Erwin Lutzer describes Pelagius's view:

> When faced with a choice of whether to sin or not to sin, man can choose one direction or another. To quote Pelagius, man has "the absolutely equal ability at every moment to do good or evil." Therefore, man can, if he so wishes, live sinlessly. If we could not keep every one of God's commands, he would be unfair in giving them. Pelagius' slogan was, "Whatever I ought to do, I can do."
>
> Both Pelagius and Augustine agreed that Adam was created morally neutral and so chose freely when he sinned. But Pelagius went on to maintain that Adam's fall hurt only himself and no one else. Children do not have original sin, nor are they born under the condemnation of Adam's sin. They are born neutral and, theoretically at least, have the ability to live sinlessly. As might be expected, Augustine disagreed with these conclusions.[6]

(2) *The Nature of Sin.* Pelagius affirmed that a person who sins does so simply because he has made a choice to sin, not because he is predisposed to sin by nature. He reasoned that if Adam had that choice, then so has everyone else. Pelagius believed that Christ would not have commanded anyone to respond to Him unless God had first given him the ability to respond to such commands. If it were beyond a person's ability to respond, how could he be held accountable or judged for not responding? He said, "As often as I have to speak concerning moral improvement and the leading of a holy life, I am accustomed

6. Erwin Lutzer, *The Doctrines That Divide: A Fresh Look at the Historic Doctrines That Separate Christians* (Grand Rapids: Kregel, 1998), 155.

first to set forth the power and quality of human nature and to show what it can accomplish."[7]

One of Pelagius's students, Celestius, made the following points on the nature of sin and human freedom:

1. Adam was created mortal and would have died even if he had not sinned.
2. Adam's fall injured himself alone, not the human race.
3. Children come into the world in the same condition in which Adam was before the Fall.
4. The human race neither dies because of Adam's fall, nor rises again because of Christ's resurrection.
5. Unbaptized children, as well as others, are saved.
6. The law, as well as the gospel, leads to the kingdom of heaven.
7. Even before Christ's death there were sinless men.[8]

(3) *The Understanding of Grace.* Pelagius believed that these views were not inconsistent with the grace of God. He did not believe that God needed to intervene directly in the heart of man in order to save him, and he believed that man's own natural ability to keep God's law was itself an expression of God's grace. Thus, he taught that God's grace was showcased in man's freedom to respond rightly to God. Cairns explains Augustine's opposition to these ideas:

> Augustine . . . opposed what he believed was a denial of the grace of God by insisting that regeneration is exclusively the work of the Holy Spirit. Man was originally made in the image of God and free to choose good and evil, but Adam's sin bound all men because Adam was the head of the race. Man's will is entirely corrupted by the Fall so that he must be considered totally

7. Ibid.
8. Ibid., 155–56.

depraved and unable to exercise his will in regard to
the matter of salvation. Augustine believed that all
inherit sin through Adam and that no one, therefore,
can escape original sin. Man's will is so bound that he
can do nothing to bring about his salvation. Salvation
can come only to the elect through the grace of God in
Christ. God must energize the human will to accept His
proffered grace, which is only for those whom He has
elected to salvation.[9]

(4) *The Ground of Justification.* Obviously, for Pelagius, the
ground of the sinner's justification is his own merit. How could
he teach anything different, given his view of man's innate ability to choose either to sin or not to sin? But for Augustine, the
unconverted do not have any freedom of the will, because their
wills are enslaved to sin. The only way someone can be right
with God is if the Holy Spirit supernaturally intervenes in his
heart by the work of regeneration, thereby granting him repentance and faith as a gift. Only Christ's righteousness—through
both His life and death—applied to the sinner by God, can produce any valid ground for the sinner's salvation.

The debate between Augustine and Pelagius set the stage
for further debate down through history: Does the sinner get
right with God because of his own effort or because of God's
effort? The issue for both of these men was a matter of eternal
life or death. "Augustine believed that Pelagianism was a threat
to the very heart of the gospel and therefore wrote extensively
against this heresy."[10] Ultimately, Pelagius's teaching was condemned as heresy at the Council of Ephesus in 431. This council was uncomfortable with Augustine's view as well, and John
Cassian, himself a monk, attempted to reach a mediating position between Pelagius and Augustine. However, "the view of

9. Cairns, *Christianity Through the Centuries,* 131–32.
10. Lutzer, *The Doctrines That Divide,* 157.

Cassian was condemned at the Synod of Orange in 529 in favor of a moderate Augustinian view."[11]

Martin Luther and Desiderius Erasmus

The second major debate on the doctrine of salvation was between Martin Luther (1483–1546) and Desiderius Erasmus (1469–1536). Luther had rediscovered from Augustine's writings and from an intensive study of Paul's letter to the Romans the doctrine of justification by faith alone, which had been largely lost by the church during the Middle Ages. As an Augustinian monk, Luther was selected by his superiors to lecture in theology at the new University of Wittenberg in 1508. In 1518, after years of study and struggle, Luther finally saw that he was justified by faith, apart from any human righteousness (Rom. 1:18). At the Diet of Worms in 1521, he refused to recant, thus setting the stage for the Reformation.

Desiderius Erasmus was also an Augustinian monk. Initially he admired Luther, standing with him against the indulgences and other corruptions of the Roman Church. But when Luther sought a wholesale reformation of the church, Erasmus turned against him. The two became bitter rivals, specifically over the doctrine of the freedom of the will. "Goaded by Rome to strike out at the Lutheran heresy, Erasmus wrote a treatise *On the Freedom of the Will* in 1524, which took Luther to task on the thorny issue of predestination and human freedom."[12] Luther likewise wrote his own treatise, called *The Bondage of the Will* (annotated in Part Three of this work).

The issue, once again, was the ability of man to respond to God—whether one becomes right with Him by faith or by a

---

11. Cairns, *Christianity Through the Centuries*, 132.

12. N. P. Feldmeth, "Erasmus, Desiderius," in *New Dictionary of Theology*, ed. Sinclair B. Ferguson, David F. Wright, and J. I. Packer (Downers Grove, Ill.: InterVarsity Press, 1988), 227.

combination of faith and effort (good works). Sproul writes of this dispute:

> The question we face is how we as unjust sinners can become just in the sight of God. The two competing theories in answer to this question that have fueled such serious controversy are the Roman Catholic and Protestant Reformation theories. These are not the only theories that have been advanced in history but they are the chief views that have clashed. The controversy over the doctrine of justification in the sixteenth century was surely the most volatile and divisive in church history. In simple terms the issue boils down to this: Are we justified by a process by which we become actually just or are we justified by a declarative act by which we are counted or reckoned to be just by God? Are we declared just or are we made just by justification?[13]

John Calvin and Jacopo Sadoleto/Jacob Arminius

John Calvin closely followed Luther, both in time (1509–1564) and in theology. Calvin was a Frenchman who pastored in Geneva, Switzerland (from 1541 until the end of his life, except for a short interlude). Calvin was raised, as was Luther, in the Roman Catholic Church. He was genuinely converted to Christ and broke away from Rome. Calvin was one of the leaders of the Reformation, and his tremendous influence began to spread throughout Europe. His influence continues to this day. Calvin's main theological influence came through his book *The Institutes of the Christian Religion* (first published in 1536, and annotated in Part Three). Calvin became the most

---

13. R. C. Sproul, "Justification by Faith Alone: The Forensic Nature of Justification," in *Justification by Faith Alone!* ed. Don Kistler (Morgan, Pa.: Soli Deo Gloria, 1995), 25.

respected and articulate defender of the doctrine of justification by faith alone (known by the Latin phrase *sola fide*).

One of Calvin's staunchest opponents was Jacopo Sadoleto (born in 1477), a Roman Catholic cardinal in southern France. In March 1539, Sadoleto addressed a letter to Calvin and the Genevan Reformers, asking them to return to the Catholic faith. The following August, John Calvin replied to Sadoleto, defending the Reformation. Again, the theocentric and anthropocentric views of God's sovereignty and man's free will became the nexus of the debate. John Olin writes:

> An extensive commentary on St. Paul's Epistle to the Romans was the most ambitious and controversial [of his writings]. In this . . . work Sadoleto grappled with the question of justification and sought to reconcile the action of divine grace and man's own free will. His overemphasis on man's freedom and his neglect of prevenient grace, however, provoked the censure of both the Sorbonne and Rome in 1535, although subsequent clarifications by Sadoleto apparently satisfied his critics.[14]

The background of this debate and the debate itself are covered in the above-cited work. Again, the emphasis in this debate was on the work of God and man in salvation. Calvin held that since man's will was in bondage to sin, man himself had no capacity to respond to God apart from divine grace. Sadoleto believed that man was capable of responding by both God's grace and human effort.

It should be noted that Calvin had another ongoing theological battle with the Dutch Roman Catholic, Albert Pighius (although the debate was cut short by Pighius's death in 1544). This battle was also over the freedom of the will. After Pighius wrote a critique of Calvin's 1539 edition of the *Institutes* on

14. John C. Olin, ed., *A Reformation Debate: Sadoleto's Letter to the Genevans and Calvin's Reply* (1966; reprint, Grand Rapids: Baker, 1976), 9–10.

this subject, Calvin responded in 1543 with his *Defence of the Sound and Orthodox Doctrine of the Bondage and Liberation of Human Choice Against the Misrepresentations of Albert Pighius of Kampen.*[15]

The most famous adversary of later Calvinism was Jacob Arminius (1560–1609). In the late 1500s and early 1600s, the controversy over divine sovereignty and human will became very apparent in the Netherlands. Arminius became convinced that the will of man was free to choose Christ, and that God was obligated to dispense His grace freely to all. He did not go as far as Pelagius, and so his views are rightly characterized as semi-Pelagian.

Arminius called for an official church synod to discuss these theological issues, but he died before it was convened. However, in 1610, one year after his death, his followers presented a summation of his teaching in five articles of faith to the State of Holland in the form of a "Remonstrance," or protest (see the discussion in Part One).

Lutzer briefly summarizes these Arminian principles (as we have done in the chart in Part One) as follows:

1. God decreed to save all who believe and persevere in the faith; all others are left in sin and damnation.
2. Christ died for all men, "so that he has obtained for them all, by his death on the cross, redemption and forgiveness of sins; yet that no one actually enjoys this forgiveness of sins except the believer."
3. Man has not saving grace of himself, nor of the energy of his free will, "inasmuch as he, in the state of apostasy and sin, can of and by himself neither think, will, or do

15. For the English translation of this debate, see John Calvin, *The Bondage and Liberation of the Will: A Defence of the Orthodox Doctrine of Human Choice Against Pighius,* ed. A. N. S. Lane, trans. G. I. Davies (Grand Rapids: Baker, 1996).

anything that is truly good . . . but that he be born again of God in Christ."

4. Without the operation of grace, man cannot do anything good, but grace is not irresistible since men have resisted the Holy Spirit.

5. Believers partake of eternal life and have power to strive against Satan. However, whether they can fall away and be lost is a matter "that must be more particularly determined out of Holy Scripture before we ourselves can teach it with the full persuasion of our minds."[16]

As was noted early in this volume, a response to these principles of Arminianism was fashioned by the Church of Holland at the Synod of Dort—the name coming from the place of the meeting in Dordrecht, Holland. From November 1618 to May 1619, the Synod of Dort wrestled with these Arminian theories. The synod consisted of eighty-four members, including eighteen political delegates. Cairns writes:

> It was really an international Calvinistic assembly because 28 of the 130 present were Calvinists from England, Bremen, Hesse, the Palatinate, Switzerland, and France. The Arminians came before the meeting in the role of defendants. Five Calvinistic articles, the *Canons of Dort*, opposing the *Remonstrance* of 1610 were drawn up, and the clerical followers of Arminius were deprived of their positions.[17]

The Synod of Dort responded to Arminianism with what became known as "the five points of Calvinism." The issues were the same as they were in the previous three historical sketches. The issues of God's sovereign choice to save and man's inability to respond to God were being vigorously pur-

16. Lutzer, *The Doctrines That Divide*, 178.
17. Cairns, *Christianity Through the Centuries*, 318.

sued because both sides believed that the gospel was being polluted and that lives were being plunged into perdition. Theology mattered a great deal to them. It was a matter of life and death! How right Paul was when he penned the words of Galatians 1:6–9:

> I am amazed that you are so quickly deserting Him who called you by the grace of Christ, for a different gospel; which is really not another; only there are some who are disturbing you and want to distort the gospel of Christ. But even if we, or an angel from heaven, should preach to you a gospel contrary to what we have preached to you, he is to be accursed! As we have said before, so I say again now, if any man is preaching to you a gospel contrary to what you received, he is to be accursed!

Asahel Nettleton and Charles G. Finney

Asahel Nettleton (1783–1844) and Charles G. Finney (1792–1875) provide another example of the continuing theological controversy about God's and man's work in salvation. A passage about Finney's theology by John Thornbury explains the disagreement:

> Finney found the commonly accepted doctrines of grace not only intellectually unacceptable but also functionally intolerable. If these views were irrational, they were false, and if false, deleterious. He believed that a vibrant and thriving Christianity could not co-exist with such concepts as inherited depravity and "constitutional" regeneration. Those beliefs, though hoary with age and loved by thousands, were, according to Finney, inimical to godliness and damaging to evangelism. Successful preaching, he maintained, must be based on the

proposition that men have the full ability to convert themselves.[18]

Rick Nelson remarks:

Widely regarded as the father of modern revivalism, Finney represents the watershed in the shift from Calvinism to Arminianism as the dominant theology of evangelism. . . . Finney's legacy shaped the theology and methodology of evangelism generally, and Southern Baptist evangelism particularly. The publication of his major works, *Lectures on Revivals of Religion* and *Lectures on Systematic Theology*, left an impact upon evangelism which reaches to the present. Southern Baptist emphases such as simultaneous crusades, crusade preparation, the public invitation system, and the use of the revival meeting as an evangelistic strategy are at least in part attributable to Finney's considerable influence on the evangelicalism of his day.[19]

What exactly did Charles Finney believe and teach? First of all, Finney denied the orthodox doctrine of election, which he called "an exercise of arbitrary sovereignty."[20] He also denied that conversion is wholly a work of God. He taught that faith is fundamentally a human decision, and that salvation is secured by the sinner's own movement toward God. John MacArthur summarizes other aspects of Finney's theology:

18. John Thornbury, *God Sent Revival* (Durham: Evangelical Press, 1977), 161.

19. Rick Nelson, "How Does Doctrine Affect Evangelism? The Divergent Paths of Asahel Nettleton and Charles Finney," *The Founders Journal*, no. 33 (Summer 1998), 5.

20. Charles G. Finney, *Systematic Theology* (reprint, Whittier, Calif.: Colporter Kemp, 1944), 489, cited in John MacArthur Jr., *Ashamed of the Gospel: When the Church Becomes like the World* (Wheaton, Ill.: Crossway Books, 1993), 158.

He concluded that people are sinners by *choice,* not by nature. He believed the purpose of evangelism should therefore be to convince people to *choose* differently—or as many would say today, "make a decision for Christ." The sinner's choice—not God's—therefore became the determinative issue in conversion. The means of moving out of darkness into light was in Finney's opinion nothing more than a simple act of the human will. The preacher's task was to secure a decision of faith, applying whatever means proved useful. Finney introduced "new measures" (unconventional methodology) into his ministry, often using techniques whose sole design was to shock and intrigue apathetic churchgoers. He was willing to implement virtually any means that would elicit the desired response from his audiences.[21]

Regarding the doctrine of total depravity, Finney wrote in his *Systematic Theology,* "Moral depravity as I use the term does not consist in nor imply a sinful nature. It is not a constitutional sinfulness; moral depravity consists in a state of voluntary committal of the will to self-gratification."[22] Again, "The doctrine of original sin is an anti-scriptural and non-sensical dogma. It is a monstrous and blasphemous dogma that a holy God is angry with any creature for possessing a sinful nature."[23] Once more: "The Bible defines sin to be a transgression of the law. What law have we violated in inheriting this [sin] nature? What law requires us to have a different nature from that which we possess? Does reason affirm that we are deserving of the wrath and curse of God forever, for inheriting from Adam a sinful nature?"[24] The notion that people have sinful natures "is a

21. MacArthur, *Ashamed of the Gospel,* 158–59.
22. Charles G. Finney, *Finney's Systematic Theology* (1878; reprint, Minneapolis: Bethany House, 1994), 264–65.
23. Ibid., 265.
24. Ibid., 339.

relic of heathen philosophy, and was foisted in among the doctrines of Christianity by Augustine."[25]

As MacArthur found to be the case,[26] Finney concluded that God's justice demanded that he extend grace equally to all. He reasoned that God could not righteously hold mankind guilty for Adam's disobedience. In his opinion, a just God would never condemn people for being sinners by nature. Thomas Schreiner says, "Finney believed that all people possess the ability, apart from grace, to choose what is good. Contrary to Wesleyans he rejects the idea that people are born morally depraved because of Adam's sin. Thus, it is not surprising to learn that Finney repudiated the doctrine of prevenient grace."[27] Finney was discarding the clear teaching of Scripture in favor of human reason. He denied that a holy God would impute people's sins to Christ or impute Christ's righteousness to believers. Indeed, he concluded that Paul's great treatise on justification and the imputation of Christ's righteousness was "theological fiction."[28]

Regarding regeneration, Finney elsewhere writes:

> The actual turning to God is the sinner's own act. . . . There is nothing in religion beyond the ordinary powers of nature. Religion is the work of man. It consists entirely in the right exercise of the powers of nature. It is just that and nothing else. When mankind become religious, they are not *enabled* to put forth exertions which they were unable to put forth. They only exert powers which they had before, in a different way, and use them for the glory of God. A revival is not a mira-

---

25. Ibid., 263.

26. MacArthur, *Ashamed of the Gospel,* 231–32.

27. Thomas Schreiner, "Does Scripture Teach Prevenient Grace in the Wesleyan Sense?" in *The Grace of God, the Bondage of the Will,* ed. Thomas R. Schreiner and Bruce A. Ware (Grand Rapids: Baker, 1995), 368.

28. Charles G. Finney, *An Autobiography* (reprint, Old Tappan, N.J.: Revell, n.d.), 56–58.

cle, nor dependent on a miracle, in any sense. It is a purely philosophical result of the right use of constituted means.[29]

Finally, in possibly the most damaging portion of his *Systematic Theology*, Finney writes, "Representing the atonement as the ground of the sinner's justification has been a sad occasion of stumbling to many." Still others, he writes, "regarding the atonement as the ground as opposed to a condition of justification have held the atonement to be the literal payment of the debt of sinners and the nature of a commercial transaction."[30] Later he writes, "Neither is the atonement, nor anything in the mediatorial work of Christ, the foundation of our justification, in the sense of the source, moving, or procuring cause."[31] And he says, "The doctrine of an imputed righteousness is another gospel."[32]

Unlike Finney, Asahel Nettleton had a God-centered theology. He was used mightily by God to bring revival and spiritual awakening to North America. Nelson summarizes Nettleton's theology:

> Man, being totally depraved in nature and by choice, cannot save himself. By God's grace, some have been chosen unto eternal life. For those chosen by God (the elect), Jesus provided a penal, substitutionary atonement for their sins on the cross. The elect, for whom alone Jesus died, will be drawn by the triumphant grace of God to repentance and saving faith in Christ. They will be kept by God unto eternal salvation.

29. Charles G. Finney, *Revivals of Religion* (Old Tappan, N.J.: Revell, n.d.), 4–5.

30. Finney, *Finney's Systematic Theology*, 322.

31. Ibid., 375–76.

32. Ibid., 362.

Human beings must be divinely regenerated, or have their sinful nature negated, before they can repent and trust Christ. In Nettleton's system, human ability to respond at every stage of salvation comes from a sovereign act of God. Unless God moves, humans remain hopelessly lost. The methodology of Nettleton matched his theology. He used preaching as a means of bringing sinners to conviction of their sinfulness. He bathed all evangelistic efforts in fervent, humble prayer to the God who alone can effect the regeneration of a lost person. For those who responded to a call for the awakened to meet outside stated services, Nettleton offered inquiry meetings where individuals could receive personal assistance without public pressure to respond.

Few men have approached the level of expertise Nettleton demonstrated in personal evangelism. He was a skillful surgeon of the soul. He urged those who had been awakened to settle the matter of salvation privately before God. Multitudes came to saving faith in Christ as a result of his ministry in "waste places" and churches of all sizes and types. Few of his converts ever abandoned their profession to return to the world.[33]

THE CONTEMPORARY DEBATE OVER SOVEREIGNTY AND FREE WILL

The theological debate rages on. The current questions are the same as they have always been: How does a man get right with God? What is the ground of his justification? What is the responsibility of man in salvation? Several recent examples prove that these issues are not soon to go away.

33. Nelson, "How Does Doctrine Affect Evangelism?" 6–7.

"Evangelicals and Catholics Together" and "The Gift of Salvation"

In 1994, a consultation of evangelicals and Roman Catholics produced the statement "Evangelicals and Catholics Together: The Christian Mission in the Third Millennium." It proposed that evangelicals and Catholics were "brothers and sisters" in Christ.[34] Is this another example of the continuing battle between theocentrists and anthropocentrists to define salvation? Shortly after this document was released, several Protestants responded.[35] A second document was released in 1998 by those who authored the original document, entitled "The Gift of Salvation."[36] The men who coauthored and arranged the release of these documents were prominent evangelical Charles Colson (the president of Prison Fellowship) and the Roman Catholic priest Richard John Neuhaus (a former Lutheran, who is the editor of *First Things*). Colson and Neuhaus have continued to publish widely on these and other subjects, including *Evangelicals and Catholics Together: Toward a Common Mission*[37] and *Your Word Is Truth: A Project of Evangelicals and Catholics Together.*[38] These two volumes seem to blur the line of demarcation between evangelicals and Catholics—and thus the demarcation between theocentrists and anthropocentrists.

One noted evangelical theologian who has opposed these documents is R. C. Sproul of Ligonier Ministries. Sproul has worked tirelessly to respond to the efforts to join evangelicals and Roman Catholics together. For instance, he has written several books that seek to deal directly with some of these issues:

34. It was published in *First Things* 43 (May 1994): 15–22.
35. For a summation of several Protestant responses, see John Ankerberg and John Weldon, *Protestants and Catholics: Do They Now Agree?* 2d ed. (Eugene, Oreg.: Harvest House, 1995).
36. *First Things* 79 (January 1998): 20–23.
37. Dallas: Word, 1995.
38. Grand Rapids: Eerdmans, 2002.

Faith Alone: The Evangelical Doctrine of Justification;[39] *Willing to Believe: The Controversy over Free Will;*[40] *Grace Unknown: The Heart of Reformed Theology;*[41] *Getting the Gospel Right: The Tie That Binds Evangelicals Together.*[42] Sproul and others have responded to these and other issues by forming a ministry called the Alliance of Confessing Evangelicals (ACE).[43] While meeting in Cambridge, Massachusetts, in April 1996, they issued a declaration that speaks powerfully to the anthropocentric mind-set of modern Christendom. Called "the Cambridge Declaration," the document and subsequent materials are designed to show how the evangelical church has drifted, but also to detail a return to a biblical path for God's glory. The text of the Cambridge Declaration can be found below in appendix H.

The Freedom or Bondage of the Will

The anthropocentric view of theology continues with the writings of many, most notably Clark Pinnock. Pinnock is helping to lead a number of others to affirm "neo-Arminian" theories about God and man. These ideas are most readily seen in *Grace Unlimited,* edited by Pinnock,[44] and *The Grace of God, the Will of Man: A Case for Arminianism,* also edited by Pinnock.[45] While Pinnock represents a new brand of Arminianism, the theocentric position is equally represented by a team of well-known and respected Calvinistic scholars and pastors. The two books listed above are answered point by point in *The Grace of*

39. Grand Rapids: Baker, 1995.
40. Grand Rapids: Baker, 1997.
41. Grand Rapids: Baker, 1997.
42. Grand Rapids: Baker, 1999.
43. For a perspective on why ACE was formed, see *Here We Stand! A Call from Confessing Evangelicals,* by James Montgomery Boice and Benjamin E. Sasse (Grand Rapids: Baker, 1996).
44. Minneapolis: Bethany House, 1975.
45. Grand Rapids: Zondervan, 1989.

God, the Bondage of the Will, a two-volume work edited by Thomas Schreiner and Bruce Ware.[46]

Pinnock's works prove that the anthropocentric/Arminian arguments live on. The historical link to Pelagius, Erasmus, Sadoleto, and Arminius can be clearly deduced. For instance, Pinnock writes:

> I have to suppose that it was the bitter controversy with Pelagius that drove him [Augustine] to place such a strong emphasis on divine sovereignty in grace and to accept the harsh notions which accompany it, including soteriological predestination, total depravity, everlasting conscious torment in hell, strict limitations on who can be saved, forbiddingly high ecclesiastical walls, the importance of living within the Catholic church, and pessimism for anyone beyond its borders.[47]

Pinnock and his associates attack the theocentric view with repeated volleys, and don't mind saying so. Later in the same section of this same work, he writes:

> It [Augustine's theology] was a tragic development in many respects. For, however we explain it, something ugly entered Christian theology through Augustine. . . . What makes this especially sad for Protestants is that even if one could rescue Augustine's reputation on this point it would not be possible to rescue the reputations of others in our tradition, such as Luther and Calvin and others who voiced opinions every bit as severe and harsh as Augustine's. Calvin, after praising the clarity of general revelation, concludes that, "It is impossible for any man to obtain even the minutest portion of right and

46. Grand Rapids: Baker, 1995. For more on this work, see above, p. 98.
47. Clark H. Pinnock, *A Wideness in God's Mercy* (Grand Rapids: Zondervan, 1992), 39.

sound doctrine without being a disciple of Scripture." Luther declared: "Those who remain outside Christianity, be they heathens, Turks, Jews or false Christians (Roman Catholics), although they believe on only one true God, yet remain in eternal wrath and perdition." What can be said about this development? First, remember that the attitude of harsh exclusion was once a novelty in the history of doctrine, being the view neither of Scripture nor the first theologians. We are free to deny that God is glorified by saving as few as possible, or by excluding the majority from salvation.[48]

In the introduction to *The Grace of God, the Will of Man*, Pinnock characterizes the two approaches (Arminianism and Calvinism) in this distorted way: "The question can be put this way: Is God the absolute Monarch who always gets His way, or is God rather the loving Parent who is sensitive to our needs even when we disappoint Him and frustrate some of His plans?" He goes on to write, "Above all, God is love, and therefore expresses his power, not by having to control everything like an oriental despot, but by giving humanity salvation and eternal life under the condition of mutuality."[49]

On God's sovereignty, Pinnock takes this position:

Insisting that God's will accounts for everything that happens creates tremendous intellectual and practical difficulties for Christians and almost insurmountable hurdles for seekers to jump over. So we think it is very important that people be made aware of an alternative theology that does not have these effects.[50]

48. Ibid., 40–41.
49. Pinnock, *The Grace of God, the Will of Man*, ix.
50. Ibid.

Likewise, Pinnock asserts this:

> Having created human beings with relative autonomy alongside Himself, God voluntarily limits His power to enable them to exist and to share in the divine creativity. God invites humans to share in deciding what the future will be. God does not take it all onto His own shoulders. Does this compromise God's power? No, surely not, for to create such a world in fact requires a divine power of a kind higher than merely coercive.[51]

Further, regarding human depravity, Pinnock says:

> I was drawn . . . to question total depravity itself as a possible ambush designed to cut off non-Augustinians at the pass. . . . Scripture appeals to people as those who are able and responsible to God (however as we explain it) and not as those incapable of doing so, as Calvinian logic would suggest. The gospel addresses them as free and responsible agents, and I suppose it does so because that is what they are.[52]

Still again, Pinnock believes this regarding Christ's substitutionary atonement:

> Christ's death on behalf of the race evidently did not automatically secure for anyone an actual reconciled relationship with God, but made it possible for people to enter into such a relationship by faith. Gospel invitations in the New Testament alone make this clear.[53]

51. Ibid., 21.
52. Ibid., 22.
53. Ibid., 23.

Pinnock thus makes his position clear: (1) He denies total depravity. (2) He disapproves of unconditional election. (3) He repudiates an actual substitutionary atonement of Christ on the cross. (4) He loathes the idea of irresistible grace. (5) He disdains the doctrine of the perseverance of the saints. His is the view of anthropocentricity at its clearest!

CONCLUSION

We have seen that theocentrism and anthropocentrism have remained throughout the history of the church. In each period, the two positions have been recycled in new dress and terminology. It is hoped that this study has awakened in you a desire to discern which position you take—and why. In the end, truth really does matter, because our eternal destiny depends on it!

Appendix H

THE CAMBRIDGE DECLARATION OF THE ALLIANCE OF CONFESSING EVANGELICALS[1]

April 20, 1996

Evangelical churches today are increasingly dominated
by the spirit of this age rather than by the Spirit of Christ.
As evangelicals, we call ourselves to repent of this sin
and to recover the historic Christian faith.

I n the course of history words change. In our day this has happened to the word "evangelical." In the past it served as a bond of unity between Christians from a wide diversity of church traditions. Historic evangelicalism was confessional. It embraced the essential truths of Christianity as those were defined by the great ecumenical councils of the church. In addition, evangelicals also shared a common heritage in the *"solas"* of the sixteenth-century Protestant Reformation.

1. Reproduced here by permission of the Alliance of Confessing Evangelicals, 1716 Spruce Street, Philadelphia, PA 19103, *www.alliancenet.org.*

Today the light of the Reformation has been significantly dimmed. The consequence is that the word "evangelical" has become so inclusive as to have lost its meaning. We face the peril of losing the unity it has taken centuries to achieve. Because of this crisis and because of our love of Christ, his gospel and his church, we endeavor to assert anew our commitment to the central truths of the Reformation and of historic evangelicalism. These truths we affirm not because of their role in our traditions, but because we believe that they are central to the Bible.

SOLA SCRIPTURA: THE EROSION OF AUTHORITY

Scripture alone is the inerrant rule of the church's life, but the evangelical church today has separated Scripture from its authoritative function. In practice, the church is guided, far too often, by the culture. Therapeutic technique, marketing strategies, and the beat of the entertainment world often have far more to say about what the church wants, how it functions and what it offers, than does the Word of God. Pastors have neglected their rightful oversight of worship, including the doctrinal content of the music. As biblical authority has been abandoned in practice, as its truths have faded from Christian consciousness, and as its doctrines have lost their saliency, the church has been increasingly emptied of its integrity, moral authority and direction.

Rather than adapting Christian faith to satisfy the felt needs of consumers, we must proclaim the law as the only measure of true righteousness and the gospel as the only announcement of saving truth. Biblical truth is indispensable to the church's understanding, nurture and discipline.

Scripture must take us beyond our perceived needs to our real needs and liberate us from seeing ourselves through the seductive images, cliches, promises and priorities of mass culture. It is only in the light of God's truth that we understand ourselves aright and see God's provision for our need. The Bible, therefore, must be taught and preached in the church. Sermons must be expositions of the Bible and its teachings, not expressions of the preacher's opinions or the ideas of the age. We must settle for nothing less than what God has given.

The work of the Holy Spirit in personal experience cannot be disengaged from Scripture. The Spirit does not speak in ways that are independent of Scripture. Apart from Scripture we would never have known of God's grace in Christ. The biblical Word, rather than spiritual experience, is the test of truth.

Thesis One: Sola Scriptura

> *We reaffirm* the inerrant Scripture to be the sole source of written divine revelation, which alone can bind the conscience. The Bible alone teaches all that is necessary for our salvation from sin and is the standard by which all Christian behavior must be measured.

> *We deny* that any creed, council or individual may bind a Christian's conscience, that the Holy Spirit speaks independently of or contrary to what is set forth in the Bible, or that personal spiritual experience can ever be a vehicle of revelation.

SOLUS CHRISTUS: THE EROSION OF CHRIST-CENTERED FAITH

As evangelical faith becomes secularized, its interests have been blurred with those of the culture. The result is a loss of absolute values, permissive individualism, and a substitution of wholeness for holiness, recovery for repentance, intuition for truth, feeling for belief, chance for providence, and immediate gratification for enduring hope. Christ and his cross have moved from the center of our vision.

Thesis Two: **Solus Christus**

We reaffirm that our salvation is accomplished by the mediatorial work of the historical Christ alone. His sinless life and substitutionary atonement alone are sufficient for our justification and reconciliation to the Father.

We deny that the gospel is preached if Christ's substitutionary work is not declared and faith in Christ and his work is not solicited.

SOLA GRATIA: THE EROSION OF THE GOSPEL

Unwarranted confidence in human ability is a product of fallen human nature. This false confidence now fills the evangelical world; from the self-esteem gospel, to the health and wealth gospel, from those who have transformed the gospel into a product to be sold and sinners into consumers who want to buy, to others who treat Christian faith as being true simply because it works. This silences the doctrine of justification regardless of the official commitments of our churches.

God's grace in Christ is not merely necessary but is the sole efficient cause of salvation. We confess that human beings are born spiritually dead and are incapable even of cooperating with regenerating grace.

Thesis Three: **Sola Gratia**

We reaffirm that in salvation we are rescued from God's wrath by his grace alone. It is the supernatural work of the Holy Spirit that brings us to Christ by releasing us from our bondage to sin and raising us from spiritual death to spiritual life.

We deny that salvation is in any sense a human work. Human methods, techniques or strategies by themselves

cannot accomplish this transformation. Faith is not produced by our unregenerated human nature.

SOLA FIDE: THE EROSION OF
THE CHIEF ARTICLE

Justification is by grace alone through faith alone
because of Christ alone. This is the article by which the church
stands or falls. Today this article is often ignored, distorted
or sometimes even denied by leaders, scholars and pastors
who claim to be evangelical. Although fallen human nature
has always recoiled from recognizing its need for Christ's
imputed righteousness, modernity greatly fuels the fires of
this discontent with the biblical gospel. We have allowed this
discontent to dictate the nature of our ministry and what it
is we are preaching.

Many in the church growth movement believe that socio-
logical understanding of those in the pew is as important to the
success of the gospel as is the biblical truth which is proclaimed.
As a result, theological convictions are frequently divorced from
the work of the ministry. The marketing orientation in many
churches takes this even further, erasing the distinction between
the biblical Word and the world, robbing Christ's cross of its
offense, and reducing Christian faith to the principles and methods which bring success to secular corporations.

While the theology of the cross may be believed, these movements are actually emptying it of its meaning. There is no gospel
except that of Christ's substitution in our place whereby God
imputed to him our sin and imputed to us his righteousness.
Because he bore our judgment, we now walk in his grace as those
who are forever pardoned, accepted and adopted as God's children. There is no basis for our acceptance before God except in
Christ's saving work, not in our patriotism, churchly devotion or
moral decency. The gospel declares what God has done for us in
Christ. It is not about what we can do to reach him.

Thesis Four: Sola Fide

We reaffirm that justification is by grace alone through faith alone because of Christ alone. In justification Christ's righteousness is imputed to us as the only possible satisfaction of God's perfect justice.

We deny that justification rests on any merit to be found in us, or upon the grounds of an infusion of Christ's righteousness in us, or that an institution claiming to be a church that denies or condemns sola fide can be recognized as a legitimate church.

SOLI DEO GLORIA: THE EROSION OF GOD-CENTERED WORSHIP

Wherever in the church biblical authority has been lost, Christ has been displaced, the gospel has been distorted, or faith has been perverted, it has always been for one reason: our interests have displaced God's and we are doing his work in our way. The loss of God's centrality in the life of today's church is common and lamentable. It is this loss that allows us to transform worship into entertainment, gospel preaching into marketing, believing into technique, being good into feeling good about ourselves, and faithfulness into being successful. As a result, God, Christ and the Bible have come to mean too little to us and rest too inconsequentially upon us.

God does not exist to satisfy human ambitions, cravings, the appetite for consumption, or our own private spiritual interests. We must focus on God in our worship, rather than the satisfaction of our personal needs. God is sovereign in worship; we are not. Our concern must be for God's kingdom, not our own empires, popularity or success.

Thesis Five: Soli Deo Gloria

We reaffirm that because salvation is of God and has been accomplished by God, it is for God's glory and that we must glorify him always. We must live our entire lives before the face of God, under the authority of God and for his glory alone.

We deny that we can properly glorify God if our worship is confused with entertainment, if we neglect either Law or Gospel in our preaching, or if self-improvement, self-esteem or self-fulfillment are allowed to become alternatives to the gospel.

A CALL TO REPENTANCE AND REFORMATION

The faithfulness of the evangelical church in the past contrasts sharply with its unfaithfulness in the present. Earlier in this century, evangelical churches sustained a remarkable missionary endeavor, and built many religious institutions to serve the cause of biblical truth and Christ's kingdom. That was a time when Christian behavior and expectations were markedly different from those in the culture. Today they often are not. The evangelical world today is losing its biblical fidelity, moral compass and missionary zeal.

We repent of our worldliness. We have been influenced by the "gospels" of our secular culture, which are no gospels. We have weakened the church by our own lack of serious repentance, our blindness to the sins in ourselves which we see so clearly in others, and our inexcusable failure to adequately tell others about God's saving work in Jesus Christ.

We also earnestly call back erring professing evangelicals who have deviated from God's Word in the matters discussed in this Declaration. This includes those who declare that there is hope of eternal life apart from explicit faith in Jesus Christ, who claim that those who reject Christ in this life will be annihilated rather than endure the just judgment of God through eternal suffering, or who claim that evangelicals and Roman Catholics are one in Jesus Christ even where the biblical doctrine of justification is not believed.

The Alliance of Confessing Evangelicals asks all Christians to give consideration to implementing this Declaration in the church's worship, ministry, policies, life and evangelism.

For Christ's sake. Amen.

ACE Executive Council (1996)

Dr. John Armstrong

The Rev. Alistair Begg

Dr. James M. Boice

Dr. W. Robert Godfrey

Dr. John D. Hannah

Dr. Michael S. Horton

Mrs. Rosemary Jensen

Dr. R. Albert Mohler Jr.

Dr. Robert M. Norris

Dr. R. C. Sproul

Dr. Gene Edward Veith

Dr. David Wells

Dr. Luder Whitlock

Dr. J. A. O. Preus III

INDEX OF SCRIPTURES QUOTED

INDEX OF PERSONS

243

David N. Steele (1926–1991) served as pastor of several Baptist churches in Arkansas until his retirement in 1978. In addition to the present work, he coauthored *Romans: An Interpretive Outline*. At the time of his death, Steele was working on a manuscript dealing with the terms "all" and "world" throughout the New Testament. His wife, Ruth, is also deceased.

Curtis C. Thomas served as pastor of Baptist churches in Arkansas. More recently, for fourteen years he was the executive pastor of The Bible Church of Little Rock, an independent Reformed congregation. He retired after having spent forty-four years in the ministry. Along with Mr. Steele, he coauthored *Romans: An Interpretive Outline*. He is also the author of *Practical Wisdom for Pastors: Words of Encouragement and Counsel for a Lifetime of Ministry*. He continues to write and is a frequent guest speaker in churches throughout central Arkansas and the surrounding area. He and his wife, Betty, have three grown sons and several grandchildren.

S. Lance Quinn is the pastor-teacher of The Bible Church of Little Rock. He received the M.Div. and Th.M. degrees from The Master's Seminary, and the Drs. degree from the Evangelische Theologische Faculteit in Leuven, Belgium. Prior to coming to The Bible Church of Little Rock, he served as manager of ministries at the Grace to You radio ministry, and for ten years was the senior associate pastor and personal assistant to John F. MacArthur at Grace Community Church in southern California.

In addition to his pastoral ministry, Quinn serves on several boards, including Grace to You, the Fellowship of Independent Reformed Evangelicals, and the National Association of Nouthetic Counselors. He has written many articles and has contributed chapters to various books, including the trilogy *Rediscovering Expository Preaching*, *Rediscovering Pastoral Ministry*, and *Introduction to Biblical Counseling*. He and his wife, Beth, have eight children.